Laptops
FOR
DUMMIES®
3RD EDITION

Laptops
FOR
DUMMIES®
3RD EDITION

by Dan Gookin

Wiley Publishing, Inc.

Laptops For Dummies®, 3rd Edition

Published by
Wiley Publishing, Inc.
111 River Street
Hoboken, NJ 07030-5774
www.wiley.com

Copyright © 2008 by Wiley Publishing, Inc., Indianapolis, Indiana

Published by Wiley Publishing, Inc., Indianapolis, Indiana

Published simultaneously in Canada

For general information on our other products and services, please contact our Customer Care Department within the U.S. at 800-762-2974, outside the U.S. at 317-572-3993, or fax 317-572-4002.

For technical support, please visit www.wiley.com/techsupport.

Wiley also publishes its books in a variety of electronic formats. Some content that appears in print may not be available in electronic books.

Library of Congress Control Number: 2008934175

ISBN: 978-0-470-27759-1

Manufactured in the United States of America

10 9 8 7 6 5 4 3 2 1

WILEY

About the Author

Dan Gookin has been writing about technology for way, way too long. He has contributed articles to numerous high-tech magazines and written over 110 books on personal computers, many of them accurate.

Dan combines his love of writing with his gizmo fascination to create books that are informative, entertaining, and not boring. Having sold more than 14 million titles translated into over 30 languages, Dan can attest that his method of crafting computer tomes seems to work.

Perhaps his most famous title is the original *DOS For Dummies*, published in 1991. It became the world's fastest-selling computer book, at one time moving more copies per week than the *New York Times* #1 bestseller (though, as a reference, it could not be listed on the NYT bestseller list). That book spawned the entire line of *For Dummies* books, which remains a publishing phenomenon to this day.

Dan's most popular titles include *Word 2007 For Dummies*, *Laptops For Dummies*, and *PCs For Dummies* (all published by Wiley). He also maintains the vast and helpful Web page www.wambooli.com.

Dan holds a degree in communications/visual arts from the University of California, San Diego. Presently, he lives in the Pacific Northwest, where he enjoys spending time with his sons playing video games inside while they watch the gentle woods of Idaho.

Publisher's Acknowledgments

We're proud of this book; please send us your comments through our online registration form located at www.dummies.com/register/.

Some of the people who helped bring this book to market include the following:

Acquisitions and Editorial

Senior Project Editor: Mark Enochs

Executive Editor: Greg Croy

Copy Editor: Rebecca Whitney

Technical Editor: Mark Justice Hinton

Editorial Manager: Leah Cameron

Editorial Assistant: Amanda Foxworth

Sr. Editorial Assistant: Cherie Case

Cartoons: Rich Tennant
(www.the5thwave.com)

Composition Services

Project Coordinator: Katie Key

Layout and Graphics: Claudia Bell, Joyce Haughey, Stephanie D. Jumper, Ronald Terry

Proofreaders: Jessica Kramer, Toni Settle, Amanda Steiner

Indexer: Broccoli Information Management

Publishing and Editorial for Technology Dummies

    Richard Swadley, Vice President and Executive Group Publisher

    Andy Cummings, Vice President and Publisher

    Mary Bednarek, Executive Acquisitions Director

    Mary C. Corder, Editorial Director

Publishing for Consumer Dummies

    Diane Graves Steele, Vice President and Publisher

Composition Services

    Gerry Fahey, Vice President of Production Services

    Debbie Stailey, Director of Composition Services

Contents at a Glance

Introduction 1

Part 1: Getting Your Very Own Laptop 5

Chapter 1: The Quest for Portable Computing 7

Chapter 2: A Laptop Just for You 23

Part 11: Discover Your Laptop 31

Chapter 3: Out of the Box and into Your Lap 33

Chapter 4: The Chapter about Turning a Laptop On and Off 41

Chapter 5: Around Your Laptop in 18 Pages 61

Chapter 6: Windows on Your Laptop 79

Chapter 7: Behold the Tablet PC 97

Chapter 8: You and Your Laptop 113

Chapter 9: Power Management Madness 129

Chapter 10: Expanding Your Laptop's Universe 145

Part 111: Your Laptop Talks to the World 161

Chapter 11: Fear Not Networking 163

Chapter 12: Doing the Internet 187

Chapter 13: That Modem Thing 197

Chapter 14: Internet Security 213

Chapter 15: Portable Internet Stuff 225

Chapter 16: The Desktop–Laptop Connection 235

Part 1V: Hit the Road, Jack 249

Chapter 17: On the Road Again 251

Chapter 18: Laptop Security 267

Chapter 19: Meeting Expectations 281

Part V: Troubleshooting 291

Chapter 20: Major Trouble and General Solutions 293

Chapter 21: Upgrading Your Laptop 305

Part VI: The Part of Tens 311

Chapter 22: Ten or So Battery Tips and Tricks 313
Chapter 23: Ten Handy Laptop Accessories 321
Chapter 24: Ten Things to Throw in Your Laptop Case 327
Chapter 25: Ten Tips from a PC Guru 331

Index 337

Table of Contents

Introduction *1*

About This Book.. 2
And Just Who Are You? 3
Icons Used in This Book 3
Where to Go from Here... 4

Part 1: Getting Your Very Own Laptop *5*

Chapter 1: The Quest for Portable Computing 7

Making It Mobile 7
    The Xerox Dynabook... 8
    The Osborne 1.. 9
    The loveable luggables 10
    The Model 100.. 11
    The lunch buckets 12
    Early PC laptops 13
    The search for weightlessness 14
    From laptop to notebook..................................... 15
    The modern notebook 17
    The tablet computer 17
    The future of the laptop...................................... 18
Why You Need a Laptop... 19
Why You Don't Need a Laptop 21

Chapter 2: A Laptop Just for You. 23

Buy That Laptop!... 23
    Things to ignore when buying a laptop................ 23
    Things to heed when buying a laptop................... 24
    Other important, computery stuff........................ 25

Optical disc, oui or nyet?..27
Communications choices 28
Energy management hardware..28
Docking stations and port replicators 29
Service, Support, and Warranty 29
The Final Step: Buying Your Laptop 30

Part II: Discover Your Laptop..................................*31*

Chapter 3: Out of the Box and into Your Lap.................33

Box Unpacking 101 33
Making piles for the various items in the box.....................34
"How long should I keep the box?" 36
Knowing when to send in the warranty................................36
Setting Up Your Laptop 37
Find a place for the laptop 37
Charge the battery!..38
"Should I plug the laptop into a UPS?"..................................39
Figuring Out What to Do Next..40

Chapter 4: The Chapter about Turning a Laptop On and Off....41

Turning On a Laptop..41
Open the lid..42
"Where's the power button?"..43
Punch the power button 44
It's Windows!..45
Windows for the first time...46
Logging in to Windows...46
Other ways to log in to Windows 47
Behold the desktop 49
Various Options for Turning Off (or Not) the Laptop 51
Properly shutting down your laptop......................................51
"I need to restart Windows"...52
The bliss of Sleep mode...52
Better than sleep is hibernation..54

The software power button......................................55

Logging off 55

Locking Windows..56

"What happens when you just shut the lid?".........................56

Shutting down when the laptop doesn't want to 58

Power Button, What's Your Function? 58

Commanding the power button to do something 58

Controlling the software power button 59

Chapter 5: Around Your Laptop in 18 Pages **61**

The Basic Laptop Tour 61

Removable storage spots 62

Removable storage storage.................................62

The PC Card garage.................................63

Holes of mystery.................................64

A place for the old ball and chain.........................66

The thing's gotta breathe 67

Look at the Pretty Lights!.................................67

This Isn't Your Daddy's Keyboard 68

The general keyboard layout 68

Where did the numeric keypad go? 70

The Fn key is the Fun key! 71

Mind these specific keys.................................72

This Isn't Your Momma's Mouse.................................73

The touchpad.................................74

Where is the wheel button?.................................75

The "happy stick" keyboard mouse.........................75

Manipulating the mouse pointer 76

Get a real mouse! 77

Chapter 6: Windows on Your Laptop **79**

Windows on the Face of It.................................79

The desktop.................................80

The Start thing 80

Goodies in the notification area 82

Storage Devices 83

A Place for Your Stuff..84
    Accessing your home folder 85
    Placing the home folder on the desktop..............................86
    Special folders for your stuff.......................................86
Where the Programs Lurk..87
    "Where is Windows?"...87
    "Where are the programs and other software?".................87
Out on the Network..88
The Control Panel...89
    Visiting the Control Panel...89
    The Control Panel on the Start menu 90
    Fun places to visit in the Control Panel........................92

Chapter 7: Behold the Tablet PC 97

Sing to Me, O Tablet PC Muse..97
Discover Your Tablet PC...99
    Touring special tablet hardware 99
    Settings in the Control Panel.....................................102
The Pen Is Mightier than the Mouse.....................................104
    Training the pen 104
    Using the Input Panel..106
    Taking advantage of gestures and flicks....................109
    Giving your laptop the finger 110
Special Tablet PC Software 111
    Windows Journal 111
    Sticky Notes...112
    InkBall 112

Chapter 8: You and Your Laptop 113

Make Windows Yours 113
    Configuring your user account 114
    Setting up your laptop's display................................115
    Dealing with User Account Controls (UACs) 116
The Software Side...117
    Adding new software..117
    Removing old software 120

The Laptop and the Printer.. 121
    Displaying the Printers window............................... 122
    Connecting a printer to your laptop 123
    "What is the default printer?" 124
    Using the Print dialog box 124
    Considering options for when you don't have a printer ... 125
Keep It Clean 126
    Sprucing up the case.. 126
    Grooming the keyboard 127
    Cleansing the screen 127

Chapter 9: Power Management Madness................. 129

The Battery Will Get a Charge Out of This!.................... 129
    Types of batteries... 130
    Locate the laptop's battery 131
    Monitor the battery 132
    What happens when the power gets low 134
    Adjust low battery warnings 135
    To charge the battery 137
    Love that spare battery 137
    Should you keep the battery in the laptop when
        you use AC power all the time? 138
    RIP, battery.. 139
Managing Your Laptop's Power 139
    Power-saving tricks and tips 139
    Using a power management plan 141
    Creating your own power management plan........... 142

Chapter 10: Expanding Your Laptop's Universe............. 145

USB Expansion Options 145
    The miraculous expandability options of the USB port 146
    That USB thing 148
    The USB cable 149
    Plug in that USB gizmo.. 149
    USB-powered devices... 150
    Here a hub, there a hub 150

Adding external USB storage 152
Removing external USB storage............................... 153
Plugging in the PC Card 154
Parking a PC Card in the PC garage............................ 154
Using the PC Card.. 155
Backing a PC Card out of the PC garage 156
Reading Media Cards 157
Adding Some Big-Boy Toys 158
"I want an external keyboard!"....................................... 158
Connecting a second monitor... 159
Gotta getta mouse 160

Part III: Your Laptop Talks to the World 161

Chapter 11: Fear Not Networking 163

Basic Networking... 164
Network hardware overview... 164
Network software overview 166
Connecting to a peer-to-peer network 169
Finding other computers on the network 170
Accessing network storage 171
Accessing network printers 172
Sharing a folder from your laptop 175
It's a Wireless Life 176
Wireless networking protocol.. 177
Wireless networking hardware...................................... 178
Connecting to a wireless network 179
"What if I don't know the SSID?" 182
"What's my computer's MAC address?"........................ 183
Renewing your lease 184
Accessing a pay-service wireless network 185
Disconnecting the wireless connection........................ 185

Chapter 12: Doing the Internet. 187

Mobile Internet Tips.. 187

Broadband Internet Access.. 189
   Broadband access overview 189
   Watch out! That network is public 190
   Disconnecting from broadband access 192
Dialup Internet Access.. 192
   Configuring a dialup connection 193
   Making the dialup connection 194
   Don't forget to disconnect the dialup connection! 195
Shared Internet Access.. 196

Chapter 13: That Modem Thing 197

Introducing Mr. Modem.. 197
Modem Setup 199
   You'll find the modem deep in the Control Panel jungle... 199
   Setting modem properties.................................... 200
   Silencing the modem.. 202
   Adding special modem-command settings 202
Dialing Out of Strange Places...................................... 203
   Location, location, location.................................. 203
   Area code madness! To dial or not to dial 205
   Calling card info.. 207
The Various Disconnect Timeouts 207
   The general timeout 208
   Timeouts for each session 208
Putting the Fax in Fax/Modem 208
   Finding the fax modem 209
   Sending a fax 210
   Visiting Fax Central 211
   Receiving a fax 212

Chapter 14: Internet Security. 213

The Four Horsemen of the Internet Apocalypse 214
Behind the Firewall 214
   Using Windows Firewall....................................... 215
   Monitoring Windows Firewall............................... 217

Antivirus Software 218
    Checking for an antivirus program 219
    Scanning for viruses 220
    Disabling the antivirus program..................................... 221
    Protecting your laptop from the viral scourge.................. 221
Sneaky Spyware 222
More Malware: Hijacking and Phishing 223

Chapter 15: Portable Internet Stuff.........................225

Web Browsing When You're Out and About................................ 226
E-Mail Tips Galore 227
    Read your e-mail on the Web... 228
    Get a Web-based e-mail account...................................... 229
    Access your e-mail from a friend's computer.................... 229
    Forward your e-mail 230
    Disconnect after picking up e-mail.................................. 231
    Disable automatic checking 231
    Send everything in one batch 232
    Skip messages over a given size 233

Chapter 16: The Desktop–Laptop Connection. 235

Can We Talk?... 235
    Sneakernet 236
    Ugly octopus net... 236
    Ethernet 237
The Bliss of Synchronization 238
    Visiting the Sync Center 238
    Reviewing your syncs 240
    Synchronizing files 241
    Accessing synced files 242
    Syncing a new file 242
    Scheduling automatic synchronization 243
    Ending a sync 243
Your PC from Afar 243
    Setting up for Remote Desktop 244
    Accessing Remote Desktop on the network...................... 245

Part IV: Hit the Road, Jack............................249

Chapter 17: On the Road Again 251

Nancy Drew and the Case of the Laptop Case............................ 251
  Avoid the manufacturer's case 252
  Things to look for in a case 253
  Recommended brands 254
I'm Leaving on a Jet Plane Checklist 255
  Things to do before you go 255
  Things to pack in your laptop bag 256
Looming Questions at the Airport 257
  Is your laptop case one carry-on bag or half
    a carry-on bag? 257
  Laptop inspection.. 257
  All aboard! 258
  Airplane mode... 259
  Up, up in the air 260
  Air power 260
Café Computing 261
  Where to sit? 262
  Be a socket sleuth... 262
  Other tips 'n' stuff... 263
Laptopping in Your Hotel Room.. 264
Mind the Laptop's Temperature 265

Chapter 18: Laptop Security. 267

Laptops Are Easy to Steal.. 267
What to Do before Your Laptop Is Stolen 268
  Mark your laptop 268
  Avoid using an obvious laptop carrying case....................... 269
  Register the laptop and its software 269
  Be mindful of your environment.. 270
  Attach the old ball-and-chain.. 270
Protecting Your Data 271
  Avoid the Setup password 271
  Use a password on your account 272

Tell Windows not to memorize Internet passwords..........273
Disable the Guest account................................274
Lock Windows...275
Having the Laptop Phone Home...............................275
Your Fingerprint, Please..................................276
Backing Up Your Data.....................................276
Preparing for backup....................................277
Doing an initial backup.................................277
Restoring from a backup.................................280

Chapter 19: Meeting Expectations **281**

Presentation Information.................................281
The dog-and-pony show..................................282
Setting up your presentation...........................283
Close Encounters of the Laptop Kind......................285
Annoying people near you...............................286
Starting Windows Meeting Space.........................287
Getting people to join a meeting.......................288
Doing a meeting.......................................289

Part V: Troubleshooting *291*

Chapter 20: Major Trouble and General Solutions **293**

The Universal Quick-Fix.................................294
System Restore to the Rescue!...........................294
Enabling System Restore................................295
Setting a restore point................................296
Restoring your system..................................297
Safe Mode..299
Entering Safe mode.....................................299
Testing in Safe mode...................................300
"My laptop always starts in Safe mode!"................301
Common Problems and Solutions..........................301
"The keyboard is wacky!"...............................301
Touchpad touchiness....................................302
Making the mouse pointer more visible..................302

"My laptop won't wake up" 302
Power-management woes 303
"The battery won't charge" 303
Maintenance 303

Chapter 21: Upgrading Your Laptop **305**

How 'bout Some New Software? 305
Upgrading your software 305
Updating Windows 306
Upgrading to a new version of Windows 308
Giving Your Laptop New Hardware 308

Part VI: The Part of Tens *311*

Chapter 22: Ten or So Battery Tips and Tricks **313**

Don't Drop the Battery, Get It Wet, Short It, Play Keep-Away
with It, Open It, Burn It, or Throw It Away 313
Every Few Months, Drain the Battery All the Way 314
Turn Down the Monitor's Brightness 314
Power Down the Disk Drives 315
Add RAM to Prevent Virtual Memory Disk Swapping 315
Keep RAM Empty 316
Guard the Battery's Terminals 317
Avoid Extreme Temperatures 317
Store the Battery If You Don't Plan to Use It 317
Understand That Batteries Drain Over Time! 318
Deal with the Low-Battery Warning 318

Chapter 23: Ten Handy Laptop Accessories **321**

Laptop Bag or Travel Case 321
Spare Battery 322
Docking Station or Port Replicator 322
Cooling Pad 323
Minivac 324
USB Lamp 324
Full-Size Keyboard 324

External Mouse 325
ID Card or Return Service Sticker 325
Theft-Prevention System 326

Chapter 24: Ten Things to Throw in Your Laptop Case 327

Power Cord and Brick..328
Spare Battery 328
Mouse...328
Screen Wipes and Cleaner...328
Laptop Lock 328
Removable Media 329
Headphones 329
Some Necessary Utensils 329
Cables, Cables, Cables 329
Not the End of the List..330

Chapter 25: Ten Tips from a PC Guru 331

Remember That You Control the Computer...............331
Realize That Most Computer Nerds Love
    to Help Beginners..332
Use Antivirus Software 332
Understand That Upgrading Software Isn't
    an Absolute Necessity 333
Don't Reinstall Windows 333
Perfectly Adjust Your Monitor 334
Unplug Your Laptop When You Upgrade Hardware..................334
Subscribe to a Computer Magazine 334
Shun the Hype..335
Don't Take It So Seriously 335

Index *337*

Introduction

You hold in your hands something lightweight, high-tech, and portable. It's the product of years of research, a long-time dream of engineers and scholars, something people hunger for all over the world. It's wireless. It's about communications. And it will help you become the ultimate mobile computer user. Yes, of course, I'm talking about this book. Welcome to the third edition of *Laptops For Dummies*.

Laptop computers are all the rage. Sales are exceeding those of desktop PCs year after year. Whether you're merely interested in laptop computing or you need a laptop for your job or you already have a portable PC, this book holds those answers you desperately seek. It's full of tips, suggestions, examples, information, good advice, and plenty of quality humor and attitude. You won't find any desktop bias here. Everything cuddled between this book's yellow covers is all about portable computing, PC style.

You doubtless are reading this introduction because your laptop came with nothing. Perhaps you got a thin pamphlet or some foldout roadmap. That's it. The Internet doesn't help. And, although desktop users may think that they understand laptops — nay, they are but fools! If you've felt frustrated at the lack of good laptop information, rest assured: Your days of second-class citizenship are over!

This book covers your portable computer from laptop to lap-bottom, inside and out, on the road or resting at home. The information here runs the gamut, from introducing your laptop to making your first wireless connection at some swanky cybercafé. You'll find this book useful whether you're just out laptop shopping or consider yourself an old hand.

New to this third edition is coverage of the Tablet PC. It has been around a while, and though it isn't as popular as its laptop brethren, I feel that Tablet PC users should be neglected no more. After all, a Tablet PC is nothing more than a standard laptop with a useful neck injury.

About This Book

This book covers all aspects of laptop computing: from buying and setting up to going on the road to networking and the Internet to power management to security and everything in between. There's a lot of laptoppy advice to be had, and you'll find it right here in this book.

This book is organized as a reference; it's not intended for you to read each chapter one after the other. Instead, merely find the tidbit of information, the knowledge nugget you need to know, and then be on your merry way. Everything is cross-referenced, so if you need to look elsewhere in the book for more information, you can easily find it.

In writing this book, I assume that you may know a bit about computers, as most folks do today. But you may be utterly fresh on the idea of *portable* computing. Despite what they tell you, a laptop computer isn't merely a desktop computer with a handle attached. There's more to it, and this book is here to show you the ropes — and let you take full advantage of what the laptop has to offer.

I divide the laptop experience into six handy parts:

Part I contains an overview of laptop computing, plus a handy how-to guide for buying a laptop to sate your portable computing lusts.

Part II discusses how to use your laptop's basic features and how Windows works with a laptop, plus important information on power management (a subject you won't find in a desktop computer book or reference).

Part III is about networking and the Internet and getting your laptop to communicate with the rest of the world.

Part IV deals with taking your laptop on the road, and includes a special chapter on the hot topic of laptop security.

Part V covers laptop troubleshooting as well as various ways to upgrade your laptop's hardware and software.

Part VI is the traditional *For Dummies* Part of Tens — various lists for review or to help you get on your way.

And Just Who Are You?

Let me jump to the conclusion that you're a human being, not a robot or an alien living on Earth in disguise. Furthermore, you either own a laptop PC or want to buy one. You may already have a desktop computer, or perhaps you had a laptop a long, long time ago and noticed that things have changed.

I use the word *laptop* to refer to all types of portable computers, including traditional laptops, notebooks, and Tablet PCs. Where they have individual differences, I note it in the text. For example, Chapter 7 talks completely about Tablet PCs and their unique features and abilities. Otherwise, a laptop is a notebook is a laptop in this book.

This book assumes that you have a PC-compatible laptop, one that runs the Windows operating system; specifically, Windows Vista. This book doesn't cover Windows XP (though the Second Edition does). I don't cover the Apple line of Macintosh laptop computers. And the mere thought of addressing any PC laptops running the Linux operating system or any other operating systems known or unknown, from this or any parallel universe or dimension, has never occurred to me.

This book doesn't describe the basic operations of a computer, Windows, or your software. I've tried to keep the information here specific to the portable aspects of the laptop computer. Beyond that, if you need more information about running your computer, any standard PC or Windows reference works fine.

Icons Used in This Book

The Tip icon notifies you about something cool, handy, or nifty or something that I highly recommend. For example, "Just because there's a dancing clown out front doesn't mean that it's the best restaurant on the block."

Don't forget! When you see this icon, you can be sure that it points out something you should remember, something I said earlier that I'm repeating because it's very important and you'll likely forget it anyway. For example, "Always check your fly before you walk out on stage."

Danger! Ah-oogah! Ah-oogah! When you see the Warning icon, pay careful attention to the text. This icon flags something that's bad or that could cause trouble. For example, "No matter how pressing the urge, no matter how well you know these things, *do not* ask that rather large woman next to you when she is 'due.'"

This icon alerts you to something technical, an aside or some trivial tidbit that I just cannot suppress the urge to share. For example, "It would be as ludicrous for me to recommend the 802.11q standard as it would be for me to insist that 1 is a prime number." Feel free to skip over this book's technical information as you please.

Where to Go from Here

You can start reading this book anywhere. Open the table of contents and pick a spot that amuses you or concerns you or has piqued your curiosity. Everything is explained in the text, and stuff is carefully cross-referenced so that you don't waste your time reading repeated information.

You can visit my Web site at:

```
www.wambooli.com
```

If there's any specific information for this book on my Web site, it can be found at

```
www.wambooli.com/help/laptops/
```

Finally, I enjoy hearing feedback. If you want to send me e-mail, my personal address is dgookin@wambooli.com. I'm happy to answer questions specific to this book or just say "Hello." Please be aware that I am not listing my e-mail address here to provide free troubleshooting or support for your computer. If you need support, contact your laptop dealer or manufacturer. Thank you for understanding.

Enjoy your laptop computer. I'll see you on the road!

Part I

Getting Your Very Own Laptop

The 5th Wave — By Rich Tennant

"You know if we can all keep the tittering down, I, for one, would like to hear more about Ken's new pointing device."

In this part . . .

May the computer that lands in your lap actually fit your lap. Of course, a laptop computer isn't really designed to be used atop your lap. In all my years of using a laptop, I've never set one on my knees. It's unstable! Besides, I read a news story a few years ago about how the heat generated from a laptop perched on a male's lap could endanger his progeny. Because I am easily prone to injuries, I always use my laptop on a tabletop, thank you.

A laptop computer provides you with the freedom to take your high-tech habit on the road. Yea verily, the desire to own a portable computer is deep-rooted and sincere, like mankind's longing for freedom or the occasional good cheeseburger. To sate your thirst, this part of the book introduces the concept of the laptop computer. Included are the many reasons why you should get yourself a laptop, as well as a handy shopping guide to help you discover which laptop is just right for your lap.

Chapter 1

The Quest for Portable Computing

In This Chapter

▶ Understanding portable computing

▶ Looking back at laptop history

▶ Recognizing the Tablet PC variation

▶ Deciding whether you need a laptop

*T*echnology is the eternal driving force behind the urge for humans to improve upon their existence. Thousands of years ago, the primitive people of this planet craved barbecue, so they invented fire. Then there was a need for more food, so the organic farmers' market was born.

Fast-forward thousands of years and you'll find bespectacled proto-nerds craving to bask their alabaster skin in the sunlight — or at least under a tree in the quad. Using the primitive technology of the wheel (in the form of castors) and an extension cord, they could well have wheeled the hulking computers of the early 1950s outside and improved upon the existence of all mankind by marking the dawn of the portable computing era. But it didn't happen.

Indeed, it's been a long road, but the portable computing device you have or are looking toward obtaining didn't just happen overnight. To help you better understand the concept of a *laptop* I present this chapter: a brief and informative history of portable computing.

Making It Mobile

Here's a handy technology tip: To make anything portable, just attach a handle. *Presto!* It's portable! Such marketing gimmickry makes a 19-pound television or a 25-pound table saw instantly portable. Wow! I suppose that even a handle on an elephant would make it portable. (Oh, but the legs! Right.)

The ancient portable computer

Long before people marveled over (solar powered) credit-card-size calculators, there existed the world's first portable, human-powered calculator. Presenting the *abacus,* the device used for centuries by merchants and goatherds to rapidly perform calculations that would otherwise cause painful headaches.

Abacus comes from the Greek word meaning "to swindle you faster." Seriously, the abacus, or *counting board,* is simple to master. Many kids now learn to use the abacus in elementary school. In the deft hands of an expert, an abacus can perform all the same operations as a calculator — including square and cubic roots.

In his short story *Into the Comet,* science fiction author Arthur C. Clarke wrote of stranded astronauts using multiple abacuses to plot their voyage home when the spaceship's computer wouldn't work because the Internet was down and their version of Windows couldn't be validated.

Real portability implies more than bolting on a handle. It means that the item has three characteristics:

- ✔ Light weight
- ✔ No power cord
- ✔ Practical

Sadly, not all those things happened at once.

The Xerox Dynabook

The desire to take a computer on the road has been around a long, long time. Back around 1970, long before the notion of the personal computer existed,

Xerox PARC developed the Dynabook concept. Today, you'd recognize it as a Tablet PC: The Dynabook was to be the size of a sheet of paper and only one half-inch thick. The top part would be a screen; the bottom would be a keyboard.

The Dynabook never left the lab, remaining only a dream. Yet the desire to take a computer on the road wouldn't go away. For the next three decades after the Dynabook concept, many attempts were made to create truly portable computers.

The Osborne 1

The first successful portable computer was the Osborne 1, created by computer book author and publisher Adam Osborne in 1980. Adam believed that for personal computers to be successful, they would have to be portable.

His design for the Osborne 1 portable computer was ambitious for the time: The thing would have to fit under an airline seat — and this was *years* before anyone would dream of actually using a computer on an airplane.

The Osborne 1 portable computer (see Figure 1-1) was a whopping success. It featured a full-size keyboard, two 5¼-inch floppy drives, but a teensy, credit-card-size monitor. It wasn't battery powered, but it did have a handy carrying handle so that you could lug around the 24-pound beast like an overpacked suitcase. Despite its shortcomings, 10,000 units a month were sold; for $1,795, you got the computer plus free software. Unlike today, it was useful software too.

Figure 1-1: A late-model Osborne.

The loveable luggables

The Osborne was portable, but not conveniently so. Face it: The thing was a *suitcase!* Imagine hauling the 24-pound Osborne across Chicago's O'Hare airport. Worse: Imagine the joy expressed by your fellow seatmates as you try to wedge the thing beneath the seat in front of you.

Computer users yearned for portability. They wanted to believe the advertising images of carefree people toting the Osborne around — people with arms of equal length. But no hip marketing term could mask the ungainly nature of the Osborne: Portable? Transportable? Wispy? Nope. Credit some wag in the computer press for dreaming up the term *luggable* to describe the new and popular category of portable computers.

Never mind its weight. Never mind that most luggable computers never ventured from the desktops they were first set up on — luggables were the best the computer industry could offer in the arena of portable computing.

In the end, it wasn't the Osborne computer's weight that doomed it. No, what killed the Osborne was that the world wanted IBM PC compatibility. The Osborne lacked that. Instead, the upstart Texas company Compaq introduced luggability to the IBM world with the Compaq 1, shown in Figure 1-2.

Figure 1-2:
The luggable Compaq 1.

The Compaq 1, introduced in 1983 at $3,590, proved that you could have your IBM compatibility and haul it on the road with you — as long as a power socket was handy and you had good upper-body strength.

Yet the power cord can stretch only so far. It became painfully obvious that for a computer to be truly portable — as Adam Osborne intended — it would have to lose that power cord.

The Model 100

The first computer that even remotely looks like a modern laptop, and was fully battery powered, was the Radio Shack Model 100, shown in Figure 1-3. It was an instant, insane success.

The Model 100 wasn't designed to be IBM PC compatible, which is surprising considering that PC compatibility was all the rage at the time. Instead, it offered users a full-size, full-action keyboard, plus an eensie, 8-row, 40-column LCD display. It came with several built-in programs, including a text editor (word processor), communications program, scheduler, and appointment book, plus the BASIC programming language, which allowed users to create their own programs or buy and use BASIC programs written by others.

Figure 1-3:
The Radio
Shack
Model 100.

Portability and communications

Long before the Internet came around, one thing that was deemed necessary on all portable computers was the ability to communicate. The laptop computer had two communications duties. First, it had to be able to talk with the desktop computer, to exchange and update files. Second, it needed a *modem* to be able to communicate electronically over phone lines.

Nearly every portable computer, from the Radio Shack Model 100 onward, had to have a modem, or at least an option for installing one. This was before the Internet era, back when a modem was considered an optional luxury for a desktop computer. On the road, a portable computer required a modem in order to keep in touch with its companion desktop systems.

The Radio Shack Model 100 was really all that was needed for portability at the time, which is why the device was such a resounding success.

- ✔ The Model 100 provided the *form factor* for laptops of the future. It was about the size of a hardback novel. It ran for hours on standard AA batteries. And, it weighed just 6 pounds.

- ✔ So popular was the Model 100 among journalists that it was common to hear the hollow sound of typing on its keyboard during presidential news conferences.

- ✔ Despite its popularity and versatility, people wanted a version of the Model 100 that would run the same software as the IBM PC. Technology wasn't ready to shrink the PC's hardware to Model 100 size in 1983, but the Model 100 set the goal for what users wanted in a laptop's dimensions.

The lunch buckets

Before the dawn of the first true laptop, some ugly mutations slouched in, along with a few rejects from various mad scientists around the globe. I call them the *lunch bucket* computers because they assumed the shape, size, and weight of a typical hard-hat's lunchbox. The Compaq III, shown in Figure 1-4, was typical of this type of portable computer.

- ✔ The lunchbox beasts weighed anywhere from 12 to 20 pounds or more, and most weren't battery powered.

- ✔ The lunch bucket portables were the first PCs to use LCD monitors. (The Osborne and Compaq portables used glass CRTs.)

✔ Incidentally, around the same time as the lunch bucket computers became popular, color monitors were becoming standard items for desktop PCs. All portables at the time, even those with LCD monitors, were monochrome.

✔ Honestly, the lunch buckets did offer something over the old transportable or luggables: less weight! A late-model lunch bucket PC weighed in at about 12 pounds, or half the weight and about one-eighth the size of the suitcase-size luggables.

Early PC laptops

The computer industry's dream was to have a portable computer that had all the power of a desktop computer, plus all the features, yet be about the same size and weight as the Model 100. One of the first computers to approach that mark was the Compaq SLT, back in 1988, as shown in Figure 1-5.

The Compaq SLT was the first portable computer that resembles one of today's laptops: A hinged lid swings up and back from the base, which contains the keyboard. This design is known as the *clamshell.*

Figure 1-4:
The Compaq
III.

Figure 1-5:
The Compaq
SLT.

Feature-wise, the SLT had what most PC desktop users wanted in a portable system: a full-size keyboard, full-size screen, floppy drive, and 286 microprocessor, which meant that the computer could run the then-popular DOS operating system. The computer lacked a hard drive.

Weight? Alas, the SLT was a bowling ball, at 14 pounds!

What the Compaq SLT did was prove to the world that portability was possible. A laptop computer was designed to feature everything a desktop computer could, plus run off batteries for an hour or so. Yeah, believe it or not, people were *delighted.*

The search for weightlessness

Just because the marketing department labeled the computer a "laptop" didn't mean that it was sleek and lightweight. For a while there, it seemed like anyone could get away with calling a portable PC a laptop, despite the computer's weight of up to 20 pounds — which is enough to crush any lap, not to mention kneecaps.

In the fall of 1989, NEC showed that it could think outside the laptop box when it introduced the UltraLite laptop, shown in Figure 1-6.

Figure 1-6:
The NEC
UltraLite.

The UltraLite featured a full-size screen and keyboard, but no disk drives or other moving parts! It used battery-backed-up memory to serve as a *silicon disk*. The silicon disk stored 1 or 2MB of data — which was plenty back in those days.

As was required of all laptops, the UltraLite featured a modem, and it could also talk with a desktop computer by using a special cable. Included with the UltraLite was software that would let it easily exchange files and programs with a desktop PC.

The weight? Yes, the UltraLite lived up to its name and weighed in at just under 5 pounds — a feather compared to the obese laptops of the day. And, the battery lasted a whopping two hours, thanks mostly to the UltraLite's lack of moving parts.

From laptop to notebook

The UltraLite marked the line between what was then called a *laptop* to what is now called a *notebook*. Although manufacturers had perverted the term *laptop* to include heavy, bulky portables that were anything but lap-friendly (such as the cannonball-heavy Compaq III), the UltraLite raised the bar and created the notebook category.

Any laptop that weighs under 6 pounds and is less than an inch thick is technically a notebook. Some even lighter units earned the moniker *subnotebook*. Keep in mind that all these terms are for marketing purposes; all these computers, regardless of weight, size, or what the brochure says, are now called *laptops*.

Calculating laptop weight: The missing pieces

When computer companies specify the weights of their laptops, I'm certain that they do it under ideal conditions, possibly on Venus or at some other location where gravity is weak. The advertised weight is, like they say, "for comparison purposes only."

Commonly left out of the laptop's weight specs is the *power brick,* the AC adapter used to connect the laptop to a wall socket. When the laptop isn't running on batteries, you need the power brick to supply the thing with juice, so the power brick is a required accessory — something you have to tote with you if you plan to take the laptop on an extended trip.

In the old days, what they didn't tell you in the advertisements was that the power brick often weighed half as much as the laptop itself! Either that, or the power brick was even bulkier than the laptop, as shown in the figure, in the Dell 320LT's obnoxiously big power brick (and heavy 30-minute batteries). Lugging around such items isn't convenient. Things are better today.

The modern notebook

As technology careened headlong into the 1990s, it became apparent that users were desperate for three things from their laptop computers — in addition to the basic PC compatibility, portability, and communications features that were long ago deemed must-haves —

- ✔ Light weight
- ✔ Long battery life
- ✔ Full hardware compatibility with desktop systems

Over time, all these qualities were achieved — at a price. Today, the holy grail of a lightweight, PC-compatible laptop that boasts a long battery life isn't elusive; it's just expensive!

- ✔ **Weight:** Depending on how much you want to pay, your laptop can be anywhere from a half-inch thick to just under an inch thick and weigh between 2 to 6 pounds. The weight and size also depend on the features you want in your laptop, with more features adding more weight.

- ✔ **Battery life:** Although the batteries themselves haven't improved much in the past several years, thanks to power-management hardware and software, modern laptops can extend battery life from the once-standard two hours to about three or four hours.

- ✔ **Hardware compatibility:** Since the late 1990s, all laptops come with color screens, just like desktop systems do. Most also sport CD-ROM or DVD drives, just like desktops. Laptops feature modems, networking (wired and wireless), and expansion options. Special laptop microprocessors and other types of hardware have been developed over the years, keeping laptop hardware small and energy efficient.

The tablet computer

Computer manufacturers have long attempted to create the electronic equivalent of a pencil and pad of paper — a very *expensive* pencil and pad of paper. Basically, what they're after is a portable computer with a monitor but no keyboard. Data is input by writing directly on the screen using a digital stylus.

Over the years, this digital triptych has had various names attached to it: the PenGo computer, the Apple Newton, Pen Windows, and eventually the Tablet PC.

The *Tablet PC* began life a few years back as its own computer category. The machine was about the same size as a laptop, but it didn't fold open; the monitor was "face up" all the time. But that model failed miserably. The Tablet PC now exists as a laptop hybrid: The machine can be used like any other laptop, but the display can be pivoted and laid flat over the keyboard, as shown in Figure 1-7. The result is a flexible computer system that is a laptop with Tablet PC features.

Figure 1-7:
A Tablet PC.

✔ Even as a hybrid, Tablet PC sales haven't taken off. Apparently, writing on the screen isn't a feature that laptop users are eager to have.

✔ Tablet PCs are discussed throughout this book and specifically in Chapter 7.

✔ The ancients used something called a *tabulae ceratea* to write temporary messages. Every Greek or Roman schoolboy took with him to class a folding wooden tablet. The insides were coated with a black wax. Using a stylus (basically a stick), the student would write into the wax, again and again. Oh, we've truly come such a long way.

The future of the laptop

Human laps aren't getting any smaller. Human eyes can only comfortably read text that's so big. Most importantly, human fingers have trouble with keyboards that are too tiny. Because of these limitations, the laptop of the future will probably remain about the same size as a laptop of today. (Even though scientists could make the keyboard and screen smaller, the human form wouldn't appreciate it.)

On the horizon are the UMPCS or Ultra-Mobile PCs, as well as the so-called *NetBook* computers. Both are smaller types of laptops designed specifically for light computer usage: Internet, e-mail, word processing, and other mundane purposes. I predict a coming price war over these new types of laptops, which may eventually make them the most popular types of PC ever.

In the long run, the laptop won't completely replace the desktop computer system. The current trend is to use both a laptop and a desktop computer. Smaller portable devices exist, such as the popular BlackBerry or Palm Treo, but the laptop holds its own as a fully functional, truly portable computer.

Technology continues to make laptop hardware smaller, more energy efficient, and better able to handle the portable environment. But one area that needs vast improvement is battery technology.

The battery of the future is the *fuel cell,* which is like a miniature power plant directly connected to your laptop PC. Fuel cell technology promises power that lasts for weeks instead of hours, which will prove a boon to portable gizmos of every kind — but only when the fuel cell makes sense economically. Although fuel cells are available now, they're just too expensive and bulky for laptops. Scientists and other people in white lab coats are predicting that the first practical fuel cell will be widely available by the end of the decade. Until then, laptop users will have to slug it out with rechargeable batteries and power packs.

(See Chapter 9 for more information on batteries as well as on other power-management issues.)

Why You Need a Laptop

Obviously, Adam Osborne was right: Computers need to be portable! The question should really be "Why buy a desktop computer that's stuck in one spot all the time?"

Naturally, a desktop computer is more powerful, expandable, and cheaper than a laptop. *But you can't take it with you!* Well, you could, but hauling around all that desktop stuff would make you look like a dork.

On the other hand, it's impossible to look like a dork with a laptop. Imagine yourself sitting in that trendy coffee shop and sipping some overpriced caffeinated beverage while poring over your e-mail and chatting on a cellphone — that's hip! That's so five-minutes-from-now!

Seriously, you want a laptop for one of the following reasons:

✔ **As your main computer**

Why dither over saving money with a desktop when you really want the portability of a laptop?

A desktop computer cannot pretend to be a laptop, but a laptop can certainly fake being a desktop: You can use a full-size keyboard and monitor with your laptop. You can also connect any number of popular desktop peripherals, such as a printer, a scanner, or an external hard drive. But, unlike with a desktop system, you're free to disconnect the laptop and wander the world whenever you want.

✔ **As a space-saving computer system**

Unlike with desktops, you don't have to build a tabletop shrine to your laptop computer — that is, you don't need a computer desk. If space is tight in your house, apartment, or dorm room, keep the laptop on the shelf or in a drawer. Then set it up on the kitchen table or coffee table whenever you're ready to work. Forget about the constant mess and clutter that orbit the typical desktop computer station. Viva Adam Osborne!

✔ **As a second computer**

Why buy a second desktop computer when you can get a laptop and enjoy not only the presence of a second computer but also the ability to make that computer system portable? Furthermore, you can network the two computers, allowing them to share the Internet connection and printers as well as each other's data and files. And, you still have the luxury of having one system that's portable.

✔ **As your on-the-road computer**

Laptops let you take your work on the road. After a few moments of *synch* (transferring current files between your desktop and laptop, covered in Chapter 16), you're off and running to anywhere you like (although being in direct, bright sunlight can make it difficult to see the laptop screen).

When you return from your "road warrior" trip, you perform another synch, and both computers get all caught up for the day.

- Laptops let you escape the confines of your office and do work anywhere you like for a few hours. Or, if there's power at your location, you can plug in and work all day.

- The laptop lets you take your work with you when you travel. It lets you experience the reality of using a computer on an airplane (which isn't as smart as it sounds).

Taking that laptop off to school

It was hard to deny being a computer nerd back in the old days. At school, you would see these guys, not known for their muscle, struggling to tote several pounds of serious PC equipment up the hard concrete stairwell to their dorm rooms. Today, *everyone* uses a laptop at school. No one considers it geeky, any more than an iPod is considered geeky. In fact, it's practically an insult if your college-bound high school senior doesn't get a laptop as a graduation present. Some parents. . . .

Laptops allow students to take full-powered computers with them anywhere on campus. Students can get work done in a dorm just as easily as they can in the library, under a tree, or anywhere else that their feet can take them (or anywhere that they can find a power outlet to

mooch from). Laptops were meant for college.

Most colleges and universities state their laptop requirements either in the registration or orientation packet or online. That information tells you which type of hardware you should look for when purchasing a laptop to use at that school. But it doesn't happen often enough.

Laptops at college are subject to two of the nastiest assaults on computer users: various ugly programs that can infiltrate a PC over the Internet and theft. See Chapter 14 for vital information regarding online security, and Chapter 18 for preventing theft. That stuff is required reading for parents *and* their children who are taking laptop computers to school.

Why You Don't Need a Laptop

Laptops aren't cheap. They're also expensive to fix. Forget about upgrading the hardware. They can easily get stolen. The battery life never lives up to the printed specifications. It's tough to get work done on a jet or in a café because people either look over your shoulder or ask you questions about the laptop. *Ack!* But those are minor quibbles.

Thanks to their light weight, long battery life, and increasing computing power, laptops make ideal computers for just about anyone. If you don't own a laptop now, you will someday.

Chapter 2

A Laptop Just for You

In This Chapter

▶ Buying a laptop

▶ Ignoring things when buying a laptop

▶ Paying attention to things when buying a laptop

▶ Mulling over specific laptop options

▶ Expanding your laptop

▶ Considering your networking and communications options

▶ Finding service, support, and warranty

▶ Buying your laptop

An educated consumer is a wise and thrifty consumer. The more you know about laptops and your needs, the better you can make an informed buying decision. Even if you're an old hand at purchasing PCs, I recommend that you do a little research and investigation before you go shopping for a new laptop. Many issues are unique to laptops, such as weight, battery life, and wireless networking options. Therefore, I present this chapter to help you make the best possible laptop purchase decision.

Buy That Laptop!

The best computer you can buy is the one that does what you need it to do. To find that computer, you have to familiarize yourself with some issues and deliberately ignore others.

Things to ignore when buying a laptop

Don't be fooled by the slick marketing campaigns. When it comes to spending your money on a useful computer, especially a laptop, feel free to ignore these items:

Brand name: Too many people consider brand name first and don't even know which components they need. Similarly, you don't need to buy a laptop from the same manufacturer as your desktop PC. As long as the laptop runs Windows (or the Mac OS, if you're getting a Mac laptop), you're fine.

Low price: An abundance of cheap laptops are available. In haste, you may buy a laptop thinking that you're getting a deal — but get stuck with a brick instead.

High price: It's easy to be duped into thinking that the most expensive laptop is the best. Buying too much is not a wise buying decision.

Service plan: Warranties are good to have, but the service plan? Forget it! You're just lining the salesman's pocket. I go over this topic in more detail later in this chapter.

Internal expansion: You can ignore internal expansion options on your laptop because in all likelihood it won't have any. Only a few of the very large laptops might have an internal expansion slot or allow you to upgrade the video adapter or processor or to add memory. This lack of internal expansion is one reason you need to be very thoughtful when you initially purchase your laptop.

Things to heed when buying a laptop

In addition to all the regular hardware that comes with a computer (see the following section), you need to consider four key items when choosing a laptop:

Weight: Nearly all laptops weigh between 2 and 7 pounds. The heavier laptops have more features, such as a larger display. The lighter models may have fewer features or merely more advanced features, plus they're more expensive. Oddly enough, you pay more for less weight, and you pay more for extra weight. Then again, there's nothing wrong with buying a 7-pound laptop that does everything you want.

Size: Most laptops are less than 1 inch thick and about as tall and wide as a small coffee table book. They could get smaller than that, but there's a limit based on the size of the keyboard and the size of the display. The smallest (and lightest) laptops often lack an optical drive.

Display: Recently, manufacturers have discovered that people love a larger LCD display on a laptop — even though the larger display adds to the laptop's size and weight (and consuming more battery power). For a laptop being used at one location and only rarely going on the road, a huge display is wonderful. If you want portability, though, and a longer battery life, consider a smaller display.

Battery life: Despite the claims on the brochures, most PC laptops run anywhere from two to three hours unplugged. Some models manage five or more hours. But power can be managed; see Chapters 9 and 22.

✔ Stuff that's important to the overall weight of the laptop — the power brick and cord, extra batteries, discs, and manuals — aren't included in the basic tonnage calculation. Keep that in mind when weight is important to you.

✔ Tablet PCs are thicker than standard laptops because of the extra circuitry required in the monitor. See Chapter 7.

✔ A popular trick that's used to make the battery life seem longer is to specify the time used by two batteries. On some laptops, you can swap a drained battery with a fresh one, thereby extending your portable time. Although there's nothing wrong with that trick, the extended battery time shouldn't be used for comparison, *and* the extra battery's weight needs to be added to the total laptop weight.

✔ Avoid any so-called laptop computer that doesn't run on batteries. Spurn it! Point, scream, and run away!

Other important, computery stuff

Beyond weight, size, and battery issues are three core parts of a computer that play a special role in choosing a laptop:

Processor: It's worth the extra money now to invest in a fast processor, or *CPU*. Doing so extends the useful life of your laptop by ensuring that you can run tomorrow's software before tomorrow comes, but not before yesterday. You'll be thankful later.

Memory: *Memory* is where the action happens in a computer, where the work gets done. Not having enough memory in your laptop limits its performance. Having enough (or way too much) memory makes Mr. Laptop very happy indeed.

Mass storage: The laptop's *hard drive* is the electronic closet where the laptop stores your stuff. The hard drive must have room for the computer's operating system, all the software you get and later install, all the data files and junk you collect, plus room (lotsa room) to grow.

The laptop buzzword jungle

When you go laptop shopping, you discover a bewildering bazaar of various technical terms and such. Most of them are marketing terms, invented by nontechnical types to describe technical things. This is okay because technical people tend to overuse the words *keen* and *neato.* Here's a roundup of some laptop technical terms you may encounter during your shopping exercises:

Processor M/Mobile: You often find the suffix M (or Mobile) appended to the name of a specific laptop CPU, such as the Celeron M or Pentium M. The M stands for *mobile.* These mobile CPUs are the laptop-specific counterparts to the standard desktop processors. The Celeron M is the low-cost alternative to the Pentium M.

Centrino: Intel uses this term to describe various laptop technology — specifically, stuff designed for a mobile computer that you won't find in a desktop. The Centrino technology includes a special chipset (or the main circuitry on the laptop's motherboard), a specifically designed laptop processor, and wireless networking technology.

Centrino Duo: The Duo suffix describes a newer version of Centrino technology, specifically with an Intel dual-core processor.

Core Duo: This term refers to the Intel replacement processor for the Pentium. The Core Duo chip contains two CPU cores, like getting two processors on one chip.

GB: The acronym for *gigabyte* means 1 billion characters of computer storage. A GB is approximately 1,000MB.

GHz: An acronym for *gigahertz*, or billions of cycles per second, this speed measurement is used to gauge CPUs. The actual speed, of course, varies, and in mundane tasks it's often difficult to tell the difference between a processor running at 2.0 GHz versus 2.4 GHz. But that doesn't stop the manufacturers from boasting about their chips' speed.

MB: This term is the acronym for *megabyte*, or 1 million characters of computer storage. One MB stores about one minute of music or a 3-by-4-inch digital photo of low quality.

Mobile Sempron: An AMD processor designed for laptop (mobile) computing. It's the economy version of the Turion flavor chip.

Pentium M: The M stands for *mobile,* and the Pentium M chip is the Intel processor specifically designed for use in laptops.

Turion 64: This term refers to the AMD version of Intel's Pentium M, a powerful 64-bit mobile processor that comes in single- and dual-core models. The dual core is named Turion 64 X2. The Turion was formerly named the Mobile Athlon 64.

How do you know how much memory or storage is enough? Easy: Look at the software you'll use.

For example, if the software states that it wants more than 1GB of memory, get a laptop with at least that much RAM. If the software requires at least 100GB of disk space, factor that amount into your laptop's mass storage capacity requirements.

✓ The processor, or central processing unit (CPU), is the main chip inside a computer. It's not the computer's "brain." The computer's brain is the software you run. No, the processor is more like the computer's muscle.

✓ Laptop CPUs are more expensive than their desktop counterparts. That's because the laptop processors must be designed to use less power and generate less heat. That takes time, so their development cycle is longer; hence, the added cost.

✓ The more RAM your computer has, the happier it appears to be and the more your software enjoys the computer. If you cannot afford a faster CPU, you can afford to buy more RAM. Pack your laptop with as much RAM as you can afford now.

✓ I recommend a laptop with at least 2GB of RAM in it. If you can afford more, buy more.

✓ The things that consume huge amounts of hard drive space are graphics image files (such as digital photographs), music or audio files, and video files. If you plan on collecting any of these files on your laptop, get a humongous hard drive!

✓ I recommend a laptop with at least a 40GB hard drive. A *humongous* hard drive would be one with over 80GB capacity.

✓ By investing in the latest, fastest CPU, lots of RAM, and copious amounts of mass storage space now, you're extending the life of your laptop. That's a good thing. You want your laptop investment to last for years to come. Pay more now, and you'll earn it back down the road, when you're still using your laptop while others are forced to buy a new one.

Optical disc, oui or nyet?

Quite a few laptops don't have optical drives. No, the manufacturers aren't being cheap. The optical drive — a DVD or CD-ROM — adds weight. Often times, adding that weight, combined with the battery power required to spin the drive, makes the laptop slightly less than portable. It's a trade-off.

✓ If your laptop lacks an optical drive, you can buy an external USB drive as an alternative. Yes, this strategy adds weight. But if you're like me, you don't need to take your laptop everywhere with you. Or, if you need it on a trip, toss it in your luggage. (Well, toss it *gently*.)

✓ A DVD drive can read CDs. You don't need two separate drives.

✓ You may not need a recordable optical drive. That's one place you can save money. If you don't need to burn discs on the road, all you need is a standard optical drive.

Your knees are alive with The Sound of Music

Laptops almost always come with the cheapest, worst, tiny stereo speakers. Ugh. Fortunately, your laptop may have a headphone jack. It may also have a microphone jack. Remember to check for those items because not every laptop has them. The tinny speakers? Oh, laptops have —'em in spades!

When sound is important to you, look into a laptop that offers decent sound hardware. One way to tell is to see whether the laptop has digital audio output. Don't despair when you can't find anything, though. You can add PC Card sound adapters to your laptop or add USB sound solutions, like the Creative Sound Blaster Audigy.

Communications choices

Your laptop computer must have gizmos that quench its communications thirst. This includes several, if not all, of the following gizmos:

Modem: It's the traditional telecommunications device, not a broadband or satellite modem. Laptops come with a dial-up modem. Discover how to use it in Chapter 13.

Networking: As with desktops, every laptop comes with a standard networking hole, called an Ethernet port by people who play *For Dummies Computer Trivia.* General networking information is found in Chapter 11.

Wireless networking: It's a given that your laptop must come with some type of wireless Ethernet adapter. If not, you can add a wireless networking adapter by using a USB or PC Card adapter, but it's not something you should neglect! The current wireless networking standard is 802.11g or 802.11n. You can read more about that topic in Chapter 11.

Infrared communications: Granted, this option isn't as popular as it once was. Come to think of it, the infrared option wasn't ever popular, but it was available on many laptops as a way to communicate with desktops — or to change channels on the TV.

Energy management hardware

Although desktop computers come with some energy management features — the ability to suspend or sleep the computer, or the "hibernate" option — these features are far more necessary on laptops. Primarily, energy management on the laptop is concerned with controlling the power drain on the battery.

Ensure that your future laptop has the ability to merely sip power when necessary. Chapter 9 has more information on various tricks to make this happen, but it helps to look for this ability in your laptop before you buy.

When power is really important to you, consider getting one of the power-miser or "mobile" processors, as opposed to a high-speed, top-of-the-line model. This option saves a tad on battery life, but keep in mind that a high-end processor works better for extending the laptop's lifespan.

Docking stations and port replicators

One optional item you can purchase for your laptop is the docking station or port replicator. Despite these items being optional, I highly recommend them.

Port replicator: A port replicator may be nothing more than an extra attachment that plugs in to a special expansion jack (or hole) on a laptop. The port replicator then lets you plug in standard desktop peripherals to the laptop, such as an older printer or serial device.

Docking station: Docking stations are more sophisticated than port replicators. They offer all the connections found on port replicators and include such items as extra memory, optional expansion cards, and other desktop-like features. Docking stations are more expensive than port replicators — and smell better.

The docking station or port replicator serves as a base for your laptop when it's not on the road. In fact, you can keep the full-size keyboard and monitor connected to the docking station or port replicator and just pop off the laptop when you're ready to go on the road.

Service, Support, and Warranty

The issue of service and support is much more important for a laptop than for a desktop computer. A laptop is a unit. It lacks the components of a desktop. As such, it's not an item anyone can fix. Off-the-shelf replacement parts just can't be found in the Nerd Bin at Fry's Electronics.

Determine where your laptop will be repaired. Odds are really good that it won't be in the back room at the local MegaPrice where you purchased the thing. The laptop will probably take a trip through the mail. If that's not what you want, ensure that you get an on-site support option when you buy the laptop. (Yes, some manufacturers offer that service.)

Research how the support for your laptop is offered. Most manufacturers offer phone support. Is it good? Terrible? In English? Maybe a superior support option is available for an extra price. If you need it, consider buying that type of support with the laptop.

Finally, definitely get a long-term warranty with your laptop. Most manufacturers offer a standard one-year warranty — I recommend at least a three-year warranty. That's because when the laptop breaks, generally it's the *entire unit* that must be replaced. That's not cheap!

✔ Some manufacturers offer you a replacement laptop while yours is being fixed by way of mail-in service. That's a bonus.

✔ A lack of service and support is one reason that some dealers (and large department stores and discount houses) offer laptops at ridiculously cheap prices. Don't ever expect the employees in such a place to be able to help you, and the guy who cuts meat in the back can't fix your laptop, either.

✔ Avoid the service contract! It's not the same thing as a warranty. A service contract is basically a way for your dealer to make *even more* money from suckers. The extended warranty that I recommend you purchase will cover your laptop just fine and dandy. Don't get a service contract. It's a pure waste of money.

The Final Step: Buying Your Laptop

When you're ready to buy your laptop, buy it!

Don't sit and wait for a better deal or a lower price. That's because you can *always* find a better deal and a lower price. Hardware gets better and better. The price always comes down. Therefore, when you're ready to buy, take the plunge and buy! Waiting gets you nowhere.

✔ If possible, pay for your laptop by using a credit card. The law offers far more protection to credit card users than to people who pay by check or — don't even think about it — cash.

✔ When you're buying from the Internet or some other nonlocal dealer, verify that it doesn't charge your credit card until the order ships. This is standard practice, but some dealers apparently haven't gotten the word yet.

Part II
Discover Your Laptop

The 5th Wave
By Rich Tennant

"You can lay on it if you want, but my channeling energy through your body's chakras isn't going to increase your laptop's battery life."

In this part . . .

It's a strange new creature. We treat it with awe and reverence, plus a little delight. Just look at it and admire the beauty, and merry yourself over the thoughtfulness of its design. Then sit back in eager anticipation of its potential and the wondrous things it can accomplish. But enough about babies — this book is about laptop computers.

This part of the book answers the question "You have your laptop — now what do you do?" The chapters here provide a general introduction to your laptop and its features, plus important stuff you need to know and remember. Because laptops don't come with manuals or getting-started booklets any more, consider the chapters in this part as your handy laptop-survival guide.

Chapter 3

Out of the Box and into Your Lap

In This Chapter

▶ Unpacking the laptop

▶ Knowing what to keep and what to throw away

▶ Setting up your laptop

▶ Finding a place to put your laptop

▶ Plugging it in

▶ Using an uninterruptible power supply (or not)

*L*aptop manufacturers have consulted with leading physicists, and the answer always comes back the same: You cannot make a box smaller than the laptop it contains. No matter how slender and lithe, your laptop will most likely arrive inside a box the size of a doghouse. Relax: It's almost all padding. That protective polymer padding is designed to shield your laptop from the brutality of our modern-day package delivery system. But there's more in that laptop box than your new portable computer and a multitude of foam peanuts.

Opening the laptop box is the first step you take on your long portable-computing journey. The second step, however, remains a mystery. Long gone are the days when any computer came with a fat manual, a getting-started booklet, or even a foldout roadmap showing how to hook things up. Oh, those items might be in the box, and other helpful goodies may be nestled betwixt the foam and cardboard. How do you know what's what? Why, may I present this handy chapter, specifically designed to help your laptop make it out of the box and into your lap?

Box Unpacking 101

Watching my late grandmother open gifts was an exercise in patience. She carefully plowed the seams on the wrapping, deftly slicing through the Scotch tape with her finger. The festive paper was removed intact, with far more care than it was applied. Having lived through the experience of the

Great Depression, Grandma would save the paper wrapping, folding it up and setting it aside for use again later. It drove us grandkids nuts!

Later generations understood that there's no point in being polite or patient when opening anything. Removing wrapping has such a speed these days that it makes me wonder whether future generations will even bother to wrap anything. But I digress.

There's no point in my telling you how to open the box your laptop comes in. Odds are pretty good that anyone able to read this book has mastered his or her box-opening skills. Despite that guess, here are some tips I have gathered specifically for opening that cardboard contraption containing your laptop:

✔ If you see instructions on how to unpack the box, heed them! I refer specifically to labels like "Open other side" or "Remove first."

✔ Be sure to open and free the packing slip (if any) attached to the outside of the box. The slip contains the shipping invoice, which you should look over to confirm that what was shipped is exactly what you ordered. (The invoice might be inside the box.)

✔ Be sure to look for boxes within boxes. Also be on the lookout for items stuck in the sides or ends of the foam packing material.

✔ Do not eat the foam packing material. When people say that rice cakes taste like foam packing material, they're being facetious.

✔ Don't fill out any warranty or registration cards until you're certain that the laptop works.

✔ Always open computer equipment boxes with your hands. Never use a box cutter, because you can slice into something important.

✔ Beware of those big, ugly staples often used to close cardboard boxes. They can go a-flyin' when you rip things open, poking out eyeballs or just lying in wait on the floor for a bare foot to stomp on by.

Making piles for the various items in the box

Laptops, like all computers, come with lots of bits and pieces. Some of that stuff isn't junk, and you want to keep it for as long as you own the laptop. Other stuff is junk, and you can throw it away. The problem: It's difficult to determine what's worth keeping and what to toss. My advice is to keep everything for now. I suggest creating piles for the stuff that comes with the laptop.

Here's a handy way to approach this unpacking and pre-setup stage of your laptop's introduction to your lap:

1. **Unpack the laptop.**

   Remove the laptop from any plastic bag or shrink-wrap. Don't worry about opening the laptop's lid yet (though the temptation may be great). Just set the thing on a table by itself. When you do this, say "There."

2. **Find all the various hardware pieces that came with the laptop.**

   Look for the power adapter, power cord, battery, extra batteries, phone cord, adapters, cables, connectors, weird, tiny gizmos that you'll probably lose eventually, and other mystery chunks and nuggets.

3. **Make a pile for any optical discs that came with the laptop.**

   Some laptops come with discs; most don't. The discs may contain programs that are already installed or ready for installation. Some discs might contain *device drivers* or special software required to run your laptop's hardware. Plus, you may see an operating system disc or system recovery disc. All these discs are important!

4. **Make a pile for all the paperwork.**

   There are four categories of paperwork: manuals, warranties, special offers, and weird pieces of paper, the importance of which cannot be determined.

5. **Place all packing material back into the box.**

   This material includes plastic bags, twist-ties from the cables, and those silica pouches they tell you not to eat (probably because the stuff inside would give you superhuman powers).

Later, after your laptop is all set up and you're starting to get familiar with it, you can further organize the detritus from the box. As you work, you need to keep various items with the laptop at all times — for example, the power cord, extra batteries, and other objects, depending on how you use the laptop. You need a place, such as a laptop case, for those items.

Other stuff that came with your laptop you might want to keep for a while, such as the discs and any manuals. Those things don't need to stay with the laptop all the time, so setting them in a drawer or on a shelf is okay.

Only after using the laptop for a while should you consider throwing some stuff away, such as the special-offer cards you don't use. Often times, you can just toss those things in the laptop box. See the next section to find out what to do with the box.

- ✔ If the laptop came with a how-to manual, consider yourself lucky. Most laptops don't come with any how-to material whatsoever.

- ✔ Sometimes, the only manuals that come with the laptop are directories listing the locations where you can get it fixed.

✔ Software discs are included even though the software may already be installed on the laptop. Don't toss away the discs! They were given to you so that you can reinstall the software if you need to.

✔ See Chapter 17 for information on finding the best laptop case. Even though your laptop may have come with a genuine imitation-leatherette case, you want to see what else is out there.

✔ I have a shelf in my office where I keep containers for each computer I own. The container holds all the stuff included with the computer that I want to keep: spare parts and the manuals and other documentation. I suggest that you have a similar shelf or location for a container or special box for your laptop's extra stuff.

"How long should I keep the box?"

I recommend keeping the box and the packing material for as long as you own the laptop. That way, if you need to ship the laptop to a repair center or return it to the dealer, you have the original box.

When the laptop dies, you can then bury it in its original box and throw them both out at the same time.

✔ Many dealers and repair centers don't accept a laptop unless it's packed in its original box.

✔ If you don't have the original box, you can order another one — but why pay for that when you can just save the original?

✔ Note that many communities have disposal standards for electronic equipment, such as laptops. Check with your municipal refuse-disposal people before blithely throwing a laptop in the trash.

✔ No, you don't need to pack the laptop in a box when you take it on the road; slipping the laptop into a briefcase or any quality carrying case is fine for that. You need the boxes only if you plan to mail or ship the laptop.

Knowing when to send in the warranty

Wait a week to ensure that the laptop works and that you have everything you ordered. When you're satisfied, fill out and send in the warranty card.

Often times, when you order a computer directly from the manufacturer, you don't need to fill in and return a warranty card.

In some cases, filling out and returning the warranty card sets the start date for the warranty period. Otherwise, the warranty may start on the day the laptop was manufactured, which could have been three months ago! Read the card to be sure.

Setting Up Your Laptop

Features vary from laptop to laptop: Not every laptop has the same keyboard layout; the optical drive may eject forward or to the left or right, or it might not even exist; connectors and holes may be on the sides or back or both. The power button? Well, it could be *anywhere!*

Beyond the differences, if you squint your eyes tightly enough, all laptop computers look basically the same. The setup for each one is similar, so this section addresses issues that are the same for all laptop owners.

When you find any specific instructions regarding setup inside the laptop box or — should you be so lucky — if you find a manual, heed its instructions first. Then look back here for a gentle review.

Find a place for the laptop

Yes, you can put the laptop in your lap. But what happens to your lap when you stand up?

Ah-ha!

Unlike a desktop PC, a laptop can go anywhere or be put anywhere. No wonder they're popular! With a fully charged battery, your laptop has a home wherever you are. Beyond that, you can place your laptop anywhere you like: on the kitchen table, the coffee table, a real desk, or a computer desk or in bed with you.

Here are some general laptop-location tips:

- ✔ Use the laptop on a flat, steady surface.
- ✔ Keep the laptop away from the sun, if possible. Heat isn't good for any computer, and you can't see the screen in direct sunlight (or else you'll waste battery power turning up the screen brightness level).
- ✔ Likewise, use your laptop in a well-ventilated area. Don't cover the laptop while it's on.
- ✔ Keep Mr. Laptop away from, or out of spilling range of, any drinks or food you might be consuming.

✔ If possible, try to find a place to plug in the laptop while you use it.

✔ Have a place to store your laptop when it's not in use: in a drawer or on a shelf. Keeping it in the same place means that you can always find it when you need it.

✔ When the laptop has a docking station or port replicator, try to keep that part in the same place all the time. Set up a desk and put the docking station or port replicator in one spot. You might also keep various peripherals — such as a printer, big keyboard, mouse, full-size monitor, scanner, and other toys — ready to go and plugged in. Call this location your Laptop Shrine.

✔ Although you can use the laptop anywhere, be aware of ergonomics! For example, when you're using the laptop on a coffee table, if you start to feel a pain in your back from hunching over, stop! Find a better, more comfortable place to work.

Charge the battery!

When you choose your laptop's final resting place — even if it's final only until you find a new resting place — plug it in, as illustrated in Figure 3-1.

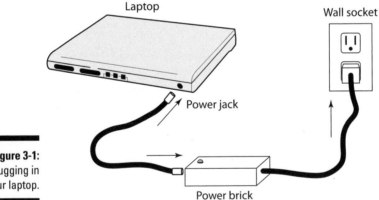

Figure 3-1:
Plugging in
your laptop.

Attach the power cord to the laptop's back or side: The power cord connector may be color-coded yellow; the yellow hole is where the power cord plugs in.

Attach the power cord to the power brick, if necessary. Plug the power brick into the wall. Note that the power brick may also contain the plug that connects directly to the wall.

That's it. The laptop is now ready for use.

- ✔ Plugging in the laptop automatically charges the battery. Even if you're unsure whether the battery has a charge (and it probably doesn't), follow the preceding steps.

- ✔ Each laptop has a different method for inserting, installing, or attaching the battery. Clues can be found on the laptop's case or on the battery itself. You might even find an instruction sheet, but don't count on it.

- ✔ It usually takes a few hours to charge a laptop's battery. The length of time depends on the type of battery and power management hardware and on whether you're using the laptop at the time. The good news is that you can start using your laptop right away, just keep it plugged in so that the battery can charge.

- ✔ Refer to Chapter 9 for more information on using the laptop's battery and power-management system.

"Should I plug the laptop into a UPS?"

I advise my desktop computer readers in *PCs For Dummies* (Wiley Publishing, Inc.) to consider investing in an uninterruptible power supply, or a UPS — specifically, one with both surge and spike protection. This device serves to protect the computer from nasty things that can come through the power lines as well as to provide emergency power if the electricity goes bye-bye.

A UPS for a laptop is unnecessary. The main reason is that your laptop already has a battery for backup power. If you're running your laptop from an electrical outlet and the electricity goes off (or some doofus unplugs it), the laptop quickly and happily switches its power source over to the internal battery. Nothing is lost!

- ✔ Although you don't need a UPS for your laptop, I still highly recommend plugging your portable 'puter into a power strip with surge protection and line filtering. Such a gizmo helps keep the power your laptop uses clean and steady.

- ✔ Generally speaking, if there's a lightning storm nearby, don't plug your laptop (power or modem cord) into the wall unless you're using a spike protection filter. If not, just run the laptop from its battery until the storm passes.

Figuring Out What to Do Next

My guess is that after setting up your laptop, you'll want to turn it on and see how it works. That's covered in Chapter 4, which also contains details on using the Windows operating system on a laptop. That chapter also describes the many different ways to turn off your laptop computer — which can be confusing if you've never used a battery-powered computer.

On the subject of batteries, I also recommend that you read Chapter 9 to bone up on how to treat your laptop's battery in a fair and just manner.

And, before taking your laptop on the road, read Chapter 17, which covers a few nifty things you might want to consider before you venture out into the cold, cruel world with your new computer companion.

Chapter 4

The Chapter about Turning a Laptop On and Off

In This Chapter

▶ Turning on the laptop

▶ Finding the power button

▶ Logging in to Windows

▶ Shutting down the laptop

▶ Putting the laptop into Sleep mode

▶ Hibernating the laptop

▶ Dealing with shutdown issues

▶ Changing the power button's function

A re you old enough to remember when electronic gizmos came with *real* On–Off switches? If so, you're probably *really* old. Back in the days when PCs were called *microcomputers,* they truly did sport an On–Off switch, as did your TV, dishwasher, and maybe even your car. Today, things are on all the time. What was once the On–Off switch is now dubbed a *power button.* Sure, it turns the thing on, but does it actually turn it off? That's why I need a whole chapter to explain the concept.

Turning On a Laptop

Despite having only three seconds of memory, a goldfish can be trained to turn on a laptop computer: Just push the power button. The only thing that prevents legions of goldfish from escaping the confines of their aquariums and powering up laptops across the globe is that it takes considerably longer than three seconds to even *find* the power button on most laptops. May the hunt begin!

It's a *power button,* not an On–Off switch.

Open the lid

Believe it or not, the laptop must be in an open position for you to use it. It's difficult to see the screen and nearly impossible to use the keyboard with the lid closed. Many have tried. They all have failed and, after giving up in frustration, returned the laptop to the store and written the whole thing off as a high-tech folly.

Here's the catch: The lid has a catch, or possibly two! The catch is either a button that you push in or a little slider that you push sideways to release the lid. After you release the catch (or catches), the laptop's lid pops up slightly. You can then raise it to an angle best suited for viewing; use Figures 4-1 and 4-2 as your guide.

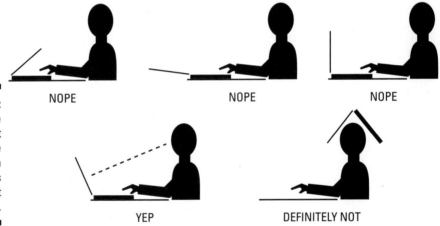

Figure 4-1: Adjust the lid so that you view the screen at an angle that's just right for you.

NOPE   NOPE   NOPE

YEP   DEFINITELY NOT

✔ The front side of the laptop is the side away from the lid's hinge.

✔ It's possible to configure the laptop to be on without opening the lid — for example, when you're using a docking station or an external monitor. See Chapter 10 for the details.

✔ Some laptops allow you to play a music CD when the lid is closed and even sport special buttons to control the CD player.

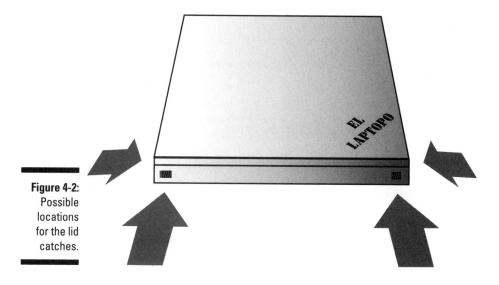

Figure 4-2:
Possible
locations
for the lid
catches.

"Where's the power button?"

Laptop designers have grown adept at hiding or masking the power button. The most recent trend is to put the power button under the laptop's lid; you must open the laptop to find and press the power button, turning the laptop on.

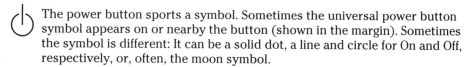 The power button sports a symbol. Sometimes the universal power button symbol appears on or nearby the button (shown in the margin). Sometimes the symbol is different: It can be a solid dot, a line and circle for On and Off, respectively, or, often, the moon symbol.

✔ That rare laptop may have the power button along one of the laptop's sides: front, left, right, or back.

✔ The power button may be a spring-slide switch that you must push in one direction and then release.

✔ Some power buttons are tiny push buttons, or what I call *pray-and-press* buttons. There's no click or bump to the button's feel; you just press it in with your finger and pray that the laptop obeys you.

✔ On a Tablet PC, the power button is most likely located on the monitor. That way, it can be accessed when the monitor is folded flat, when the laptop is in "tablet" mode. In that case, look for a special power-button lock. The lock prevents the power button from being punched accidentally when the tablet laptop is in full Tablet mode.

✔ On some laptops there is both a power button and a moon button. In that caste, the moon button is the *sleep* button.

✔ You can put a red-dot sticker near the power button's location, in case the button is easy to overlook. Even so, I find that after opening the case and turning the system on a few times, I remember where the button is. Of course, this doesn't help you use anyone else's laptop, because the power button is never in the same location twice.

Punch the power button

To turn on your laptop, press the power button.

Sometimes you can turn on the laptop by opening the lid. Sometimes you can *wake up* a laptop by tapping a key on the keyboard. Whether those tricks work depends on how the laptop was shut down. But for all intents and purposes, punching the power button does the job most of the time.

✔ Refer to the previous sections if you need help finding the power button.

✔ If nothing happens when you punch the button, the battery is most likely dead: Plug the laptop into a wall socket by using its AC adapter cord (or module or power-brick thing).

✔ Be sure to check all the power cables! The power brick may wiggle loose from the wall socket cable.

✔ When everything is plugged in and nothing happens, you have a problem. Contact your dealer or laptop manufacturer for assistance.

Nerdy terms for starting a computer

Despite years of effort to come up with better words, the computer industry continues to use antique and obscure jargon to say "starting a computer." Among the lingo, you will find

Boot: The oldest and most mysterious computer term; it basically means to turn the thing on, or to "pull it up by its bootstraps." In fact, *boot-strap* is an even older version of this term.

Cold boot: To turn the computer on when it has been off for a while. See *warm boot.*

Cycle power: To turn the computer off, wait a few seconds, and then turn it on again. This process is often required when you're trying to fix something.

Das Boot: Not a computer term at all, but rather the title of a German film about a U-boat in World War II.

Power up / power on: More human terms for turning the computer on.

Restart / reboot / reset: To shut down a computer and then start it up again without turning off the power.

Start / turn on / switch on: Again, more human terms for turning the computer on.

Warm boot: Another term for a restart, reboot, or reset.

It's Windows!

When your laptop starts up, you see some initial messages and perhaps a logo or graphic, and then the computer's operating system — its main program — comes to life. For PC laptops, this program is Windows.

The version of Windows used on laptops is identical to the one used on desktop computers. Some extra options are included for laptops, specifically for power management and battery monitoring. Plus, some other utilities and fun junk may have been installed by the laptop manufacturer. Otherwise, it's the same Windows you know and hate.

- ✔ This book covers Windows Vista.

- ✔ Chapter 6 covers a few of the places in Windows that laptop computer owners should be familiar with.

- ✔ Some messages may appear before Windows starts, especially when the laptop was improperly shut down or the laptop's battery expired the last time you used it. These messages are expected as the laptop recovers from mishaps and improper shutdowns.

- ✔ For more information on Windows, visit a bookstore near you and purchase a good Windows book. If you enjoy reading my stuff, check out *Find Gold in Windows Vista* (Wiley Publishing).

The laptop's Setup program

All modern PCs, laptops included, have a *Setup program*. This program isn't a part of your computer's operating system (Windows). Instead, Setup is built in to the computer's circuitry, or *chipset*, and it might also be referred to as the *BIOS Setup program*.

What the Setup program does is configure your laptop's hardware. It keeps track of such things as how much memory (RAM) is installed, the type of hard drive, whether the laptop has an optical drive, plus other hardware settings and options.

Be sure that you know how to open your laptop's Setup program. The method used to access it differs from computer to computer. Commonly, to open the Setup program, you press a specific key or key combination on the keyboard when the computer first starts (and before Windows starts). On most laptops, the special key is Del or F1. If your laptop uses a different key, be sure to make a note of it on this book's Cheat Sheet.

One important category in the Setup program is security — specifically, the startup password option. I don't recommend setting that password when you're just getting used to your laptop). Instead, see Chapter 18, which covers laptop security, for more information.

Windows for the first time

When you first turn on a brand-new laptop, Windows goes through some gyrations and prompts you to set up Windows on your computer. Yes, Windows is installed. You just need to finish the job.

Various questions are asked. They aren't trivia questions such as "What was the name of Woodrow Wilson's dog." Nope, they're customization questions, such as which language you use, the time zone you live in, and so on. You also create a *user profile* for yourself, which includes an account name and a password.

After you answer the questions, Windows is fully installed. More configuration may be necessary, such as networking options and customizing the desktop. You can mess with these options later.

✔ When you're asked to create user accounts, just create one for yourself. Don't bother creating one yet for each member of the whole fam-damily as well as your pets. You can do that later, and then only when other people *really* need to use the computer.

✔ The main Windows account is known as *Administrator.* That account is the one used to modify the computer, add new software, and do other administrative chores. Even when you don't intend it, when you're the only person using the computer, *you* are the administrator.

✔ Do not forget the administrator's password! Refer to the nearby "Passwords, passwords, passwords" sidebar for more information.

✔ Entering an organization name is optional, though it's fun to specify fictitious organizations or something juvenile, like Central Intelligence Agency.

Logging in to Windows

After the initial setup, and every time you start your laptop after that, you're greeted with the graphical fun and folly of the Windows operating system.

The first step is to log in to windows. *Log in* is computer jargon for identifying yourself to the warden, er, to Windows. It involves supplying a user account name and a password to verify that you are who you claim to be.

If you're the only person using your computer, the login screen appears with your account picture on it, as shown in Figure 4-3. Type your password in the box. Press the Enter key. When the stars are aligned in your favor, you're granted access to Windows.

Figure 4-3:
The main
Windows
Vista login
screen.

For other ways to log in to Windows, read the following section.

- ✔ The term *log on* means to identify yourself. A *logon* is the name of your account or the word you use to log on.

- ✔ The terms *log in* and *login* can be used instead of *log on* and *logon*. They did that just to keep you confused.

- ✔ By the way, it's *log,* as in *to write down.* It has nothing to do with timber.

Other ways to log in to Windows

On laptops with multiple accounts, you have to choose your account name and then enter the password before you can behold the glory that is Windows. Multiple accounts appear when Windows first starts, each identified by the account picture, as shown in Figure 4-4.

To choose an account, click on it with the mouse. You then see a login screen (refer to Figure 4-3) where you type your account's password.

Figure 4-4:
Choosing
a specific
account for
logging in.

Perhaps the most nifty way to log in to a laptop is by using your thumb. Some laptop models sport a fingerprint reader right next to the keyboard. On Tablet PCs, the fingerprint reader is near the monitor. Simply swipe the proper finger across the reader to log in; no need to type anything.

- ✔ When your laptop lacks a fingerprint reader, you can buy a handy, external, USB fingerprint reader.

- ✔ All fingerprint readers must be trained. After you initially set up Windows, software specific to your laptop's fingerprint reader is used to configure the thing. Configuration must be done before you can use the fingerprint reader to log in to your laptop. It also sets which finger is the "proper" one to use as a login ID.

- ✔ Yes, the fingerprint reader works whether your finger is attached or not. And, yes, you watch too many spy movies.

- ✔ On some laptops, the ability to log in using a fingerprint reader is obvious at the logon screen: you see a Fingerprint Login or similar icon or a message prompting you to swipe your finger.

- ✔ A fingerprint reader is a *biometric* device.

Passwords, passwords, passwords

Passwords seem to be everywhere these days. Yep, it's all part of computer security. Although passwords may have been optional in the past, they are no more.

On your laptop, Windows requires that you have a password on your main account. Yes, it might be optional, but for a laptop computer I highly recommend that you not only use a password but also chose one that's an effective, *strong* password.

Of course, the natural problem with passwords is that people forget them. So, the idea is to do two things: First, choose a password that you can easily remember, and second, write down that password in an obvious location but in a secure manner. It's called "concealed in plain sight."

For example, a good password contains a combination of numbers and letters. For example, if you once lived at 4870 Elsa Road, `elsa4870` is a suitable password. Capitalizing one of the letters makes the password stronger: `elSa4870`. Making it longer makes it stronger still: `elSa4870road`.

Another technique is to use two obnoxiously unrelated words and connect them with a number, such as `stinky7teetH` or `pirate3Diaper`.

When you have a good password, write it down in a handy, obvious place. Just write it in a manner that doesn't say "My password is." For example, write the password on a recipe card or in your address book or portfolio. Stick it in a list of otherwise innocent information, a place where you can recognize it but a snoop would easily miss it.

See Chapter 18 for more information on passwords and Windows security issues.

Behold the desktop

Eventually the Windows desktop appears on your laptop's screen, similar to what you see in Figure 4-5. Note the important items that are called out in the figure.

Here's what you need to find:

- ✔ **The desktop:** This area is the starting point for all your adventures in Windows. The main screen. Home plate.

- ✔ **Wallpaper or background:** The desktop is the image you see on the desktop, or it may be just a solid color. The desktop background, also known as *wallpaper,* is optional and can be changed by using the Windows Control Panel. (More on that in Chapter 6.)

- ✔ **Icons:** These tiny pictures represent files, folders, or programs inside Windows.

✔ **Sidebar:** This area contains small icons or *gadgets* that serve to distract you from getting work done.

✔ **The Start button:** This button is the main control on the desktop. Clicking the Start button pops up a menu that contains options for controlling the computer or for starting programs.

✔ **The taskbar:** This doohickey displays a host of buttons used to switch between windows and programs that are open on the desktop.

✔ **The notification area:** This annoying little thing contains teensy icons that pester you with pop-up balloons from time to time. The icons can also help you do things or monitor events, plus show the date and time.

Take a moment to find each of those items on your laptop screen right now. Don't touch the display to point them out! Just find them and point (and maybe even say "Oh, there it is!").

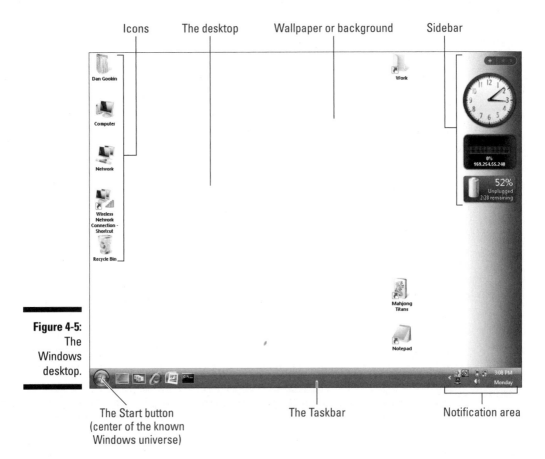

Figure 4-5:
The
Windows
desktop.

Various Options for Turning Off (or Not) the Laptop

There are scant questions regarding turning on a laptop. On the other hand, there are a multitude of questions about turning the thing off. It's not an unanswerable puzzle, like the existence of the afterlife or whether the cat really wants to go outside, but it is a question worth looking into.

Properly shutting down your laptop

Here are the not-so-obvious steps you need to take to properly shut down Windows and turn off your laptop when you're done for the day:

1. **Save your work and close all your programs.**

   The generic Save command is Ctrl+S. The command to close most windows is Ctrl+W, although often the weirdly obscure Alt+F4 is needed.

2. **Click the Start button.**

   Up pops the Start menu thing.

3. **Click the right-pointing triangle next to the Padlock icon.**

   A pop-up menu appears with various shutdown options, as shown in Figure 4-6.

Figure 4-6:
Shutdown
options on
the Start
menu.

Switch User
Log Off
Lock
Restart
Sleep
Hibernate
Shut Down

4. **Choose the Shut Down menu item.**

   The laptop turns itself off.

Yes, that's correct: The laptop turns itself off. When the screen goes dark and the power lamp is dimmed, you can shut the laptop's lid and put away the laptop.

When you still have unsaved files, first, you didn't follow all the instructions, and second, you have an opportunity to save them before the laptop shuts down.

 Windows may have updates to install. If so, note the little Shield icon over the software power button on the Start menu (see the margin). In that case, the software updates are installed as the laptop shuts down. (They might continue to be installed when the laptop starts up again.)

"I need to restart Windows"

Occasionally, you're directed to reset the laptop, which is often referred to as "restarting Windows." To do so, heed these steps:

1. **Save your work and close all your programs.**
2. **Click the Start button.**
3. **Click the triangle next to the Padlock icon and choose Restart from the pop-up menu.**

    Refer to Figure 4-6 if you need help locating the pop-up menu.

After you choose the Restart command, the laptop seems to be turning itself off, but just before it does, it starts right back up again.

Sometimes, restarting Windows happens automatically, such as when installing some software, adding some hardware helpers called *device drivers*, or when performing Windows Updates. You're generally given a choice: "Would you like to restart Windows now?" If so, click the Yes button, and things happen automatically. When the process stalls, such as when you have an open and (gasp!) unsaved document, you have to interrupt your work or play, take care of business, and then manually restart Windows according to the preceding steps.

The bliss of Sleep mode

All laptops have a special low-power mode. In this mode, the computer is still on but power to certain areas is shut off. That way, you can keep the laptop ready for an extended period without wasting battery juice. This low-power mode is officially called *hybrid sleep,* but everyone calls it Sleep mode.

Your laptop can slumber in Sleep mode for quite some time, much longer than it would otherwise stay alive when it's turned on. The amount of time the laptop stays in Sleep mode depends on various power settings in

Windows. You can direct Windows to sleep for maybe 30 minutes and then have the laptop automatically turn itself off or switch into Hibernation mode (covered later in this chapter).

The method for putting your laptop to sleep varies; the following sections describe the details.

> ✔ There's no need to be quiet while your laptop is sleeping.
>
> ✔ The moon lamp might be on when the laptop is in Sleep mode. See Chapter 5 for information on this light and others on your laptop.
>
> ✔ I recommend that you save your work before your laptop enters Sleep mode, just in case.
>
> ✔ If you're going to quit all your programs before putting your laptop into Sleep mode, just shut down the laptop instead. Honestly, the laptop mysteriously benefits from being turned off every once in a while.
>
> ✔ See Chapter 9 for information on checking how much charge is left in your laptop's battery.
>
> ✔ The laptop may beep just before it goes to sleep. That's okay.

Putting your laptop to sleep by pressing the sleep button

When your laptop is blessed with a sleep button, pressing it puts the laptop to sleep instantly. But, hang on! The sleep button's function can be changed, so pressing that button may not always put the laptop to sleep. Before you use this method, see the section "Various Options for Turning Off (or Not) the Laptop," earlier in this chapter.

Putting your laptop to sleep by using the Shutdown menu

One of the items on the Shutdown menu (refer to Figure 4-6) is Sleep. To use it, heed these steps:

1. **Click the Start button.**

2. **Click the triangle next to the Padlock icon.**

3. **Choose Sleep from the pop-up menu.**

Waking up from Sleep mode

To revive a snoozing laptop, simply press a key on the keyboard or tap on the mouse pad. That wakes the sucker up, bringing it back to active duty.

If the laptop is conditioned to sleep when you close its lid, opening the lid wakes it up.

If the laptop still doesn't rouse itself, press the power button.

It just goes to sleep by itself!

Windows configures itself so that the laptop automatically goes into Sleep mode after a spell. An activity timer keeps track of what the laptop is doing. When there hasn't been any keyboard or mouse activity for a set amount of time, the laptop automatically goes to sleep. (The time interval can be adjusted.) The idea here is to save power; when the computer thinks that you're bored or off for a walk (or dead), it slips off to sleep to conserve power.

The Power Options icon in the Control Panel sets the inactivity timer value. See Chapter 9 for the details.

After waking up the laptop, you may have to log in to Windows again. That's okay — in fact, it's what you want; it's unsafe not to have the Windows logon screen appear when the laptop wakes up from Sleep mode. (See Chapter 18 for more information on laptop security.)

✔ I generally push the Ctrl key on the keyboard to wake up my sleeping laptop.

✔ One reason a laptop may not wake up is that the battery is probably dead. Check the laptop's power-on lights. If they're off, the battery is dead. Plug in the laptop and try again.

✔ If the laptop still doesn't wake up, you may have a problem with the system's power management software. Try pressing (and holding) the power button until the unit turns either off or on again. Then try starting up the laptop as you normally do. Ask your dealer or laptop manufacturer for updated power management software.

Better than sleep is hibernation

One power management feature that's sadly often ignored, despite its great benefits, is hibernation. When you *hibernate* a laptop, you're essentially turning it off. So, unlike in Sleep mode, a hibernated laptop isn't using any battery power — that laptop is off!

The secret behind hibernation is that before you turn off the laptop, everything you're doing with the computer is saved; the entire contents of memory are saved to the hard drive. When the computer is turned on again, it recovers from hibernating by reloading all the saved information and restoring your laptop to exactly the same condition it was in before it was hibernated.

Before you use hibernation, determine whether it's activated: Look for the word *Hibernate* on the Shutdown menu (refer to Figure 4-6). If you don't see that option, you can assign the Hibernate function to one of the laptop's power buttons. See the later section "Power Button, What's Your Function?" for details.

When Hibernation is available on the Shutdown menu, hibernate the laptop by choosing that option. The laptop saves everything in memory to disk and then turns itself off.

To recover from Hibernation mode, turn the laptop on, although in some cases the laptop may recover from hibernation when you press a key or touch the mouse pad. I generally try that trick first, before I punch the power button.

- ✔ I prefer to put my laptop into hibernation when I know that I won't be using it for longer than a half-hour or so.

- ✔ Hibernation saves power because it actually turns the laptop off. Sleep mode, however, is faster when you need to use the laptop quickly.

- ✔ Unlike when you put your laptop in Sleep mode, you can leave your laptop in a hibernated state for as long as you want. Even if the batteries eventually drain, the system returns to where you left it after the computer is plugged in and started again.

- ✔ You can set up the laptop to automatically hibernate when the battery power gets way too low. See Chapter 9.

- ✔ Note that Hibernation mode requires hard drive space. When hard drive space runs low, it's possible that Hibernation mode won't work. Be aware of that.

The software power button

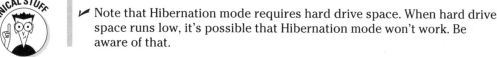

Windows features a *software* power button. It exists on the bottom of the Start menu, right next to the Padlock icon and the Shutdown pop-up menu. When you click this button, it instantly shuts down the laptop. Or, it tosses the laptop into Hibernation or Sleep mode. Yes, the button has multiple personalities.

To find out what the button does, just point the mouse at it and wait. A pop-up balloon describes the button's current mode of operation. Otherwise, you can set the button's function manually. See the later section "Controlling the software power button" for details.

Logging off

One not-quite-shutdown option for Windows is to *log off.* What that does is end your computer session without turning off the computer or restarting it.

To log off, choose the option Log Off from the Shutdown menu (refer to Figure 4-6). Windows begs you to save any unsaved documents, and then it proceeds just like it's shutting down Windows. Eventually you find yourself back at the main logon screen (refer to Figure 4-3).

✔ By the way, you can use the little Power button on the main logon screen to turn off your computer: Clicking that Power button displays a pop-up list of options, including Restart, Sleep, and Shut Down.

✔ Another option you can choose instead of Log Off is Switch User. Again, choosing that option is done primarily so that someone else can use the computer. But with Switch User, you can keep your programs and documents open until you switch back.

✔ Logging off exists as an option for when folks with other accounts want to use the computer. Because most laptops are single-user PCs, logging off is rarely necessary.

Locking Windows

The final thing of the gazillion things that you can do to end your Windows day is to lock the computer. By locking the computer, you present yourself with the Logon screen (refer to Figure 4-3 or Figure 4-4). That's a handy way to keep out prying eyes and fingers when you're away for a spell.

You can summon the Lock command from the Start menu's shutdown menu (refer to Figure 4-6). Or, you can click on the Lock icon on the Start menu (shown in the margin) to lock the computer. Or, if you're not overwhelmed with options yet, you can press Win+L on the keyboard.

✔ *Win* is the Windows key.

✔ Locking Windows is a software action. It doesn't physically lock the laptop.

"What happens when you just shut the lid?"

The laptop can be told to do a number of things when you close its lid: Shut down, sleep, hibernate, or even stay on. Determine what your laptop does when the lid slams down by obeying these steps:

1. Open the Control Panel.

Refer to Chapter 6 for information on getting to the Control Panel, if you're unfamiliar with Windows.

2. **In the Control Panel Home, choose Change Battery Settings from the Mobile PC area; or, from Control Panel Classic View, open the Power Options icon.**

   Either way, you open the Power Options window.

3. **From the list of tasks on the left, choose the option Choose What Closing the Lid Does.**

   The Power Options System Settings window is displayed, as shown in Figure 4-7. The later section "Power Button, What's Your Function?" covers this window in detail. For now, you need to pay attention to the bottom row of buttons, labeled When I Close the Lid.

Figure 4-7: Setting options for various power buttons and the lid.

4. **Choose a command from the pop-up list in the On Battery column.**

   That option determines what the laptop does when you close the lid while the laptop is running on battery power.

5. **Choose a command from the pop-up list in the Plugged In column.**

   This option determines what happens when you close the laptop's lid while it's plugged into the wall.

6. **Click the Save Changes button.**

7. **Close the window.**

On my laptop, the options are set as shown in Figure 4-7: When I close the lid on battery power, the laptop hibernates. When I close the lid while the laptop is plugged in, the system goes to sleep.

Refer to the later section "Power Button, What's Your Function?" for details on the four options available for closing the laptop's lid.

Shutting down when the laptop doesn't want to

Unlike with a desktop computer, you just can't yank that power cord from the wall to deliberately force a laptop into electronic submission. The reason it doesn't work is that with the AC power gone, the laptop immediately starts using its battery. This can be very disconcerting when the system is locked up and you really, badly, want to turn the sucker off.

If the computer just utterly seems to be ignoring you, press and hold the power button. Keep holding it down, usually for five to ten seconds. Eventually, the laptop turns itself off.

See Part V of this book for laptop troubleshooting information.

Power Button, What's Your Function?

Your laptop doesn't have an On–Off switch — it has a *power button*. That button always turns the computer on, but it doesn't always necessarily turn the computer off. Believe it or not, you should appreciate that lack of fortitude. That's because it's you, the computer's lord and master, who determines what happens when the power button is pressed while the computer is on.

Commanding the power button to do something

To exercise authority over your dominion, you must summon the Power Options System Settings window (refer to Figure 4-7). Here are the steps required to summon that window:

1. **Open the Control Panel.**

2. **In the Control Panel Home, choose Change Battery Settings from the Mobile PC area; or, from Control Panel Classic View, open the Power Options icon.**

3. **Choose the option titled Choose What Closing The Lid Does from the list of tasks on the left.**

There are two rows of options: one for the laptop's power button and a second row for the sleep button (if it's available). There are also two columns: one specifying which actions to take when the laptop is on battery power and a second column specifying what to do when the laptop is securely plugged into the local power grid. There are four options for each button and condition:

Do nothing: Pressing the button or closing the lid doesn't change anything. If the laptop is on, it stays on.

Sleep: The laptop immediately enters Sleep mode, saving vital battery power.

Hibernate: The laptop hibernates, saving important information to disk and then turning itself off.

Shut down: The laptop turns itself off.

When the laptop is off, pressing the power button turns it back on again. There's no way to change that, nor would you really want to.

Controlling the software power button

There's one additional button you can lord it over: It's the software power button, found at the bottom of the Start menu, just next to the Padlock icon. Clicking that button with the mouse can either shut down, hibernate, or sleep your laptop. To set that button's function, obey these steps:

1. **Open the Control Panel.**

   See Chapter 6 for more information about the Control Panel.

2. **In the Control Panel Home, choose Change Battery Settings from the Mobile PC area; or, from Control Panel Classic View, open the Power Options icon.**

3. **Click on one of the links that says Change Plan Settings.**

4. **Locate and click on the link that says Change Advanced Power Settings.**

   The Power Options dialog box appears, as shown in Figure 4-8. It's a treasure trove of various power-saving settings in Windows.

5. **Locate the item labeled Power Buttons and Lid.**

   Scroll down a bit in the dialog box's list to find the Power Buttons and Lid entry.

6. **Click on the + (plus sign) to open the Power Buttons and Lid branch-thing.**

Figure 4-8:
Controlling
the
Windows
Vista Start
menu power
button.

7. **Click on the plus sign (+) to open the item labeled Start Menu Power Button.**

   Two items appear: one for when the laptop is on battery power and the other for when the laptop is plugged in.

8. **Choose an option for the Start menu power button.**

   Click on the current setting (shown in blue text) to see a pop-up menu of options (refer to Figure 4-8). On my laptop, three options are available: Sleep, Hibernate, and Shut Down. Whichever option you pick becomes the new Start menu power-button setting.

9. **Click OK to close the Power Options dialog box, and then (optional) close the Control Panel window.**

The Start menu's power button thing now functions as you dictated.

Chapter 5

Around Your Laptop in 18 Pages

In This Chapter

▶ Recognizing items on your laptop

▶ Discovering connectors and holes

▶ Recognizing mystery symbols

▶ Using a laptop keyboard

▶ Understanding laptop pointing devices

*Y*our laptop has the same capabilities and most of the features of a standard desktop computer, plus a handful of its own, unique traits. All that stuff is jammed into the smallest space possible. In fact, ringing your laptop is a smattering of bumps, holes, lights, and buttons. It's festooned with a festival of features. In fact, there's so much going on about your laptop that I thought I'd cobble together this chapter to go over what's what and why it's important.

✔ *Hardware* is the physical part of a computer, the stuff you can touch.

✔ *Software* is the set of instructions that make the hardware do stuff.

✔ Not every laptop has all the gizmos and doodads mentioned in this chapter. Some laptops have even more! Consider your exploration a generic survey. For some mystery items specific to your own laptop, the world may never know!

The Basic Laptop Tour

Most desktop computers look the same. Aside from minor design differences in the case, your typical desktop PC has on its face an optical drive, a media card reader, USB and headphone connectors, a power button, plus blinking lights. Ho-hum. But forget about consistency when it comes to locating those common things on a typical laptop.

Go grab your laptop. Gently. Take a moment to look it over. Then read through this section to help you discover where some key items are located.

Removable storage spots

Locate the spot on your laptop where the optical disc is inserted. It should be obvious, unless your laptop happens to lack an optical drive. In that case, give up looking now.

The optical disc may slide right into a slot. Stick the disc into the slot. At some point the computer "grabs" the disc and pulls it all the way in. If not, your laptop has a tray-type optical drive: Push a button to eject the tray. Stick the optical disc into the tray and push it shut.

Locate the spot on your laptop where any media cards may be inserted. There are several types of media cards: Secure Digital, Compact Flash, and Memory Stick, for example. These cards slide into four general slots. Your laptop may sport one, two, or all four types of slots.

- ✔ I've used laptops where the disc ejects on the right side and laptops where the disc ejects on the front. The only place I've not seen discs eject from is the back of the laptop, which would be really silly.

- ✔ Be aware of the method by which discs are inserted into the drive: either slide in or pop-out tray. Either way, you need room around your laptop to insert or remove the disc.

- ✔ For the pop-out tray, be sure that you find and recognize the tiny button that you press to eject the disc.

- ✔ It's a good idea to use the Eject command in Windows to properly remove a disc. Refer to Chapter 6, the section about storage devices.

Removable storage storage

To keep some laptop users happy, and laptop hardware flexible, manufacturers offer a removable storage option. It's possible on some laptops to remove, say, an optical drive and replace it with a second hard drive or memory card reader. Having such an option is a quick way to expand a laptop's hardware universe.

- ✔ Not every laptop supports swappable storage options.

- ✔ One advantage to removable storage is that you can lighten the laptop's weight when you can do without the device. But ensure that the laptop is designed to operate that way (and nothing nasty gets in the empty hole).

✔ Be mindful that you remove the storage devices per the directions that came with your laptop. Sometimes the devices can be removed in the way you would eject any media; sometimes you may need to turn off the laptop before swapping storage thingies.

The PC Card garage

Locate the spot on your laptop where PC Cards are inserted. It looks like a gaping hole on the side of the laptop. A tiny "garage door" may cover the hole, or the hole might be hidden behind a panel.

 I've often seen the PC Card garage labeled with the icon shown in the margin, although I'm not sure whether there's a universal hieroglyph for a PC Card.

The PC Card is inserted into the slot "holy" end first. In fact, it fits in only one way. Push the card in all the way until it fully docks with the connectors deep down inside the laptop.

To remove the card, locate the eject button alongside the slot, right next to the door. (See Figure 5-1.) Press the eject button all the way in, and the card pops out a little bit. You can then pinch the card between your thumb and forefinger and pull it out the rest of the way.

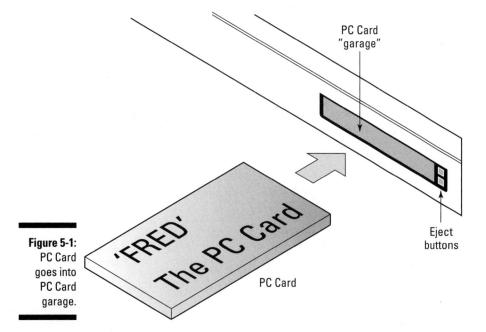

Figure 5-1:
PC Card
goes into
PC Card
garage.

An equal number of eject buttons appears alongside the spot where the card slides in.

➤ Be sure to read the instructions before inserting a PC Card the first time. Some cards might require that the laptop be turned off before inserting the card.

➤ Some laptops sport a depot for two PC Cards, stacked one atop the other. Some laptops might have room for only one PC Card.

➤ Hole too small for a PC Card? Then what you found is most likely a memory card reader, a hole that accepts Compact Flash, Secure Digital (SD), or other memory cards often used in digital cameras.

➤ Be careful of that PC Card eject button. Some of them tend to stick out beyond the edge of the laptop case. Ensure that you press it back into the laptop so that it doesn't snag on something and break off.

Holes of mystery

Laptop PCs come with most of the expandability options found in desktop computers. These options, the various holes and connectors, are referred to as *ports*. They serve to add features and attach cables to your laptop. (Although they increase your laptop's potential, they also impair the thing's mobility.)

Each part has its own type of connector with a specific shape and size. Each one is also labeled with an appropriately confusing hieroglyph. Often, it's color-coded. Bottom line: It's really difficult to plug the wrong connector into the wrong hole, but don't let that prevent you from trying.

Table 5-1 lists the name, configuration (shape), symbols, colors, and duties of the various ports you might find lingering around your laptop. Try to locate each one on your own laptop. Note that some can be hidden behind doors or panels, and your laptop may not sport all listed options. Also, not every laptop manufacturer uses the same color-coding scheme. That keeps things interesting.

Table 5-1	Laptop Ports and Their Symbols, Designs, and Colors			
Port Name	**Configuration**	**Symbol**	**Color**	**What You Can Do with It**
Custom	Nonspecific	?	None	Most likely, connect a docking station or an external disk drive or some other form of expansion.

Port Name	Configuration	Symbol	Color	What You Can Do with It
Digital Video			White	Connect a high-performance, external digital (LCD) monitor or TV.
Headphone			Forest green	Plug in headphones, which automatically disables the laptop's speakers.
IEEE			None	Connect high-speed peripherals; also called the 1394 or FireWire port.
Line In			Gray	Plug in an external audio device.
Line Out			Lime	Send sound to Audio Out jack or speakers.
Mic			Pink	Connect a microphone.
Modem/ Phone			None	Attach a modem for online communications or send or receive faxes.
Monitor			Blue	Connect an external monitor or a video display for presentations.
Power			Yellow	Plug the laptop into an AC power socket.
RJ-45/ Ethernet			None	Add your laptop to an Ethernet network or connect to the Internet.
S-Video Out			None	Attach a desktop video projector or attach the laptop to a TV or VCR.
USB			None	Add a variety of components to the laptop, including printers and disk drives.

✔ Despair not when your laptop lacks most of these ports. Ports can be added to most laptops by using a port replicator or docking station. The port replicator may also contain traditional (old-fashioned) PC ports, including the old serial, printer, keyboard, and mouse ports. See Chapter 23 for more information.

✔ Keyboards and external mice are attached to your laptop using the USB port. When you need more USB ports, you attach a portable USB hub to your laptop. See Chapter 9 for more information about USB.

✔ The RJ-45/Ethernet port might also have the icon shown in the margin labeling its trapezoidal crack.

✔ By the way, that Ethernet port and the modem port look awfully similar. Happily, one (the Ethernet port) is larger than the other (the modem port).

✔ The power jack might look different from what's shown in Table 5-1. Be sure that you don't plug the power cable into a microphone port!

✔ Another hole you may find on the monitor is a video camera. You can use that built-in camera for Web conferencing, online chatting, or taking pictures of yourself while you're using the computer. (Needs must be met, you know.)

✔ The IEEE symbol might be different on some laptops. Apparently, the Y type of symbol isn't universal.

✔ If your laptop has S-Video Out, note that the S-Video connection is video only, not sound.

✔ Check out Chapter 7 for some specific items to look for on a Tablet PC.

A place for the old ball and chain

Most laptops have a special "belt loop" through which you can snake a security cable. The belt loop's real name is universal security slot, or USS. A common icon for the USS is shown in the margin.

Another option is the Kensington Security Slot, or K-Slot. The slot looks like a tiny oval and is labeled with a Padlock icon sporting a *K* in the middle.

✔ Note that the security cable must be attached to something solid and immovable to prevent the laptop from being stolen. Just threading a cable through the security hole doesn't do the trick.

✔ See Chapter 18 for more information on laptop security.

The thing's gotta breathe

As you conclude your journey around the perimeter of your laptop, note where the breathing slots are. They might not be obvious; they might not even be there. If they are, note their locations and try to keep the vents clear.

Look at the Pretty Lights!

What would a computer be if it weren't for all the blinking lights? Even before real computers were popular, those monster computers of science fiction came equipped with banks and banks of blinking lights. Although I'm certain that a modern laptop could easily replace all the Batcomputers in Batman's Batcave, it just wouldn't be visually impressive — and believable to a 1960s television audience.

Your laptop most likely has many more lights than the typical desktop computer. I'm trying to think of a reason for this, but it honestly baffles me. Suffice it to say that Table 5-2 lists some of the common lights, lamps, and bright, blinking things you might find on your laptop and describes what they do or why they're necessary.

Table 5-2	Pretty Laptop Lights
Symbol	*What It Could Possibly Mean*
☾	The laptop is in Sleep mode.
🔋	The laptop is running on battery power. This lamp can change color when the laptop is charging.
⊲	The laptop is plugged in.
⦶	The laptop is on.
⬭	The hard drive is being accessed.
A	The Caps Lock state is on. There might also be a light on the Caps Lock key.
1	The Num Lock state is on. There might also be a light on the Num Lock key.
(((·)))	Wireless networking activity is taking place.
✷	Bluetooth wireless activity is taking place.

Other pretty lights doubtless exist, some specific to your laptop's manufacturer. Thanks to that International Symbol Law, most symbols are pretty common. In fact, consider checking with Table 5-2 to see whether any of those symbols appears on the laptop's pretty light strip as well.

Some lights can blink or change color. For example, the battery indicator might change from green to amber to red as the battery drains. The hard drive or wireless lights might flicker as access is being made.

When the laptop is off, or even in Hibernation mode, none of the lights is lit. (See Chapter 4 for hibernation information.)

This Isn't Your Daddy's Keyboard

The standard computer keyboard has 105 keys, not counting any special "Web" keys, media keys, or other buttons. That's a lot of knobs. You just can't sport that many keys on a laptop and keep it portable. Oh, sure, some of those laptops the size of an aircraft carrier — the models with the 18-inch displays — they can sport a full-size PC keyboard. But most laptops opt for portability over the need to use your laptop as a surfboard.

This section mulls over the laptop's keyboard.

The general keyboard layout

Figure 5-2 illustrates a typical laptop keyboard layout. The standard typewriter keys are normal size, but the many other keys have been miniaturized and arranged around the standard keys in a confusing and arbitrary manner. Observing your own laptop's keyboard easily confirms this.

Figure 5-2: Typical laptop keyboard layout.

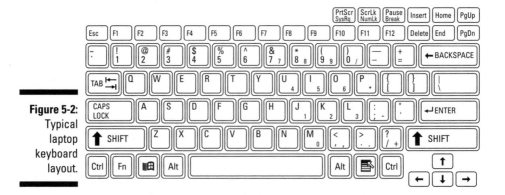

As with a desktop keyboard, you should be able to identify the following basic items on your laptop keyboard:

- ✓ **Alphanumeric, or "typewriter," keys:** These are the basic typing keys, each of which is labeled with a character (a letter, number, or punctuation symbol). When you're typing on the computer, pressing a key produces its character on the screen.

- ✓ **Shift keys:** The keyboard sports various shift keys used either alone or in combination with other keys. These include Shift, Alt, Ctrl, and the special Windows keys Win and Menu. The Win key appears in the bottom row between the Fn and Alt keys in Figure 5-2; the Menu key appears between Alt and Ctrl. Also note the Esc (or Escape) key, found at the beginning of the top row of keys.

- ✓ **Function keys:** These keys, labeled F1 through F12, are on the top row of the keyboard, right above the number keys.

- ✓ **Cursor-control keys:** These keys can be anywhere around the keyboard. In Figure 5-2, they're split; arrow keys in the bottom right corner and other cursor keys (Home, End, Pg Up, Pg Dn, Insert, Delete) in the top-right corner.

- ✓ **Numeric keypad:** This area is covered in the next section.

The alphanumeric keys are approximately the same size and have the same *travel,* or feel, as on a desktop computer keyboard.

The text on some keys is color coded. That tells you which keys are used in conjunction with each other. For example, if the Alt key is green and the Num Lock key is green, the Alt+Num Lock key combination is required in order to use Num Lock. (See the section "The Fn key is the Fun key!" later in this chapter.)

The cursor-control keys are used to move the text cursor when you're editing text in Windows. They can also be used to help navigate the Web. The keys can take on other functions in other programs as well.

Some keys are labeled with images or icons rather than with text. For example, I've seen the Caps Lock key labeled with the letter *A* and a padlock symbol.

European laptops often sport an AltGr key. That's the Alt (or Alternative) Graphic key. It's used to help produce the many diacritical marks and special characters found in various European languages.

European laptops also have the euro symbol, €, on the keyboard. It's apparently a much more valuable symbol than the $ symbol.

Your keyboard might have more or fewer keys than those shown in Figure 5-2, and the arrangement might be different.

Where did the numeric keypad go?

The first thing the laptop designers decided to sacrifice to the Space Gods was the keyboard's numeric keypad. Rather than just saw off that end of the keyboard, laptops since the Model 100 have used a combination of numeric keypad and alphabetic keyboard.

Most laptops combine the main keyboard with the numeric keypad: Examine the 7, 8, and 9 keys. Those three keys are also the top three keys on a numeric keypad. Because of this similarity, a shadow keypad can be created by using the right side of the alphabetic keyboard, as illustrated in Figure 5-3. The trick, of course, is knowing how to turn the thing on and off.

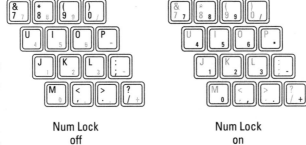

Figure 5-3:
The hidden numeric keypad.

Num Lock off   Num Lock on

The following steps help to train you in proper laptop hidden numeric keypad usage:

1. **Open a program you can type in, such as Notepad or your word processor.**

2. **Type** I just love Kimmy.

   You discover in a few steps why you adore Kimmy.

3. **Find the Num Lock light on your laptop's strip of lights.**

   The light is your confirmation that your keyboard is in Num Lock mode and that you can use the embedded numeric keypad. (See Table 5-2.)

4. **Find the Num Lock key on your laptop's keyboard.**

   Somewhere on your keyboard is a Num Lock key. It might be labeled NumLock or NumLk or Num, or it might even be labeled with a symbol, as shown in the margin. Locate that key.

5. **Attempt to activate Num Lock.**

   Press the Num Lock key. If nothing happens, try Shift+Num Lock.

   If the text *Num Lock* is shown in a different color, find the matching-color key, such as Alt or Fn. Then press that key in combination with Num Lock.

You're successful when the Num Lock light comes on. At that point, the keyboard has switched into Numeric Keypad mode.

6. **Try to type** I just love Kimmy **again.**

   It doesn't work. You see something like `14st 36ve 500y`. That's because most of the keys on the right side of the keyboard now have their numeric keypad abilities activated. It's helpful for entering numbers or working a spreadsheet, but rather frustrating at other times.

7. **Deactivate Num Lock.**

   Press whichever key combination you used to turn it on.

8. **Close the program.**

   There's no need to save the document.

Try to remember which key combination you used to activate the numeric keypad. Write it down on this book's Cheat Sheet, lest you forget.

The Fn key is the Fun key!

To make up for a lack of keys, many laptops came with a special function key, the Fn key. The Fn key is used in combination with other keys like a Shift key, giving those keys multiple purposes.

Having an Fn key is an old, old laptop trick, dating back to the prehistoric days of computer. In Figure 5-4, you see the keyboard from a Compaq SLT, similar to the one Abraham Lincoln used to type drafts of the Declaration of Independence. You can find the Fn (function) key all by itself in the lower-left corner.

In Figure 5-4, the text *Fn* on the Fn key is enclosed in a rectangle (if you can see it). On other keys, text is also enclosed in a rectangle. That's your hint that the key's function performs the rectangle text's duties when the Fn key is pressed. A similar technique is used on modern laptops with the Fn keys, though color coding is used instead of rectangles.

Sadly, there's no standard for naming the various Fn keys and their functions. But, among the many laptops out there, you find Fn key combinations that do the following:

✔ Turn the laptop's internal speaker volume up and down.

✔ Mute the laptop's internal speaker.

✔ Increase or decrease the monitor's brightness or contrast.

✔ Activate an external monitor for giving a presentation.

✔ Activate Sleep mode.

✔ Hibernate the laptop.

✔ Eject an optical disc.

✔ Enable or disable the wireless networking adapter.

✔ Play, stop, pause, rewind, and advance media playing.

✔ Lock the keyboard.

✔ Perform other special and specific tricks.

Take a moment to peruse your laptop and look over the available Fn keys.

Some Fn keys can be rather fun. For example, on one of my laptops, Fn+PgUp activates a tiny keyboard light in the laptop's lid.

Mind these specific keys

In addition to the standard keyboard, or perhaps right along with it, your laptop may have some custom keys or buttons next to the keyboard. They're totally specific to the manufacturer, and you might never end up using them. But they're keys nonetheless.

The most common location for these keys is above the keyboard, although I've seen them on the left and right sides. Some keys can be used to pick up e-mail, browse the Web, connect to a digital camera, or contact a vendor for tech support. I've also seen keys that control the display or speaker volume.

Figure 5-4:
The Compaq
SLT key-
board
(1987).

Use these keys if you will, but keep in mind that their functions are specific to your laptop. Don't expect to find similar keys on a desktop computer or even on a laptop from another manufacturer.

The special keys are controlled using specific software that must be loaded into Windows. If there's a problem with this software, or if you end up using an operating system other than Windows, don't be surprised when the special keys no longer function.

This Isn't Your Momma's Mouse

The marriage of mouse and laptop is an old idea. Even back before graphical operating systems such as Windows existed, laptop users were aware of how handy a computer mouse could be.

Figure 5-5 shows one old and funky solution to the laptop mouse problem: the thumb ball mouse. It plugged into the laptop's serial port and attached to either the lid or the side of the keyboard, giving the laptop user a primitive pointing device. Yes, using it was as awkward as combing your hair with a spoon, but it was something.

Today, nearly all laptops use a touchpad or mousepad as a pointing device. The following sections describe the various options.

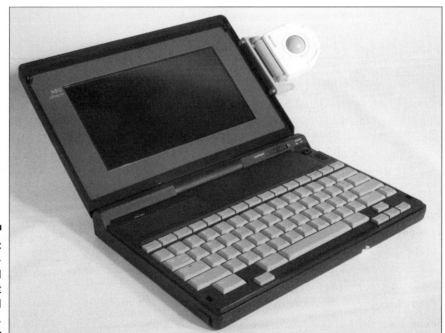

Figure 5-5:
An early-model Microsoft thumb ball mouse.

The touchpad

Nearly all of today's laptops feature a *touchpad*. It might also be called a *mousepad*. Either way, you use the touchpad to control the pointing device on the screen by gliding a thumb or finger along its flat surface. Buttons nearby emulate the left and right buttons on your typical bar-of-soap mouse, as shown in Figure 5-6.

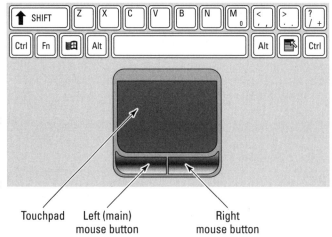

Figure 5-6: The touch-pad thing.

Touchpad   Left (main) mouse button   Right mouse button

There's an art to using the touchpad:

- ✔ It helps to use your forefinger to move the mouse pointer. Use your thumb to click the left and right buttons on the bottom of the touchpad.

- ✔ A light touch is all that's required.

- ✔ You must be careful not to touch the pad in more than one spot. If you do, the pointer on the screen jumps about in an erratic and annoying manner.

- ✔ The most difficult mouse operation is the *drag*. That's where you have to hold down a button while moving the pointer. With practice, this can be done — but you must practice! (It's another excuse to play FreeCell.)

- ✔ Try to avoid accidentally hitting the right mouse button when you mean to hit the left one. doing so causes context menus to pop up in Windows — very frustrating.

✔ On some touchpads, you can tap pad to simulate a mouse click. You can use the Control Panel in Windows to enable or disable this feature; see the section "Manipulating the mouse pointer," later in this chapter, for more information.

The latest rage in the laptop touchpad is the ability to interpret finger strokes. Apple popularized this type of technique on the iPhone and later on the MacBook Air laptop. I expect most laptop touchpads to offer special finger stroke interpretations in the future.

Where is the wheel button?

Most modern computer mice come with a *wheel button*. The button sits between the mouse's left and right buttons and is used to scroll, pan, or click for various effects. People love the wheel button, and obviously they want it on their laptops. Well, *tough!*

Sadly, the common laptop mousepad doesn't have a standard wheel-button replacement. Some manufacturers provide a button with similar features, but if you want a wheel button, you just have to end up using an external "wheel" mouse with your laptop. That's not a bad idea, anyway.

The "happy stick" keyboard mouse

Popular on IBM and Lenovo laptops is a joystick-like mouse that looks like a pencil eraser jammed between the keyboard's G, H, and B keys. It's officially called the TrackPoint, though I prefer to call it a happy stick. Regardless, the gizmo is quite handy to use.

The idea behind the happy stick is that you can manipulate it by using the index finger of either hand. You can then use your thumb (on either hand) to click the left or right "mouse" buttons, as shown in Figure 5-7.

Note that a middle button exists in Figure 5-7. That's the "wheel" button, and it can be used with the happy stick to scroll information in a window. Although the wheel button isn't a full replacement for the wheel button on a mouse, it's a pretty neat trick.

✔ As with the touchpad, using the happy stick takes some training and getting used to.

✔ Some laptop models come with both a happy stick and a touchpad. You can use either one.

Figure 5-7:
The
TrackPoint.

Manipulating the mouse pointer

The touchpad (or happy stick) is used in Windows to scurry around the mouse
pointer on the screen. Although the touchpad itself controls the mouse pointer's
position, as well as what it touches or picks up, it's up to Windows to dictate
how the mouse pointer looks and which options it features.

As with controlling many things in Windows, controlling the mouse pointer
on the screen is done in the Control Panel, which is the gateway to the Mouse
Properties dialog box, shown in Figure 5-8.

To display the Mouse Properties dialog box, follow these steps:

1. **Open the Control Panel.**

   Refer to Chapter 6 if you need directions.

2. **From the Control Panel Home, locate the Mouse link beneath the
   Hardware and Sound heading; from Control Panel Classic View, open
   the Mouse icon.**

   Behold the Mouse Properties dialog box.

In addition to finding the standard mouse information, you might find a
custom tab in the Mouse Properties dialog box, similar to the one shown in
Figure 5-8. That's where you can configure the laptop's touchpad or custom

pointing device. In Figure 5-8, the TrackPoint and touchpad mouse options are set.

- ✔ Refer to Chapter 20 for information on making the mouse pointer more visible on your laptop.

- ✔ If you're a southpaw, use the Buttons tab in the Mouse Properties dialog box to switch the functions of the left and right mouse buttons. Be aware, however, that most manuals refer to the main mouse button as being on the *left!*

- ✔ You can use the Pointers tab in the Mouse Properties dialog box to change the way the mouse pointer looks on the screen. That can be a fun waste of time.

- ✔ Items on the Pointer Options tab can be used to help you locate a lost mouse pointer. Settings such as Pointer Trails and Show Location can be used to help find hard-to-see mouse pointers on the laptop's display.

- ✔ You can disable your laptop's mousepad. Some laptops, such as some HP Pavilion models, might even have a mousepad On–Off switch. This is entirely acceptable if you plan to use an external mouse. (See the next section.)

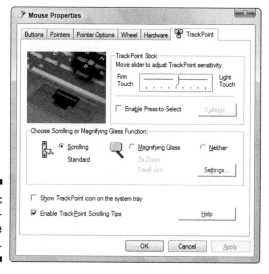

Figure 5-8:
Setting custom mouse options.

Get a real mouse!

The best type of input device you can get your laptop is . . . *a real mouse*. No, not the furry rodent kind. Silly. A desktop computer mouse.

Now you can readily use a desktop computer mouse on your laptop instead of or along with the touchpad. Yes, it's one more thing to carry. But because desktop computer mice are so familiar and people are used to them, it often makes sense for the laptop to have a "big computer" mouse.

Then again, you can get a laptop mouse, such as the wireless model shown in Figure 5-9, the Microsoft Wireless Notebook Laser Mouse 6000. It's smaller and lighter than a desktop mouse, plus it has no tangly wires to mess with.

✔ Beyond the Laser Mouse 6000 are other specialty laptop mice — some wired, some wireless, some with retractable cords.

✔ I often pause and wonder what happened to the Laser Mouse models 1 through 5999.

✔ Buy your laptop a nice wheel mouse, and you'll never again moan about your laptop missing a wheel button.

✔ I've seen people on airplanes use real mice. Even in that cramped space, people find a place to roll about the mouse. Pant legs work — yours or your seatmate's.

✔ Be careful when you install the software for your external mouse. Sometimes, doing so disables the software controlling the laptop's touchpad. Follow the installation advice that comes with the external mouse.

Figure 5-9:
Would Goldfinger use this laser mouse against James Bond?

Chapter 6

Windows on Your Laptop

In This Chapter

▶ Visiting places in Windows

▶ Locating storage

▶ Finding your home folder

▶ Discovering where programs dwell

▶ Looking out on the network

▶ Working with the Control Panel

A laptop is merely hardware, and expensive hardware at that. But it's useless.

No joke. To make your laptop computer worthwhile, you need to stir some software into the mix. The key piece of software is the *operating system*. That's the main program that controls all the hardware and all the software, organizes all the files, and interfaces with you, the human. On a PC laptop, the operating system is most likely Windows.

This chapter is about Windows; specifically, how Windows comes into play on a laptop computer. As with the rest of the book, the information here is specific to Windows Vista.

Windows on the Face of It

A lot of effort is put into making Windows look easy to use, and for the most part, it is. But Windows itself is one vast, complex program. For example, although the concept of copying a file seems easy, Windows provides 95.3 ways to copy a file. Microsoft may believe that all those options make things easier. I believe it just makes Windows overwhelming.

Rather than overwhelm you with Windows (and, indeed, that's a topic for a whole book), I decided to do a quick summary of those places in Windows where you spend most of your time, specifically with your laptop. This is the "Places to See and Things to Do" Windows tour.

The desktop

The desktop is the main thing you see when you use Windows. It contains icons, the taskbar, the Start button, the Sidebar (optional), and other elements. Review Figure 4-5, over in Chapter 4, if you need to know what's what.

- ✔ The desktop is the home to some key icons in Windows.

- ✔ Key Windows icons include your User Profile (or home) folder, Computer, Network, Control Panel, and Recycle Bin. Whether these icons show up is optional. (It's a triumph of customization over consistency.)

- ✔ The desktop may also sport shortcut icons. There are two types: One lets you run a program, and the other opens a folder, which gives you speedy access to files stored on a laptop.

The Start thing

Yes, the desktop looks pretty. But to get things done on the laptop, you need to start something. To start something, you use the aptly named but unlabeled Start button, found on the left end of the taskbar (at the bottom of the screen).

Clicking the Start button displays the Start menu, a fun slab-o-stuff that includes a list of programs, fun places to visit in Windows, and other things to start. The Start menu is illustrated in Figure 6-1.

To summon the Start menu, click the Start button with the mouse pointer or press the Windows (Win) key on your laptop's keyboard.

Take a few hours to find the following goodies on the important left side of Start-thing menu:

- ✔ **The pin-on area:** The upper-left half of the slab contains programs permanently attached, or *pinned,* to the Start menu.

- ✔ **Recently Used Programs area:** Just below the pin-on area, on the left side of the Start menu, you find the names and icons of programs you've used recently.

- ✔ **The All Programs menu:** Below the Recently Used Programs area is the All Programs link. Clicking that item displays a list of programs installed on your computer, all shoved into various menus and submenus.

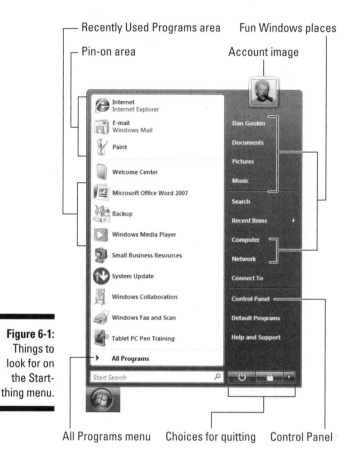

Recently Used Programs area   Fun Windows places

Pin-on area   Account image

Figure 6-1:
Things to
look for on
the Start-
thing menu.

All Programs menu   Choices for quitting   Control Panel

Find these items lurking on the right side of the Start menu panel:

- **Fun Windows places to visit:** The items on the right side of the Start menu represent places to go in Windows, where you can carry out interesting (or not) tasks and play or dawdle. These include locations where you find the stuff you create as well as general computer and networking thingies.

- **The Control Panel:** One of the most important places to visit is the Control Panel, which is accessed by choosing the Control Panel item from the right side of the Start menu's palette. You visit the Control Panel often as you set up various options for your laptop. (See "Visiting the Control Panel," later in this chapter.)

Finally, in the lower-right area of the Start button's menu, you find

✔ **Choices for quitting:** The mysterious options for ending your computer-time fun and folly appear in the lower-right corner of the Start panel.

You discover elsewhere in this chapter more about using Windows and what all this stuff means. For now, just knowing where things are is all you need to know. Take care: The Start menu is customizable. What you see may differ from what's shown in Figure 6-1 and from what's listed in this section.

You can make the Start menu go away by clicking the mouse on the desktop or by pressing the Esc key on the keyboard.

Goodies in the notification area

The *notification area* is located on the far right end of the taskbar, where the Start button cannot smell it, as shown in Figure 6-2.

Figure 6-2:
The notifica-
tion area
lurks on the
right end of
the taskbar.

The icons in the notification area serve two purposes. First, they can notify you with pop-up bubbles. Or, you can just point the mouse at an icon to view status information, such as whether the network is connected or how much battery juice is left. Second, the icons provide instant access to some common features, such as networking, antivirus, volume control, and other things to keep handy.

Some people really can't stand the notification area. They want to obliterate it with computer gaming-like destructive glee. But the thing is only there to be useful. Microsoft understands this, so if any of the items in the notification area annoy you, try right-clicking them. From the context menu that appears, choose an Exit or Quit command. If not, try finding a Properties command, or access the window that controls the little icon. You usually find a turn-me-off item there.

Storage Devices

One of the key parts of any computer system is *information storage.* The other key parts are *input* and *output,* but I shan't bore you here with prattle on computer science theory (despite the possibility that it would make you a better computer user). Leave it to say that information storage is the sun around which the laptop's planets revolve.

Storage is important because that's where all your stuff is on the laptop. Yes, the stuff is "inside there, somewhere." All the programs, the Windows operating system, and all the files you create all must be put somewhere inside the laptop.

In Windows, you can view the gamut of storage devices available to your laptop in a single, handy place. It's the Computer window, as shown in Figure 6-3.

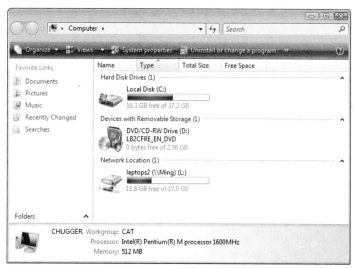

Figure 6-3:
Various
places to
store stuff.

To open the Computer window, either choose the Computer command from the Start menu (refer to Figure 6-1) or open the Computer icon on the desktop (if it exists).

The Computer window lists all storage devices available to your computer, including the hard drive, or main storage device, any removable media drives, plus network drives you may have access to. In Figure 6-3, you can see the standard laptop hard drive, `Local Disk C:`, plus an optical drive and a network drive.

- ✔ *Input* is about getting information into the computer. The input is done through the keyboard, mouse, network connection, modem, and other input devices.

- ✔ *Output* is about getting information from the computer. Output is done through the monitor, speaker, printer, network connection, modem, and other output devices.

- ✔ The Computer window is your gateway to the laptop's storage devices. When you're told to "examine drive C," for example, you open the Computer window.

- ✔ A quick shortcut to open the Computer window is pressing the Win+E combination on the keyboard.

- ✔ For more information on the various types of available disk drives, as well as to gain good background computer knowledge, refer to my book *PCs For Dummies,* published by Wiley and available at fine bookstores.

- ✔ The Computer window might also display things such as a scanner or digital camera or other toys attached to your computer.

- ✔ The icon for the optical drive may change, depending on whether you have a disc in the drive and the type of media on the disc.

A Place for Your Stuff

Your laptop uses the various storage devices to keep your stuff organized. By *stuff,* I mean the files you create, music you steal — *er,* download, videos, stuff from the Internet, pictures — all that junk has to go somewhere. By *organized,* I mean using folders on the storage devices in your laptop.

Under Windows Vista, the location set aside for all your junk is the *User Profile* folder. I prefer to use the term *home* folder.

- ✔ A *folder* is a storage container for files.

- ✔ *Files* are those things you create using your software: documents and graphics, for example. Files go in folders.

- ✔ The concept of files and folders is all basic Computer Knowledge, stuff you probably ignored in school or assumed that you knew already.

- ✔ Your programs *do not* reside in the My Documents folder. No, they go in the *Program Files* folder. See the section "Where the Programs Lurk," later in this chapter.

Accessing your home folder

Your home folder is the first place you should look when trying to find your stuff. It's the first place presented to you when you go to save your stuff. Obviously, it's important to know how to access that folder.

In Windows Vista, the home folder (officially your User Profile folder) is given the same name as the account name you use to log in to the computer. So, if your login ID is `Al Gore`, the folder is named Al Gore. On my laptop, the folder name is `Dan Gookin`, which is also my human name.

To open your home folder, look for its name on the Start menu. In Figure 6-1, you can see the name `Dan Gookin` listed on the upper-left side of the Start menu. Choosing that item opens the home folder on my laptop. Choosing the account name from the right side of your laptop's Start menu does the same thing for you.

The home folder on my laptop is shown in Figure 6-4. The window shows other folders for storing things (described in the section "Special folders for your stuff," later in this chapter), plus it may contain icons representing files. It's all my stuff — mine, I tell you!

Figure 6-4: There's no folder like home.

To close the home folder window, click on the X close box in the window's upper-right corner.

✔ The home folder is really called the User Profile folder. The home folder might also be referred to by the name `Users Files`.

✔ Your home folder has the same name as your user account ID.

Placing the home folder on the desktop

Dan Gookin

You may find on the desktop an icon representing your home folder. Whether it's there depends on how you configured the Windows desktop icons. If the icon is there, double-clicking to open it displays your home folder contents. If the icon isn't on the desktop and you want access to your home folder from the desktop, follow these easy and painless steps:

1. **Click the Start button.**

2. **Right-click on the account name item, found in the upper-right part of the menu.**

   The account name item is the one you choose to open your home folder. It's the same name as your login ID. That's Dan Gookin, for my account.

3. **From the pop-up menu, choose Show on Desktop.**

   If a check mark already appears by the Show on Desktop item, you don't need to choose it; you're done!

4. **Press the Esc key to banish the Start menu.**

You should then see your account folder's icon on the desktop, given the same name as your account. The icon lacks the traditional shortcut arrow in its lower-left corner, but it's still a shortcut.

Special folders for your stuff

The key to not losing your sanity in Windows is to organize your stuff. You get a head start on that because Windows comes out of the box with certain folders designated to hold certain types of files. In Windows Vista, these folders are found in your home folder. They include

Documents: The main place where you store documents and other, random files.

Music: A place to store all audio files, especially songs downloaded from the Internet or ripped from your friends' mix CDs.

Pictures: The folder where your graphics go. Most graphical applications automatically store your images in this folder.

Videos: A special folder for storing digital video on your computer.

You have even more custom folders: Contacts, Desktop, Downloads, Favorites, Links, Saved Games, and Searches. Each of these folders is used somehow by one or another program in Windows. You're also free to create and use your own folders or to create *subfolders* within the folders that are pre-created for you.

Where the Programs Lurk

The laptop's storage system also stores all the software installed on your computer. Software, programs, applications — same thing. Your laptop most likely came with lots of software installed, including stuff you want and need, and you doubtless will install more software as you use and enjoy (or just use) your laptop.

"Where is Windows?"

Windows installs itself on your laptop's hard drive in a folder named *Windows* or *WinNT.* The folder name depends on which version of Windows you're using. To view the folder — and I promise that this doesn't mess anything up — follow these simple steps:

1. **Click the Start button.**

2. **From the Start button menu, choose Computer.**

   The Computer window appears (refer to Figure 6-3).

3. **In the Computer window, open the icon for drive C, the laptop's primary hard drive.**

   In the Drive C window you see several folders. Each represents the main *branches* of information stored on the hard drive. One of those folders is named Windows or WinNT.

4. **Point at the Windows folder and say "There you are!"**

5. **Close the Computer window.**

Do not poke around the Windows folder. Like any piece of fine art: Don't touch! Don't delete! Don't tell!

"Where are the programs and other software?"

Windows places the programs and other software you install on the laptop into a folder named `Program Files`. As with the Windows folder, you find this folder by opening the C disk drive from the Computer window. If you desire, repeat the steps from the preceding section, but in Step 4 point at the Program Files folder and say "There you are, too!"

As with the Windows folder, do not modify or change or add anything to the `Program Files` folder. Installing and removing software is done in a specific way in Windows, as described in the sections that follow. Do not manually delete or add programs on your own!

Also see Chapter 8 for information on installing and removing programs on your laptop.

Out on the Network

When your laptop is connected to a network, it can access other computers on that network, including any resources (folders or printers, for example) shared by those computers. The place to go for that type of networking action is the Network window.

To display the folder full o' networking goodness, choose the Network item from the Start menu. Or, if you see the Network icon on the desktop, open the icon. The Network window opens, as depicted in Figure 6-5.

Figure 6-5: Things you're connected to on the network.

Each icon in the Network window represents a computer or network resource available elsewhere on the network. Using this window, and general networking information, is offered in Chapter 11.

Close the Network window when you tire of its presence.

The Control Panel

Windows is your laptop's main program. *El numero uno.* The big boss. The head cheese. The on high.

As *capo di tutti capi,* Windows controls everything. When you want to pay a call to *Don Windows* and ask for a favor (and not on the day of his daughter's wedding), you make the request in a place called the Control Panel. The following sections prepare you for that visit.

Visiting the Control Panel

There's no single, simple way to visit or view the Control Panel. I start from the simple and go on from there:

To open the Control Panel window, you can choose the Control Panel item from the Start menu.

Control Panel

If the Control Panel appears as an icon on the desktop, you can open that icon to view the Control Panel window.

Either way, the Control Panel window appears, as shown in Figure 6-6. The way it appears in that figure is called *Control Panel Home.* In that view, the things you can control are organized by category and topic. The Control Panel Home presents the easy way to view the Control Panel, but not the most efficient way.

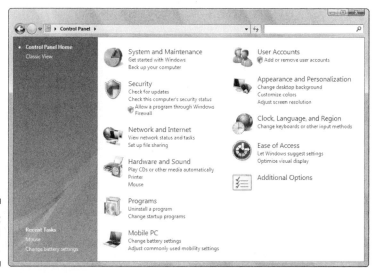

Figure 6-6:
Control
Panel Home.

In Figure 6-7 you see the Control Panel window shown with the more traditional and efficient icon view. Officially, it's *Control Panel Classic View*.

Figure 6-7:
Control
Panel
Classic
View.

To switch between Control Panel Home and Classic View, choose the proper link from the upper-left part of the Control Panel window.

- ✔ This book contains directions for using both Control Panel Home and Classic View. Personally, I prefer to use Classic View.

- ✔ Note that some of the icons you see in your laptop's Control Panel contents are different from the ones shown in Figure 6-7. Special icons exist for your laptop's custom features and software, such as the Fingerprint Sensor icon shown in Figure 6-7.

- ✔ Of all the icons in the Control Panel, only a handful play roles specific to a laptop computer. For information on icons not mentioned here, please refer to a good Windows reference, such as my book *Find Gold in Windows Vista* (Wiley Publishing), which I shall continue to plug throughout this book.

The Control Panel on the Start menu

Yes, there's a third way to view and access the Control Panel. It's the most efficient method. It's the Start menu Control Panel menu, shown in Figure 6-8. I find using this method of accessing items in the Control Panel to be very speedy, and speed makes a big difference when you're using a laptop on battery power.

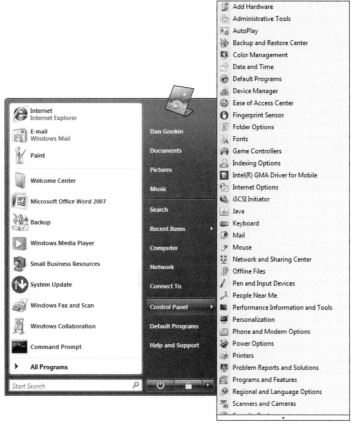

Figure 6-8:
The Control
Panel's fly-
out menu
on the Start
menu.

To configure the Control Panel as a pop-up menu on the Start menu, comply with these steps:

1. **Right-click the Start button.**

2. **Choose Properties from the Start button's pop-up menu.**

   The Taskbar and Start Menu Properties dialog box appears.

3. **Click the Start Menu tab.**

4. **Click the Customize button, by the Start Menu option.**

5. **Locate the Control Panel item in the scrolling list of Start menu items.**

6. **Select the Display As a Menu option beneath the Control Panel heading.**

7. **Click OK to close each dialog box.**

The Control Panel now dwells as a submenu on the Start-panel thing. (Well, you can still get to it by opening the Control Panel icon on the desktop.)

Fun places to visit in the Control Panel

The Control Panel contains a clutch of items, windows, dialog boxes, and so forth, where you can control various aspects of Windows. A complete Windows reference should give you all the details. The following sections highlight places in the Control Panel that are related to laptop computing.

The Windows Mobility Center

A collection of laptop, Tablet PC, and mobile computing options is kept in a special, laptop-only place in the Control Panel. That place is the Windows Mobility Center. Figure 6-9 shows what it looks like. There you can see special options, plus a few options specific to my Lenovo Tablet PC.

Figure 6-9:
The Control Panel's Windows Mobility Center window.

The Windows Mobility Center is accessed from the Control Panel Home by clicking the Adjust Commonly Used Mobility Settings link, beneath the Mobile PC heading.

From Control Panel Classic View, open the Windows Mobility Center icon to view the Windows Mobility Center.

✔ The Mobile PC heading appears in the Control Panel Home only on laptop computers.

✔ The keyboard shortcut to bring up the Windows Mobility Center is Win+X.

✔ It's the *Windows* Mobility Center, not just the Mobility Center.

Tablet PC settings

Unique to the Tablet PC is its ability to use a digital pen as an input device. To set up all that pen-input stuff, you need to access the Control Panel and display the Pen and Input Devices dialog box.

To open the Pen and Input Devices dialog box from the Control Panel Home, choose the heading Mobile PC, and then on the next screen, choose Pen and Input Devices.

From Control Panel Classic View, open the Pen and Input Devices icon to see a dialog box of the same name.

Personalization and display settings

To mess with the screen, to control the way Windows looks as well as how your laptop's monitor is configured, you need to visit the Personalization window. That's where options such as the desktop background, screen saver, and display settings are controlled.

From the Control Panel Home, items found under Appearance and Personalization help you configure the display.

From Control Panel Classic View, choose the Personalization icon. A Personalization window opens, as shown in Figure 6-10. You're not quite there yet. To *do* something, you must click one of the links. For example, to set the screen resolution, choose Display Properties. You choose the screen saver and desktop background from the appropriately named links.

You can also access the Personalization window by right-clicking on the desktop and choosing the Personalize command from the pop-up menu.

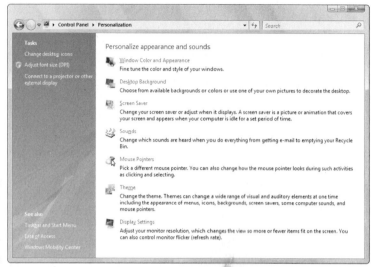

Figure 6-10:
The Person-
alization
window.

Networking things

The Network window, covered earlier in this chapter, shows network connections. But to set up and configure the network, the Network and Sharing Center window is used. To open that window, you use the Control Panel.

From the Control Panel Home, display the Network and Sharing Center window by choosing the View Network Status and Tasks link, found under the Network and Internet heading.

From Control Panel Classic View, open the Network and Sharing Center icon.

You can see a sample shot of the Network and Sharing Center window in Chapter 11, which goes into detail about its operation.

You can quickly get to the networking hardware center by clicking on the wee li'l Networking Guys icon in the notification area and choosing the Network and Sharing Center link. (The icon looks like two computer monitors, one overlapping another.)

Power management options

To control how your laptop manages power, and conserves battery life, you use the Power Options window. Details for using that window are covered in Chapter 9. To display that window, you use the Control Panel.

From the Control Panel Home, clink the Change Battery Settings link, found under the Mobile PC heading.

From Control Panel Classic View, open the Power Options icon.

Power Options

Phone and modem options

Using a laptop's modem is covered in Chapter 13. To configure things, you need to use the Control Panel.

In the Control Panel Home, choose Hardware and Sound, and then on the next screen, scroll down and choose Phone and Modem Options.

From Control Panel Classic View, open the Phone and Modem Options icon.

Phone and Modem Options

Printer and fax settings

The Printers window lists a collection of printers that your laptop is configured to use. It's the location where you can monitor printing or set up a new printer when you need to. The topic of printing on your laptop is covered in Chapter 8. To control printing, however, you need to use the Control Panel.

From the Control Panel Home, choose the Printer link, found under the Hardware and Sound heading.

From Control Panel Classic View, open the Printers icon.

Printers

User account stuff

To modify your account, login picture, and password, as well as to manage others who use your laptop (not recommended), you *could* use the Control Panel. But I don't bother writing all that stuff (because it's late and I'm tired), so let me tell you the trick I use:

Click on your account icon's picture in the upper-right corner of the Start button menu. That one-click shortcut instantly opens the User Accounts window, which displays information about your own account. Simple.

More information on customizing your account is in Chapter 8.

Chapter 7

Behold the Tablet PC

In This Chapter

▶ Understanding tablet computers

▶ Studying Tablet PC hardware

▶ Configuring a Tablet PC

▶ Working with the stylus

▶ Inputting text

▶ Using special tablet software

The Romans called it a *tabulae ceratea,* a wax writing tablet. It was *the* high-tech recording device 2,000 years ago. The wax was black, and you wrote on it using a sharp metal stick called a *stylus.* You wrote with the pointy end of the stylus while the wider, flat end served as an eraser. The *tabulae* was used for all kinds of writing, including important documents. And I'm certain that more than one Roman schoolkid used the excuse "I left my homework in the sun" once too often.

The modern equivalent of the *tabulae ceratea* is the Tablet PC. After 2,000 years, we've finally figured out how to use a digital stylus to write on a computer screen rather than use an iron stylus to write on beeswax. Such a marvel seems like a must-have extension to the whole laptop concept, and therefore this chapter covers the Tablet PC.

> ✔ A common variation on the *tabulae ceratea* was a trifold version (three tablets tied together). Medieval scholars referred to it as a *triptych.*
>
> ✔ By the way, you didn't do math on a *tabulea ceratea.* Roman schoolboys learned to do math on the abacus. (Roman girls did not go to school.)

Sing to Me, O Tablet PC Muse

Computer engineers have dreamed of something like the Tablet PC ever since the Xerox Dynabook concept, back in the 1960s. And I agree, the Tablet PC seems like a marvelous technological advance: You input data directly by writing on the screen. A Tablet PC is the electronic version of a pad of paper and a pencil, a stone tablet for the digital age. Yet mankind hasn't quite taken to the notion.

There have been many attempts to make a Tablet PC successful. Over the years, the design has been called the GRiDPad, Pentop Computer, Apple Newton, and Pen computing. Back in the early 2000s, the Tablet PC was ballyhooed with marketing and splash from many computer manufacturers and Microsoft. It was a big push, but once again the consumer was nonplussed.

Today, there are Tablet PCs to be had, but it's more of a laptop option than a unique computer category all its own. As such, the Tablet PC is a valid choice for fans of the wireless digital life.

There are three different types of Tablet PC, as shown in Figure 7-1:

- ✔ Convertible
- ✔ Slate
- ✔ Hybrid

The *convertible,* the most common Tablet PC model, is basically a laptop with a hinged, swiveling lid. When the screen is up and facing the keyboard, the computer looks like a laptop. If you rotate the screen and fold it over the keyboard, the PC becomes a tablet. This model also has the bonus feature of allowing you to write on the screen no matter which configuration is used.

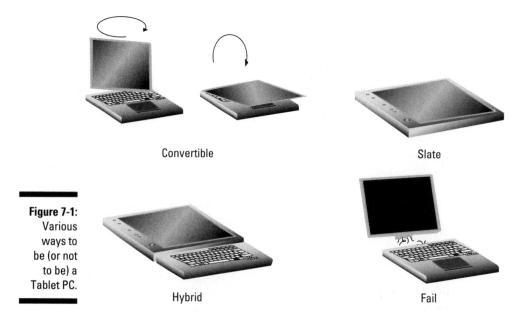

Convertible

Slate

Figure 7-1:
Various
ways to
be (or not
to be) a
Tablet PC.

Hybrid

Fail

The *slate* model is the traditional type of tablet computer. It's basically a thick laptop screen without a keyboard. Often it has buttons or options around the screen, but the slate model distinguishes itself by doing away with any type of keyboard.

The *hybrid* model is the rarest of the bunch. It's basically a slate model that features a detachable or retractable keyboard.

✔ A special version of Windows, *Pen Windows,* was introduced in 1991. It was rereleased as *Windows for Pen Computing* in 1992. In 2002, Microsoft released *Windows XP Tablet PC Edition.* In Windows Vista, Tablet PC support is provided in all releases and versions.

✔ See Chapter 1 for more information on the Dynabook.

✔ The biggest advantage of the Tablet PC is that its interface is natural. It's easier to jot down notes than to use a keyboard. Plus, the digital stylus on the screen works much better for artistic applications than does a mouse or touchpad.

✔ Tablet PCs are space-wise. It's easier to use a Tablet PC on a cramped airplane than it is to unfurl a laptop. A Tablet can lie flat on a desktop, which makes it less obtrusive during an impromptu meeting.

✔ The biggest disadvantage of a Tablet PC is cost: It's more expensive than its laptop cousins. Also, because of its digitizer screen, a Tablet PC is heavier than a typical laptop and cannot sport the larger screen sizes that are available.

Discover Your Tablet PC

If you squint really hard, you'll be casually fooled into believing that a Tablet PC is basically just a fancy laptop computer. It's not, of course. Although my portable computing advice that applies to a laptop also applies to a Tablet PC, many things make your tablet computer special.

Touring special tablet hardware

Everything you know about a standard laptop PC also applies to a Tablet PC. Aside from that, there are three main physical characteristics to note about a tablet computer.

First, if you have a convertible Tablet PC, examine how the screen turns and folds to transform between Laptop and Tablet modes. Note that the screen probably twists only one way. Practice converting the computer between Laptop and Tablet modes.

Check to see whether there's a way to secure the screen when the computer is in Tablet mode. You need to use the laptop's lid-catch release to release the screen whether the laptop is closed or open in Tablet mode.

Second, peruse the screen part of your Tablet PC. Figure 7-2 illustrates some potential features you might find on or around the screen.

Here's a smattering:

Power button: This button is often a duplicate of a convertible laptop's main power button.

Power button lock: The lock allows you to keep the laptop on or off by disabling the Power button's function. That way, the tablet doesn't accidentally turn itself on when it's jostled in its case.

Fingerprint, or biometric, reader: A standard feature on many laptops, but it's found on the lid of a Tablet PC for obvious reasons.

Cursor control pad: Some Tablet PCs offer this feature as an alternative way to control the mouse pointer, which is helpful if the stylus goes missing. You might also be able to press the control pad to simulate the mouse click.

Speaker/microphone: These features provide audio input and output in Tablet mode.

Webcam: This common feature is found on many laptops.

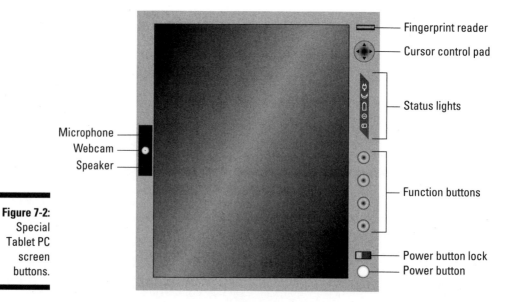

Figure 7-2: Special Tablet PC screen buttons.

Status lights: Status lights on the keyboard do no good in Tablet mode, so when you don't find them there, look on the lid.

Various function buttons: These include buttons that control certain features that might be handy or otherwise necessary but are out of reach when the keyboard isn't available. Included are an Esc key; an on-screen menu button; a button to control screen orientation; a multifunction or menu button; a button to access security features; a button to lock Windows; a button to quickly access the Windows Mobility Center; a button to contact the manufacturer for support; programmable buttons; and others.

Other standard controls: Examples of these controls are for volume control, screen brightness, external monitor activation, and wireless networking.

Finally, a Tablet PC uses a special digitizer pen that I call a stylus, as depicted in Figure 7-3.

Find the stylus. It most likely snaps or slides into a compartment somewhere on the tablet's case. Practice removing and inserting the stylus: For styluses inserted into the case, press the stylus in a little. That should pop it out so that you can grab it. The stylus is returned to its cave by inserting it all the way in until it clicks.

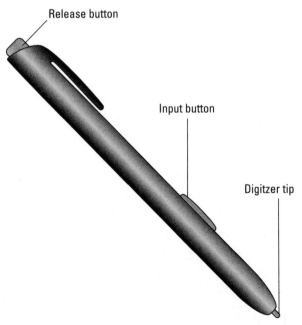

Release button

Input button

Digitzer tip

Figure 7-3:
A typical
stylus.

The stylus works by touching the tablet's screen, which is a *digitizer*. In Windows, the stylus's touch is interpreted just like mouse movement. (See the section "Training the pen," later in this chapter, for tips on using the stylus.)

You may find one or more buttons on the stylus. The button might be used as a mouse click or right-click, or its function may be programmable.

It's important to note that the stylus is *not* a stick. Although you may be able to use your finger to work the tablet computer or you find that a capped pen works sometimes, you really need the stylus. Do not lose it!

✔ On convertible tablets, the lid sports features commonly found on the keyboard part of a traditional laptop. Obviously, you cannot access those necessary features when the laptop is in tablet configuration mode.

✔ You can still use the stylus on the screen of a convertible Tablet PC when it's in a standard laptop configuration.

✔ A convertible Tablet PC lets you lock down the lid in both Laptop and Tablet modes. Don't forget to use the lid catch to release the screen in either orientation.

✔ Buttons and controls for the tablet's screen might be hidden behind a panel.

✔ When your Tablet PC lacks buttons or controls on the screen, you can often access those same features by using software. Refer to the next section.

✔ Your Tablet PC probably came with a spare stylus, or perhaps replacement parts for the stylus. Do not lose them!

✔ Some Tablet PCs feature a *pen tether,* or a place where you can attach the stylus to the tablet by using a nylon cord. That comes in handy for all us pen-droppers who loathe the awkwardness of searching underneath an airline seat for *anything.*

Settings in the Control Panel

Two special places in the Control Panel allow you to configure the Tablet PC. They're the aptly named Tablet PC Settings dialog box and the Pen and Input Devices dialog box. To visit these places, open the Control Panel window.

To open the Tablet PC Settings dialog box from the Control Panel Home, choose Mobile PC and then Tablet PC Settings. From Control Panel Classic View, open the Tablet PC Settings icon. The Tablet PC Settings dialog box is shown in Figure 7-4.

Figure 7-4:
The Tablet
PC Settings
dialog box.

The purpose of the Tablet PC Settings dialog box is to adjust settings or to control things specific to your tablet computer, some of which are covered later in this chapter.

Pen and Input
Devices

The second Tablet PC–specific place to visit in the Control Panel is the Pen and Input Devices dialog box. To open it from the Control Panel Home, choose Mobile PC and then choose Pen and Input Devices. From Control Panel Classic View, open the Pen and Input Devices icon. The Pen and Input Devices dialog box is shown in Figure 7-5.

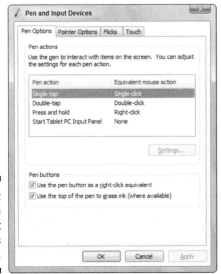

Figure 7-5:
The Pen
and Input
Devices
dialog box.

You use the Pen and Input Devices dialog box to specifically deal with the Tablet PC stylus. There you can set up the stylus-mouse equivalent actions (double-click and right-click, for example), set up feedback options, configure other stylus options, and set up the tablet for finger input.

✔ Performing finger input is covered later in this chapter.

✔ Not every tablet computer has a touch-sensitive screen. Those that don't, lack the Touch tab shown in Figure 7-5.

✔ An option to rotate the Tablet PC screen might be found in the Windows Mobility Center. You may find additional options in the Windows Mobility Center window, put there by your Tablet PC's manufacturer. (See Chapter 6 for more information on the Windows Mobility Center.)

The Pen Is Mightier than the Mouse

Not the keyboard. Not the mouse. The Tablet PC's main input device is a *digitizer pen,* which I call a stylus. It's used just like you use a computer mouse, though it's pressed directly against the screen. Yes, ignore what you learned about not touching an LCD screen; a Tablet PC's screen is designed to be touched by the stylus.

Using the stylus is easy, and Windows offers a host of features that may make you soon forget the keyboard. (Well, not for long.)

Training the pen

You don't need to train the stylus, but you probably need to train yourself how to use it, to understand its quirks. Follow these simple steps for basic stylus orientation:

1. **Remove the stylus from the tablet's clutches.**

2. **Bring the stylus near the screen, but don't touch the screen yet.**

   You should see the mouse pointer change to a target-like thing, as shown in the margin. That's the *pen cursor,* and it appears instead of the mouse pointer (or mouse cursor) when you use the stylus on your tablet.

3. **Move the stylus near the screen (but not touching the screen).**

   The pen cursor follows the movement. Don't move too far away with the pen or else the signal gets lost.

4. **Tap (touch and release) the stylus on the Start button.**

Touching the Start button with the stylus works like clicking it with the mouse.

5. **Choose your account.**

Tap the stylus on your account name on the right side of the Start menu. Your account window appears.

6. **Use the stylus to drag the window around the desktop.**

Touch the top part of the window and, keeping the stylus on the screen, drag the window around.

To move the pen cursor without dragging, just point the stylus at the screen. To drag items on the screen, touch the stylus to the screen.

7. **Double-tap on the Documents icon to open it.**

Double-tap = double-click.

8. **Press and hold the stylus on an icon.**

As you hold down the stylus, you see the pen pointer grow into a circle in a clockwise direction.

9. **Release the stylus after the circle appears.**

The *press-hold-release* operation is a "right-click." The circle is your visual clue that a right-click was successful. Well, also the shortcut menu for the icon appears when you've done a proper press-hold-release.

10. **Tap on the desktop to dismiss the shortcut menu.**

11. **Practice your tapping skills to close the window.**

12. **Put the stylus back into its garage for now.**

Table 7-1 lists a quick summary of pen and mouse equivalents.

Table 7-1	Pen and Mouse Actions
Mouse Activity	*Pen Equivalent*
Point	Point the stylus at the screen. (Don't touch!)
Click	Tap the stylus on the screen.
Double-click	Tap the stylus twice on the same spot.
Drag	Touch the stylus to the screen and move the stylus about.
Right-click	Touch the stylus to the screen, pause, and then lift the stylus; alternatively, touch the stylus while pressing its button.
Right-drag	Press and hold the stylus button while keeping the stylus touching the screen.

If the stylus sports a button, it can be used to quickly emulate a right-click. Essentially, pressing the button is the same as a right-click or right-drag operation, depending on what you're doing with the stylus.

For more help using the stylus, you can use the Tablet PC Pen Training program. From the Start menu, choose All Programs⇨Tablet PC⇨Tablet PC Pen Training. Work through the program by following the directions on-screen.

✔ In the Control Panel's Pen and Input Devices dialog box, on the Pointer Options tab, you can set the following visual feedback for the basic pen-input actions

  • Single-tapping

  • Double-tapping

  • Press-tapping

  • Pressing the pen's button

✔ Also in the Pen and Input Devices dialog box, you can click the Settings button on the Pen Options tab to refine the stylus equivalents for the double-click and right-click.

✔ Don't be too slow on the press-hold-release right-click thing. If you wait too long before lifting the stylus, the operation fails, and you have to try again.

✔ I find using the stylus button easier than the press-hold-release method for emulating a right mouse click.

✔ In some cases, the top of the stylus can be used as an input device; for example, to erase parts of an image in a graphics program. The availability of this feature depends on the graphics program software.

Using the Input Panel

To make up for the absence of a keyboard, your Tablet PC comes with something called the *Input Panel.* You can use this on-the-fly gizmo either to scribble in text or as a small on-screen keyboard for those desperate situations when typing is required.

The Input Panel is always available on a Tablet PC. It lurks on the right or left edge of the screen, looking like a window that has gone astray. Touching the Input Panel with the stylus pops it out a bit more, as shown in Figure 7-6. Touch the Input Panel again to summon it in its full-blown glory, as shown in Figure 7-7.

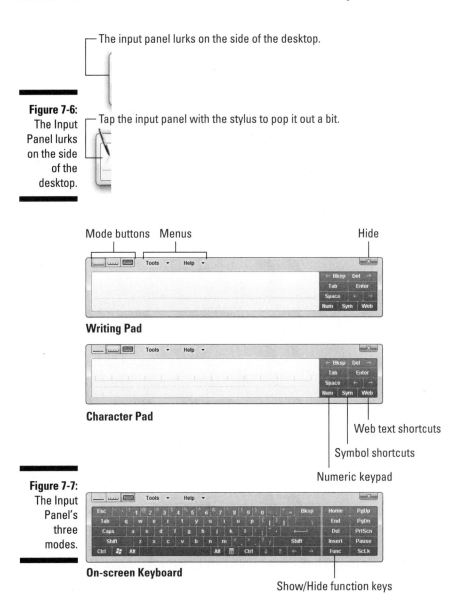

The input panel lurks on the side of the desktop.

Figure 7-6:
The Input
Panel lurks
on the side
of the
desktop.

Tap the input panel with the stylus to pop it out a bit.

Mode buttons   Menus   Hide

Writing Pad

Character Pad

Web text shortcuts

Symbol shortcuts

Numeric keypad

Figure 7-7:
The Input
Panel's
three
modes.

On-screen Keyboard

Show/Hide function keys

The Input Panel features three different modes for input:

> **Writing Pad:** In this mode, the Input Panel allows free-form text input. You can print or write in "cursive," and Windows does its best to trans-late what you type into text, as shown in Figure 7-8.

> To make a correction, click on one of the buttons that appear below your scrawl. A pop-up window appears, allowing you to edit each word indi-vidually or reenter words using a mode that resembles Character Pad.

Figure 7-8:
Working in
Writing Pad
mode.

The Input Panel expands as you write, so don't worry about running out of room.

Click the Insert button to paste your text into a document, dialog box, or Web page.

Character Pad: This mode works like Writing Pad mode, but is better for those of us with lousy handwriting; each letter must fit into its place. As you draw each letter, Windows approximates what you mean and replaces it with a best guess, as shown in Figure 7-9.

Figure 7-9:
Working in
Character
Pad mode.

To correct a mistake, point the stylus at the offending letter. Click the button that appears beneath the letter, and then choose the proper letter from the pop-up menu that appears, as shown in Figure 7-9. When there are no options, click the Clear button and try writing again.

Click the Insert button to paste in the text you've written.

On-Screen Keyboard: You can hunt and peck using the stylus in this mode, which is often times less frustrating than toiling in the other two modes.

The On-Screen Keyboard works just like typing on the keyboard. To type key combinations, the Shift, Alt, and Ctrl keys lock automatically.

 The Input Panel can also be accessed any time you click in a text box, such as in a dialog box or even on a Web page. When you click in such an area, an Input Tablet icon appears, as shown in the margin. Tap that icon to summon the Input Tablet and quickly "type" what you need.

✔ You can drag the hidden Input Panel up or down the side of the window. That way, it doesn't interfere with program windows or palettes.

✔ You can also dock the Input Panel at the top or bottom of the screen by choosing the proper option from the Tools menu.

✔ The X button in the Input Panel window doesn't close the Input Panel; clicking the X button merely sends the Input Panel hiding back to the side of the screen.

✔ You configure the Input Panel by using its Options dialog box. To summon that dialog box, choose Tools⇨Options from the Input Panel menu.

✔ Use the Options dialog box to specify whether the Input Panel appears on the left or right side of the desktop.

✔ In either Writing Pad or Character Pad mode, erase text by drawing a line back and forth over the text. That action "rubs out" what you wrote. You can customize how text is erased by using the Gestures tab in the Options dialog box.

✔ When all else fails, remember that you can convert some tablet computers into the standard laptop configuration and just use the keyboard.

Taking advantage of gestures and flicks

Some things that you can do with a stylus a mouse just can't accomplish. These include two handy shortcuts referred to as gestures and flicks.

A *gesture* is a handwriting shortcut. It's a way of inputting a special character quickly. For example, typing a Z shape over a word or letter in the Input panel erases that word. The Z shape is a gesture. Other gestures are shown in Table 7-2.

Table 7-2	Common Gestures
Character or Key	*Action*
Backspace	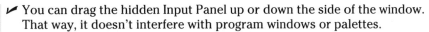
Enter	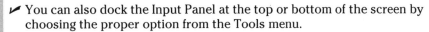
Space	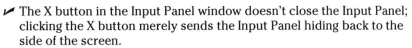
Tab	

A *flick* is another type of input shortcut, one that's growing more common, thanks to touch computer interfaces such as those found on the iPhone and the Apple MacBook line. Using the stylus, you *flick* quick and short in one direction. For example, flicking up scrolls a document or Web page up one screen. Flicking down scrolls down. Flicking left or right is the same as clicking the Back or Forward button in Internet Explorer or Windows Explorer.

✔ Gestures are enabled in the Input Panel's Options dialog box: Choose Tools➪Options from the Input Panel's window, and then click the Gestures tab.

✔ Hone your flicking skills in the Pen and Input Devices dialog box, on the Flicks tab.

Giving your laptop the finger

Many Tablet PCs allow you to use your finger as an input device, just like your nose does! Although it's not as elegant a solution as the stylus, it may do in a pinch. Honestly, I've not really gotten the hang of the finger thing (and it smudges up the monitor). You might find it handy, however.

To use your finger, extend it from the rest of your hand.

To have the laptop recognize finger input, use your extended finger to work these steps:

1. **Open the Pen and Input Devices dialog box.**

   Directions are offered earlier in this chapter.

2. **Click the Touch tab.**

   What? No Touch tab? Then your laptop doesn't have that ability. Oh, well.

3. **Place a check mark by Use Your Finger As an Input Device.**

4. **(Optional) You can click the Settings button to make adjustments or to practice.**

   Click the OK button to close the Settings dialog box if you elect to go there.

5. **Put a check mark in the Touch Pointer area to activate that feature as well.**

6. **Click OK to close the Pen and Input Devices dialog box, and also close the Control Panel window if it displeases you.**

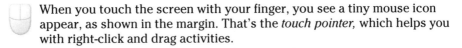 When you touch the screen with your finger, you see a tiny mouse icon appear, as shown in the margin. That's the *touch pointer,* which helps you with right-click and drag activities.

To get the most out of the Touch Pointer, as well as using your finger to work the Tablet PC, I recommend that you run the Tablet PC Touch Training program. It's found on the Start menu; choose All Programs⇨Tablet PC⇨Tablet PC Touch Training.

Special Tablet PC Software

You can do anything on a Tablet PC with a stylus that most people do on a laptop with a mouse. But you do have an edge in certain things. To exploit that edge, Windows Vista comes with a slate of useful programs and tools that Tablet PC users can exploit. This section explains some of the highlights.

Windows Journal

Finally, it's come to this: Your pricey Tablet PC serves the same function as a cheap pad of ruled paper. In fact, the Windows Journal program, shown in Figure 7-10, follows that paradigm visually.

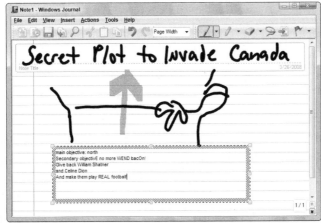

Figure 7-10:
Windows
Journal in
action.

Start Windows Journal by choosing it from the Start menu's All Programs menu. Then scribble. If you need to write text, create a text box by choosing Insert⇨Text box and then use the keyboard or Input Panel to write. Don't forget to save your work!

Sticky Notes

For taking quick notes, you can use the Sticky Notes program, shown in Figure 7-11. It's not quite a virtual Post-it Note, but the program comes close. It's simpler than using the full-blown Windows Journal, plus it offers a way to take audio notes using your computer's microphone.

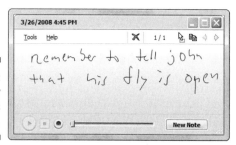

Figure 7-11:
The Sticky
Notes
program.

InkBall

Finally, what would life be like without computer games? Well, we'd probably read more books. So when the urge to enrich your mind from a good book reaches its peak, you can play a game like InkBall.

Start InkBall by choosing All Programs⇨Games⇨InkBall from the Start menu. InkBall is an arcade game that should help you hone your stylus skills. I'd put an image of it in this chapter, but I don't want the publisher to think that I'm playing games when I should be writing this book.

Chapter 8

You and Your Laptop

In This Chapter

▶ Customizing Windows

▶ Understanding the User Account Control warning

▶ Installing software

▶ Uninstalling software

▶ Using the Printers window

▶ Printing with your laptop

▶ Cleaning your laptop

O, the life of the laptop user is a vagabond one. It's kind of like the theater, but without the smell of greasepaint, the roar of the crowd, and the plethora of easy girls with low self esteem. You and your laptop will be going places, doing things, connecting to strange and dangerous networks. As a laptop user, your computing life will truly be wireless and unfettered.

Bottom line: It's *your* laptop. Microsoft may own Windows; the laptop may have been manufactured in China by some American company that prefers the flighty profits of cheap labor over invigorating the U.S. economy; but the laptop — she is yours! Despite the changing locations you may visit, when you bring along a laptop, everything is all about *you*. This chapter helps you make your laptop your own.

Make Windows Yours

I often complain that there are just too many ways to do things in Windows. I suppose it's a blessing, but when you're finding out how to do something new, having too many options is frustrating. The same holds true for the way Windows looks and acts: That's where the multiple methods are beneficial. You can indeed truly make Windows act the way you want.

Configuring your user account

I'll bet that your user account picture is a flower. Or a chess piece. Or a cat. That picture can change: You can set your account picture to anything. Likewise, you can change many things about your user account. Make it your own!

User account changes are made in the User Accounts window, shown in Figure 8-1. You can see this window by clicking and clicking through the Control Panel. That's boring. The easy way to display the User Accounts window is to click on your account image, found at the top of the Start menu. (Refer to Figure 6-1 in Chapter 6.)

Figure 8-1:
The User
Accounts
window.

The User Accounts window is the locus of all things dealing with your account. For changing your account image, act upon these steps:

1. **Choose the link Change Your Picture.**

   A slate of insipid images appears. Ignore them.

2. **Choose the link Browse for More Pictures.**

   A Browse dialog box opens, displaying files found in your account's Pictures folder.

3. **Use the Browse dialog box to find an image.**

   You can use any type of graphics file for your account image, including all standard Web page images (GIF, JPG, PNG) as well as Windows Paint program doodles and artwork.

4. **Choose a better image.**

5. **Click the Open button.**

The new picture is chosen and shows up in the window, at the logon screen, and at the top of the Start menu.

You can also use the User Accounts window to change your password, change the account name, plus manage other accounts (if you have administrator privileges). But, naturally, the most important thing you can do is change your account picture.

Setting up your laptop's display

As with a desktop computer, you can set various options for how Windows displays information on the laptop's screen. Here are the items most people want to customize:

- ✔ Screen size (resolution)
- ✔ Desktop background, or wallpaper
- ✔ Screen saver

Each of these items can be set by using the Personalization window. (It's mentioned in Chapter 6 and shown in Figure 6-10.) To sum up: You can see the Personalization window by right-clicking the desktop and choosing the Personalize command from the pop-up shortcut menu.

Resolution: To set the monitor's resolution, choose the Display Settings link in the Personalization window. Use the Display Settings dialog box to set screen resolution and colors.

Your laptop's display has certain modes and resolutions that work best — for example, 800 x 600 or 1024 x 768. These and other resolutions are known as *native* settings for the monitor. Although other resolutions might be possible, the results don't look good and can wreak havoc on the display.

You might also consider setting a lower resolution and number of colors for your monitor. The higher resolution and color settings require more video memory, which means more work for the computer, more power, and less battery life.

Background: To set the desktop background, also known as *wallpaper,* choose the Desktop Background link. You can choose a solid color or select from a raft of designs and images supplied with Windows. To use an image you created or saved (say, with a digital camera), choose Pictures from the Picture Location drop-down menu.

As with the screen resolution, you can save a modicum of battery power by choosing a solid color background rather than an image. Images must be loaded from disk, which uses more battery power.

Screen saver: The final toy, er, important display setting used by most folks is the screen saver. Choose the Screen Saver link to set things up. Because most people have no problems here, I'll let you discover things for yourself.

Note that the screen saver timeout value should be less than the timeout value used to sleep the monitor. Refer to Chapter 9 for more information on setting a sleep timeout for the laptop's display.

For more information on configuring a computer display in Windows Vista, refer to my book *Find Gold in Windows Vista* (Wiley Publishing).

Dealing with User Account Controls (UACs)

Windows Vista is all about security, and when you want security, you sacrifice freedom. Of course, security could have been done differently. But, no. All laptop users must face the consequences of having to see and deal with the various User Account Controls, or UACs, as a warning that something sneaky might be in the works.

Security Center

User Account Control warnings are predictable. You can tell when one is coming up because a link, button, or menu item is flagged with the shield icon, as shown in the margin. That means the command requires administrator privileges to continue; for example, when you change a configuration option or setting. That shield is also your assurance that a UAC warning is expected and coming.

When you're logged in as an administrator, you choose Continue or Allow to Proceed. To stop it, choose Cancel or Don't Allow.

On non-administrator accounts, the UAC looks different, as shown in Figure 8-2. To continue, you must type the administrator's password and click the OK button. To stop, click Cancel.

When faced with a UAC, instantly ask yourself: "Did I summon this warning?" If not, cancel the UAC warning.

Figure 8-2:
The User
Account
Control dia-
log box for
a "limited"
user.

The Software Side

In the realm of computers, all hardware requires software to make it go.
Your laptop is no different and, most likely, came with lots of software preinstalled. Windows is software, after all. You may also have Microsoft Office
installed, plus other software: security, antivirus, financial, plus some junk.
You may even add more software. And you probably want to remove the
junk. This section explains the details.

Adding new software

To expand your laptop's abilities, or to provide support for new hardware,
you add new software to your laptop's repertoire. Installing new programs is
one of the basic computer operator duties.

Software can be installed from two sources:

- ✔ An optical disc
- ✔ The Internet

The standard and easiest way to install new programs on your laptop is to
stick the software's optical disc into your laptop's optical drive. After inserting the disc, just sit back and watch as the installation program runs. Follow

the directions on the screen. The operation may take a while, and it may require some decisions and choices on your part. Don't fret: Eat a cookie and watch. Soon, you're done.

To install a program from the Internet, the program must first be downloaded into your laptop. This is a common and safe way to add programs to your laptop. Follow these general steps:

1. **In your Web browser, click the link to download the software.**

   Choose the EXE, or *executable,* link. Avoid ZIP, TAR, GZ, SRC, RAR, or other links because they involve more setup steps, require programs you don't have, or contain information you don't need.

   A warning might appear near the top of the Web browser window. It says, "To help protect your security, Internet Explorer blocked this site from downloading files to your computer. Click here for options."

2. **Click the warning text to display a menu of options.**

3. **Choose Download File from the menu.**

   If a problem occurs and the download doesn't start, look for a link on the page that says something like "Click here to download directly." Clicking that link should start the download.

   A File Download Security Warning dialog box appears, as shown in Figure 8-3.

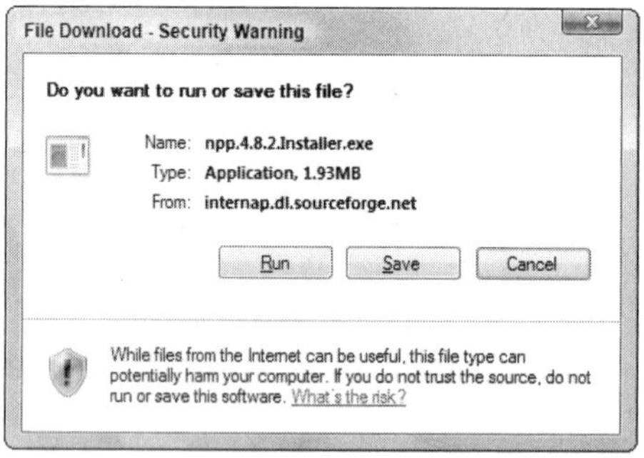

Figure 8-3: Downloading a new program from the Internet.

4. **Click Save.**

   I recommend saving the file so that you have a copy on your laptop. That makes it easier to reinstall the file later, if the need arises.

A Save As dialog box appears. It has the Downloads folder selected for you, which is the disk location in which I recommend saving down-loaded files.

5. **Click the Save button in the Save As dialog box.**

Wait while the file is downloaded. Well, actually, you can go do some-thing else if the download is lengthy; Windows continues to retrieve the file as you work on other tasks.

When the download is complete, you see a Download Complete dialog box.

6. **Click the Run button to install the program.**

You're done with the download, but not with the security warnings.

7. **Click the Run button.**

This last step confirms that you trust the software developer and are certain that you haven't downloaded something nefarious.

At this point, installing the program works the same as though you were setting things up from an optical disc: Read and obey the directions on the screen.

✔ If the program doesn't automatically install after you insert the CD, open the Computer window and then open the optical drive's icon. Look for a Setup or Install program icon. Double-click that icon to open the installer program and set up the software.

✔ You need to attach an external (USB) optical drive to install software from an optical disc on a laptop that lacks an optical drive.

✔ Install only software from the Internet that comes from a reliable source. If you question the source, use Google to search for the software name or for the software developer's name. When the software is question-able, you find many links that explain why it is or that answer questions about potential dangers.

✔ Some programs require that you restart Windows before installation is complete.

✔ The reason you occasionally have to quit all other running programs is that some programs, such as antivirus and security software, may inter-fere with the installation process. Also, if the computer automatically restarts when the installation is over, you can lose unsaved data in any running program.

✔ EXE is the filename extension for programs in Windows. ZIP is the filename extension for Compressed Folders. When you download such a file, you must first *extract* files from the folder and then install, which is a pain. The filename extensions TAR, GZ, and RAR represent archives, like ZIP does, but require special software to extract their contents. The SRC filename extension is given to downloads that also contain the programming source code.

Removing old software

Back in the days when computers were started with a hand crank, it was easy to uninstall or remove computer software: You simply deleted the program. Despite the fact that those days have been over for about 20 years, some people out there still believe — and spread the word — that you remove software by wearing a sheepskin and wool flap hat and playing Elmer Fudd: Folks, you do not remove software by hunting it down and killing it.

To rid yourself of unwanted software, obey these steps:

1. **Open the Control Panel window.**

   Refer to Chapter 6 for details on finding this important window.

Programs and
Features

2. **From the Control Panel Home, choose the link Uninstall a Program (beneath the Programs heading); from Control Panel Classic View, open the Programs and Features icon.**

   You see a list of installed programs.

3. **Click to select the program you want to remove.**

4. **Click the Uninstall or Uninstall/Change button that appears.**

5. **If you see a User Account Control warning, click the Continue button.**

   What happens next depends on the software you installed. Each program has its own Uninstall procedure, and most are easy to follow.

6. **Close the Programs and Features window when you're done.**

Some applications, such as Microsoft Office, run a special program that lets you change or repair the installation as well as remove programs. My advice: Read the screen directions *carefully*.

✔ Uninstalling a program erases its files from the laptop's hard drive. The uninstall program also resets certain options deep inside Windows, by trying to change things back to how they were before the program was first installed.

What did they preinstall this time?

Most laptops come with a bloat of software preinstalled. Don't feel compelled to use it. In fact, if that software annoys you, uninstall it. There's no point in keeping anything on your laptop's hard drive that you don't plan to use. Don't want AOL or Earthlink? Bye! Don't plan to use Disk Doctor? Bye! Bye! Bye! *Remember:* It's *your* laptop!

✔ Not every uninstall operation is successful. Sometimes, pieces of the program, or its files, remain behind. This is normal, sadly, and there's little you can do about it.

✔ If you remove a program the only way to get it back is to re-install it. That means from a downloaded file, optical disc, or from the computer's recovery or installation discs. Don't throw that stuff out!

✔ Removing a program *does not* remove its associated data files. For example, removing a graphics program doesn't delete all the graphics images you created with that program. After all, you created and own those files, and only you can remove them.

✔ Removing programs frees up space on your hard drive.

✔ Occasionally, you can find an Uninstall command on the All Programs menu (from the Start thing). Such a command sits on the same menu as the program itself. Very handy.

The Laptop and the Printer

When Adam Osborne originally proposed the portable computer, portable printing wasn't part of the big picture. He was right! How many times have you been in the *Café sans Fils* and seen someone printing from a laptop? Never! That's because printing is something that can be done later. You wait until your laptop is back home to print.

There are portable printers, of course. I've used a Canon Bubble Jet portable printer with my laptop. The printer isn't that heavy, it has full color, it's fairly fast, and it uses flashlight batteries. So, you have some on-the-road printing options, if you want them.

Whether you're printing on the road or at home, this section describes how to set up and use a printer — or even printer alternatives — with your laptop computer.

Displaying the Printers window

Printing in Windows centers around the Printers window, shown in Figure 8-4. That window lists all printers available to, or installed for, your laptop, including any printers directly connected to your laptop, network printers, and the Fax printer.

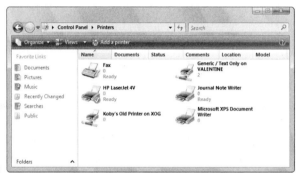

Figure 8-4:
The Printers window.

To display the Printers window, heed this procedure:

1. **Open the Control Panel window.**

2. **From the Control Panel Home, choose the Print link (beneath the Hardware and Sound heading); from Control Panel Classic View, open the Printers icon.**

The Printers window is used to set up and manage the printers available to your laptop. The icons in the window represent various printers (or printing devices, like the fax modem) available to, or installed for, your laptop. The icons appear whether the printer is available or attached to your laptop.

> ✔ The quickest way to display the Printers window is to choose Printers from the Start menu. The Printers command, however, is available only if you configure the Start menu to show it. My book *Find Gold in Windows Vista* (Wiley Publishing) has directions right on page 364 that explain how it's done.

> ✔ Connecting network printers is covered in Chapter 11.

> ✔ Using your laptop's fax modem is discussed in Chapter 13.

Connecting a printer to your laptop

To connect a standard computer printer to your laptop, follow these steps:

1. **Go back to the store and buy a USB cable.**

   True, your laptop didn't come with a USB cable. Go back to the store and buy one now. Also consider boning up on the whole USB issue by reading Chapter 10 on your way to the store. Or, better yet, be safe and bring someone else along to read Chapter 10 to you while you drive to the store to buy a USB cable.

2. **Plug the printer into the wall socket.**

3. **Ensure that the printer is turned off.**

   Also, set up the printer with ink and paper and all that other good stuff, according to the directions that came with the printer.

4. **Connect the USB cable to the printer and to your laptop.**

5. **Turn on the printer.**

   Windows should instantly recognize the printer and set everything up for you.

If you doubt the amazingly simple process by which you add a printer to your laptop's peripheral armada, simply confirm that an icon representing the printer dwells in the Printers window.

 If you're having trouble adding your printer, first open the Printers window (refer to Figure 8-4). Check the list of available printers. If you don't see your printer listed, click the Add a Printer button. Run the Add Printer Wizard to complete the printer setup task.

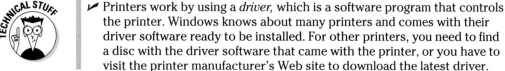

✔ You can disconnect the printer when you don't need it. Reconnecting the printer simply reactivates its support in Windows.

✔ No, it's not a good idea to unplug or turn off your printer while it's printing.

 ✔ Printers work by using a *driver,* which is a software program that controls the printer. Windows knows about many printers and comes with their driver software ready to be installed. For other printers, you need to find a disc with the driver software that came with the printer, or you have to visit the printer manufacturer's Web site to download the latest driver.

"What is the default printer?"

Your laptop can print documents to only one printer at a time. That printer can be chosen in the Print dialog box (refer to Figure 8-5), or when you don't choose a printer, Windows uses the *default* printer.

 You can determine which printer is the default by looking in the Printers window (refer to Figure 8-4). You see a tiny green circle with a white check mark flagging the default printer. In Figure 8-4, the default printer is the HP LaserJet 4V (which is an antique, but it works like a horse).

 One printer must always be chosen as the default. To change the default, choose any printer icon in the Printers window, and then click the Set As Default button on the toolbar.

Using the Print dialog box

Printing in Windows is done from within an application. The Print command is on the File menu, or often a Print toolbar button is used to print. The Print dialog box, shown in Figure 8-5, is where you control the printing of your documents. It's also where you choose which printer to use for printing that document.

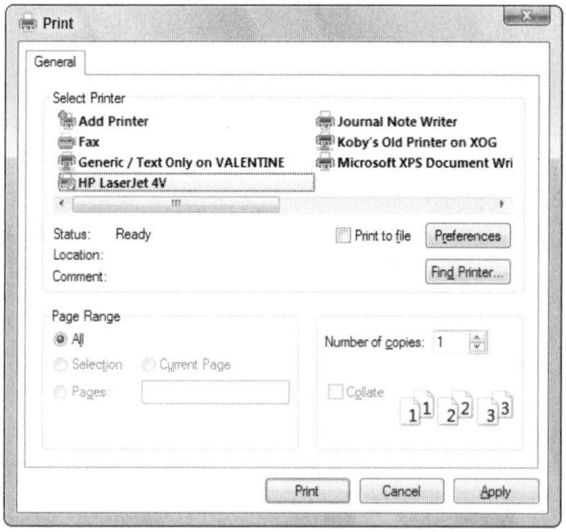

Figure 8-5:
A typical
Print dialog
box.

Clicking the Print button in the Print dialog box instantly (more or less) prints your document. Or, you can set options that allow you to change the number of copies or choose a range of pages to print.

✔ You choose paper size and set margins by using the Page Setup dialog box. Produce it by choosing the Page Setup command from an application's File menu.

✔ The keyboard shortcut for summoning the Print dialog box is Ctrl+P. [Insert overactive bladder humor here.]

Considering options for when you don't have a printer

The urge to print is often immediate. Honestly, when printing can wait, let it wait: Save a document. Then open the document again and print when your laptop is connected to the printer. Otherwise, I offer these nonprinter printing suggestions:

✔ Decent hotels and airports have business centers where you can temporarily connect to a printer and get your stuff on paper.

✔ Some office-supply stores offer printing services. Print shops and places such as FedEx Kinko's also have printers available for rent by the hour or by the sheet.

✔ Fax machines are printers. If you know of a fax machine nearby, just send your document as a fax. Note that plain-paper faxes are preferred; avoid wax-paper faxes, if possible. Note that faxes don't print in color. See Chapter 13 for more information about faxing with your laptop.

✔ You can create PDF (Adobe Acrobat) files, which can be displayed and printed on any computer with the Acrobat Reader software installed. You must, however, buy the Acrobat Writer software to create PDF files.

✔ An oddball Print to File option is found in most Print dialog boxes. Putting a check mark there means that Windows creates a file rather than prints your document. The file can be found in your account's Documents folder, but there's really little you can do with the file. I don't recommend using that option.

Keep It Clean

Laptops are robust beasts. They can go through a lot without cleaning. Well, any man will tell you that carpets can go for months without any vacuuming. But I digress.

After you've been around with your laptop a few times, you should do some cleanup. Look at those fingerprints! Yikes! If only your mother could see it. . .

 ✔ Consider washing your hands from time to time.

 ✔ Turn off the laptop before you start cleaning it.

 ✔ You need a sponge or lint-free cloth as your cleaning tool.

 ✔ Isopropyl (rubbing) alcohol is also a good cleansing agent, but not for the screen. (More on cleaning the screen in a few pages.)

 ✔ If your laptop manufacturer has any specific cleaning instructions, directions, or warnings, please refer to them first before following the information offered here.

Sprucing up the case

The best way to give the case a bath is with a damp sponge. You can use standard dishwashing liquid, by mixing it at about 1 part detergent to 5 parts water. Soak the sponge in the mixture, and then wring the sponge clean. Use it to gently wipe the laptop's case.

When you're done with the sponge, wipe off any excess moisture or dust by using a lint-free cloth.

 ✔ Ensure that the sponge is dry enough that it doesn't drip liquid into the laptop.

 ✔ You might also want to use cotton swabs to clean some of the gunk from the cracks.

 ✔ Do not clean inside any disk drive openings or the PC Card garage. Never spray any liquids into those openings, either.

 ✔ Avoid using detergent that contains strong chemicals (acid or alkaline). Don't use abrasive powders.

Grooming the keyboard

Every so often, I vacuum my laptop keyboard. I use the little portable vacuums, with either the tiny (toothbrush-size) brush or the upholstery-cleaning attachment. This effectively sucks up all the crud in the keyboard. It's amazing to watch.

Some people prefer to clean the keyboard by using a can of compressed air. I don't recommend this method because the air can blow the crud in your keyboard further inside the laptop. Instead, use a vacuum.

Cleansing the screen

I've found the techniques used for cleaning an LCD screen, whether it's for a desktop or laptop computer, to be filled with controversy! Generally, no one recommends using any liquids because they can damage the LCD's delicate surface. Even so, you gotta have something to rub with if you ever plan to get that sneeze residue off the thing.

First, for general cleaning, get a soft, lint-free cloth. Use it to wipe the dust off the monitor. For a Tablet PC, use the lint-free cloth to help wipe the finger smudges off the screen.

Second, dampen a sponge or lint-free cloth with water. Be sure to wring out all excess moisture. Rub the screen's surface gently, and don't get any excess liquid on or inside the monitor.

Let the monitor dry completely before closing the lid!

✔ Often times, the keyboard creates a shadow stain on the screen. It's difficult to avoid and impossible to clean off. To help prevent the stain, consider storing the soft, lint-free cloth that you use to clean the monitor inside the laptop, between the keyboard and screen.

✔ Office-supply stores carry special LCD screen cleaners as well as the lint-free wipes you can use to clean your screen and the rest of your laptop.

✔ One product I can recommend is Klear Screen, from Meridrew Enterprises (www.klearscreen.com). No, it's not cheap. You want *good,* not cheap.

✔ Avoid using alcohol or ammonia-based cleaners on your laptop screen! They can damage the LCD screen.

✔ Never squirt any cleaner directly on a laptop's screen.

Chapter 9

Power Management Madness

. . . .

In This Chapter

▶ Knowing various types of batteries

▶ Locating your laptop's battery

▶ Monitoring battery use

▶ Charging the battery

▶ Using a spare battery

▶ Saving power

▶ Managing battery power

▶ Creating your own power plan

. . . .

*F*orget weight. Forget size. Truly portable computing isn't possible without a robust battery. Portable power potential is what keeps you computing untethered and free. Yet, while laptop weight and size have been shrinking dramatically, battery life remains a stubborn constant. The electronics components in a modern laptop draw less power than in years past. Power management hardware and software help keep the thing going longer. But the sad bottom line is that batteries themselves remain the last limitation to an entirely wireless existence.

If the laptop's CPU is the muscle, and software the brain, then the battery is its heart. As long as that sucker keeps beating, you can use your laptop anywhere. This chapter covers the basics of laptop batteries and how to make the power last longer.

The Battery Will Get a Charge Out of This!

It's easy to understand how having a battery in a laptop is what separates the computer from the wall. Battery power means *freedom*. Most people recognize that, but relatively few really know what this *battery* thing is all about.

No, I don't go into a technical description of anything here. Heaven forfend!

You probably know that your car has a battery in it. It's a boxy thing. Scary. Only people who are comfortable with jumper cables bother with the car's battery. Then there are those cylinder batteries used in flashlights and toys. (They were developed in the 1890s, by the way.) Beyond those two trivial tidbits — well, and batteries are weakest when you need them most, and when you leave a battery in a toy for too long, it rusts out and reeks of ozone — no one wants to know anything about batteries. Hopefully, this section helps expand your battery knowledge an amp or two.

Types of batteries

Just as a good gardener knows that there's more than one type of rose, so is there more than one type of battery. They all provide electricity (*direct current,* if this were a physics class), but they go about generating that electricity in different ways, some more useful than others. Here are the knowledge tidbits:

Alkaline: This is the most common type of battery, normally used in flashlights, portable radios, remote controls, smoke alarms, and kids' toys. The advantage here is that you can find these standard-size batteries anywhere. A few portable computing devices (printers, handhelds) use them, but laptops do not. The reason is that this type of battery isn't rechargeable. You use an alkaline battery and then you throw it out (properly, according to the environmentally safe battery-disposal rules of your jurisdiction).

Lead acid: If ever two words could make an environmentalist blanch, they're *lead* and *acid.* Shocking as it may seem, millions of us drive around every day with a quantity of lead and acid nearby; those two chemicals supply the robust power of a car battery. Lead acid batteries are durable, long lasting, and rechargeable, but they're also heavy and, well, *full of lead and acid!* Yikes!

Lithium-ion: This type of battery is the one you most likely have in your laptop. Lithium-ion, or *Li-ion,* batteries are lightweight and perform better than other types of batteries. Unlike earlier types of batteries used in laptops, Li-ion batteries don't have The Dreaded Memory Effect. (See the upcoming sidebar "The Dreaded Memory Effect.") Li-ion batteries can be managed through hardware and software, controlling how they're recharged — including a rapid-charging option, which is good when you're in a time crunch. Finally, this type of battery is more environmentally friendly than the other types, plus it has a cool *Star Trek*–sounding name.

Two older types of batteries, once popular in portable computers, are nickel-cadmium (NiCad) and nickel-metal hydride (NiMH). The NiCad isn't often considered for laptops these days because it suffered unpleasantly from The Dreaded Memory Effect. A NiMH battery is longer lasting than a NiCad, but it too woefully suffers from The Dreaded Memory Effect.

✔ You can confirm which type of battery your laptop has by looking at its label. See the next section.

✔ A few laptop computers out there are still using NiMH batteries. This is fine, of course, but you might want to check to see whether you can find a battery upgrade to the Li-ion type.

✔ To prolong the life of a NiMH battery, I recommend fully discharging it every so often. For example, after you use, drain, and recharge the NiMH battery about four times (or so), do a complete drain and then recharge it again. That should help the battery last a bit longer.

✔ Your laptop might have *two* additional batteries inside. A secondary, alkaline battery inside is used to power the laptop's internal clock. An optional third battery keeps things powered for the minute or so that it takes you to swap out a spent main battery with a fresh one. See the section "Love that spare battery," later in this chapter.

✔ Using unapproved batteries in your laptop may lead to bad situations, such as, oh, the laptop catching fire and exploding. If you doubt me, look up **exploding laptop** on YouTube.

✔ *AC powered* means powered by electricity from a wall socket.

✔ *DC powered* means powered by the battery.

Locate the laptop's battery

Take a moment to locate your laptop's battery. Odds are good that it loads into the bottom of the laptop, though a few laptop models have their batteries inserted through a hole or door in the side.

The battery may be labeled, describing which type of battery it is (see the previous section) as well as other information about the charge it holds, its serial number, and its replacement information. Note that often this information may be printed on the laptop case instead of, or in addition to, on the battery. Sometimes the information may be included with the laptop's documentation. Then again, there may be no information.

✔ Know where your battery is stored in your laptop. You may need to remove or replace it in the future.

✔ Most laptops use a few sliding locks or clips to help keep the battery in place. The locks may be numbered when there's a sequence to release the battery. Don't force a battery into or out of your laptop.

✔ Batteries get warm as they're being used. That's simply their nature. However:

Fuel cells

The future of the battery looks weak. I could say *drained.* That's because electronic gizmos in a few short years will start using fuel cells rather than batteries.

Fuel cells use a magical combination of chemistry and physics that provides power for much longer periods than typical batteries do. Although a fuel cells drains like a battery does, you can refill it — add fuel similar to filling a gas tank — and keep the fuel cell power going and going until it needs refilling again.

Fuel cells are available today, but they're a bit too bulky to be used with laptop computers. The estimated time schedule states that by the year 2010, fuel cells will be small, light, and compact enough for use in laptop computers. When that time comes, power management on your laptop becomes a different creature, and battery-saving tips and techniques become a thing of the past.

 ✔ Watch out if the battery gets too hot! For example, the battery can get too hot to touch or hold for more than a few seconds. That could be a sign of a malfunctioning battery, and such a thing is *dangerous.* Phone your dealer or laptop manufacturer immediately if you suspect that the battery is running hot.

Monitor the battery

The laptop's battery drains as you use it, which is to be expected. You should plan for at least two or three hours of active computer use under battery power. The rate of drain varies, however, depending on what you're doing with the laptop. And, naturally, depending on what you're doing, that time may pass rather quickly.

You can monitor the battery in one of several ways, some of them useful.

The most popular way to check laptop battery status is by viewing the tiny battery icon in the notification area on the taskbar. The icon graphically shows how much power is left; the icon's color "drains" out as you use the laptop.

When the notification area's battery icon is too tiny for you to see properly, you can point the mouse at that icon. A pop-up bubble appears, explaining how much juice is left, similar to what's shown in Figure 9-1.

Figure 9-1:
Nearly two
hours are
left on the
battery.

In Figure 9-1, the icon shows that two hours 14 minutes remain for battery
life, and the battery has about 87 percent of its power remaining.

To ensure that the battery icon shows up in the notification area, heed these
steps:

1. **Open the Control Panel.**

2a. **From the Control Panel Home, choose Appearance and
    Personalization, and then on the next screen choose the link
    Customize Icons on the Taskbar from beneath the Taskbar and
    Start Menu heading.**

2b. **From Control Panel Classic View, open the Taskbar and Start Menu
    icon. Then click the Notification Area tab in the Taskbar and Start
    Menu window.**

3. **Put a check mark by the Power item.**

4. **Click OK.**

5. **Close the Control Panel window.**

Refer to Chapter 6 for more information on the Control Panel.

Finally, your laptop may feature a battery light on its case. The light may
change color as the laptop drains. Or the battery light may be a fancy display
that accurately tracks battery power. And, as usual, custom programs may
monitor your battery's status. For example, my laptop has a battery icon
on the 3 key. Pressing Fn+3 on my laptop displays the battery status on the
screen.

    ✔ Oops! Almost forgot: You can also monitor battery use from the Control
       Panel's Windows Mobility Center. Type Win+X on the keyboard to
       quickly summon that window.

    ✔ If you're using the Windows Sidebar, you can get a battery monitor
       widget to display the battery life. Refer to a good Windows Vista refer-
       ence for information on obtaining Sidebar gadgets.

    ✔ A different icon may appear in the notification area when the laptop is
       AC powered. For example, a power plug or other icon may show up in its
       place.

The Dreaded Memory Effect

In the old days of the NiCad, and even NiMH, batteries, the mantra was that you had to fully discharge the battery, all the way down to empty, before you even considered recharging the thing. This principle was true and necessary: If you didn't fully drain the battery, it began to lose its potency over time.

What happened, especially with the NiCad battery, was that the battery would "remember" how long it was used. So, if the battery held one hour of power when it was fully charged and you recharged it after only 30 minutes of use, the former one-hour battery would become a 30-minute battery. That's *The Dreaded Memory Effect*.

To avoid The Dreaded Memory Effect and to prolong the life of their batteries, NiCad users would insist on fully draining their batteries each and every time they were used. Laptop owners would have to wait until their machines completely shut down before recharging. Even so, some users would give up, and eventually their rechargeable one-hour NiCads would last for only ten minutes of power — not enough.

Today's lithium-ion batteries don't have The Dreaded Memory Effect. They're smart. You can use them for a minute and then recharge them, and the battery is still as good as it was when you bought it. So, boldly use your battery without fear. And the next time someone mentions The Dreaded Memory Effect, giggle with a smug laugh of confidence, secure in the knowledge that you're safe from the power problems of the past.

✔ Smart-battery technology is responsible for the ability of Windows to determine how much power is left in the battery. Be aware, however, that such a thing is an *estimate*. Different things can affect battery life, so don't bet real money on how much longer your laptop can survive on the battery.

What happens when the power gets low

Thanks to smart-battery technology, your laptop computer gives you a whit of warning before the battery poops out. So don't panic! You have enough time to finish what you're working on, save, close programs, and properly shut down the computer.

To prepare for the inevitable, you receive a series of warnings.

First, the various battery icons and lights may change color. The battery light on the laptop's case may go from green to yellow or red. The battery icons on the desktop do the same. This type of warning happens gradually as you use the laptop.

As battery life passes below the 25 percent available mark, the battery icon in the notification area may grow one of those international warning triangles: yellow with an exclamation point in the middle. Humans grow the same thing after they turn 65, though only angels and little kids can see it.

You may hear an audible warning as the battery's life grows shorter and shorter. See the next section for particulars.

When you get a low-battery bubble warning from the notification area's teensy battery icon, as shown in Figure 9-2, you can be pretty sure that time is just about up. At that point, save your stuff and shut down (or hibernate) the laptop. I'm serious because the last thing that happens when the power gets low is that the laptop shuts itself off. The screen goes dark. You're done.

Figure 9-2:
Oops!
Quitting
time!

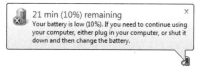

> 21 min (10%) remaining
> Your battery is low (10%). If you need to continue using your computer, either plug in your computer, or shut it down and then change the battery.

Adjust low battery warnings

You have control over what the laptop does as the battery drains. All the battery warnings and timeout values are set in one handy location. That's the good news. The bad news is that it's not the easiest place to get to. Here's how I go about it:

1. **Open the Control Panel.**

   Refer to Chapter 6 if you're bewildered by the words *Control* and *Panel*.

2. **From the Control Panel Home, choose the link Change Battery Settings, found under the Mobile PC heading; from Control Panel Classic View, open the Power Options icon.**

3. **Beneath the selected power plan setting, click the link that says Change Plan Settings.**

4. **Locate and click the link that says Change Advanced Power Settings.**

   Finally, the Power Options dialog box shows up. It's *the* happening place for all things having to do with power management in Windows Vista.

5. **Scroll through the list and locate the item labeled Battery.**

   As you would expect, it's the last item in the list.

6. **Click the + (plus sign) by Battery to display various battery notification and action options.**

   Each of the five items has two subitems, one for settings when the laptop is on battery power and a second for when the laptop is plugged in.

   In chronological order, here are the items you can set:

   A. **Low battery notification:** Sets a warning for a low battery level, before the situation gets critical. Values are *On* to set the low warning and *Off* to ignore it.

   B. **Low battery level:** Determines what exactly is the low battery level as a percentage of battery power. This value should be generous, well above the critical level (see item D).

   C. **Low battery action:** Tells the laptop what to do when the battery charge gets to the low battery level. Your options are Do Nothing, Sleep, Hibernate, and Shut Down.

   D. **Critical battery level:** Sets the battery power level at which the crucial action takes place. This is the last-gasp thing Windows can do for your laptop just before the power goes out. The level is set as a percentage of battery power.

   E. **Critical battery action:** Directs the laptop to sleep, hibernate, or shut down when the critical battery level is reached.

7. **Set each item according to your needs.**

   Click the colored text next to either the On Battery item or Plugged In item to see a pop-up menu. Choose the setting you want from the pop-up menu.

   I set the low battery action to Do Nothing and the critical battery action to Hibernate.

8. **Click OK to confirm your settings; close the remaining dialog boxes and windows.**

The battery warning settings don't have any visual effect; the low-battery display in the notification area continues to drain and appears in yellow with a warning flag, and then the pop-up message appears (refer to Figure 9-2) at the critical point.

✔ That critical-battery notice is serious. Computer time is over! If you ignore the warning, your laptop stops working. And so do you. Well, you stop working on your laptop.

✔ When the low-battery notice sounds or appears and you're blessed with a second battery for your laptop, pop it in and keep working! Refer to the section "Love that spare battery," later in this chapter.

✔ The best thing to do when power gets low: Plug in! This is why I always take my power cable with my laptop wherever I go.

To charge the battery

This task is easy to do: Plug the laptop into a wall socket, and the battery begins to charge. Nothing could be simpler. Well, dropping your new laptop on hard concrete and having it break is simpler, but not recommended.

✔ You can recharge your laptop's battery whether the battery is fully drained or not. Especially if your laptop is using a lithium-ion battery, it makes no difference.

✔ Lithium-ion batteries have a rapid-charging option. This option is available either on a custom tab inside the Power Options dialog box or from special battery software that came with your laptop. In a pinch, a rapid charge can save time. Otherwise, you want a nice, full, slow charge for your laptop's battery.

✔ I leave my laptop plugged into the wall whenever I can.

✔ There's no need to fully drain your laptop's lithium-ion battery every time you use it.

✔ The battery continues to charge even when the laptop is turned off.

✔ It doesn't take longer to recharge the battery if you use the laptop while recharging.

✔ Never short a battery to fully drain it. By *short*, I mean that you connect the two terminals (positive and negative) directly so that the battery simply drains. This is a very bad, stupid thing to do. It can cause a fire. Don't do it.

Love that spare battery

An option you probably ignored when you bought your laptop was to get a second battery. Having that spare battery is a must for anyone seriously on the road or in a remote location, where a long time is spent away from the power socket.

Before you use a spare battery, ensure that it's fully charged. Either charge it in the laptop, or use an external charger (if available). Put the fully charged spare battery in your laptop case or in any nonconducting (nonmetallic) container. Then head out on the road.

Most laptops support some type of quick-swapping ability. When the power gets low, you can just eject your laptop's original, spent battery and quickly insert the spare battery. But be sure that your laptop can survive such a heart transplant before you attempt it! Perform a test swap in a noncritical situation, just to be sure.

- ✔ Save your stuff before you attempt any battery swap.

- ✔ If your laptop doesn't have the ability to hot-swap batteries, just turn off (or hibernate) the laptop when the original battery is nearly spent. Remove the old battery, insert the fresh one, and then turn on the laptop again.

- ✔ I recommend labeling the batteries with a Sharpie so that you don't get the two (or more) confused and accidentally insert a dead battery.

- ✔ You can buy a spare battery from your dealer or from stores that sell extra batteries, such as iGo (`www.1800batteries.com`) or Batteries. com (`www.batteries.com`).

- ✔ Be wary of generic batteries! Always try to get a manufacturer's (or manufacturer-approved) battery for your laptop. Get anything less, and you run the risk of setting your laptop ablaze! It has happened!

Should you keep the battery in the laptop when you use AC power all the time?

Quite a few folks use laptops as their primary computers. If that's the case with you, and you keep the laptop plugged in all the time, there's really no need for the battery to be in the laptop.

In situations where you never use the laptop's battery, such as when it's more or less permanently docked, consider removing the battery. The laptop should run just fine without it, and by removing it, you keep the battery in good condition for when you do need it.

To store the battery when it's not in use, place it in a nonmetallic (or nonconducting) container. Keep it in a cool, dry place. Over time, the battery drains. That's just the way nature works. When the battery has been in storage a while, don't be surprised if it's dead when you retrieve it. You can recharge it by inserting it into your laptop and charging it as described earlier in this chapter. The battery should work just fine.

- ✔ Yeah, some laptops may refuse to run from AC power when the battery is missing. I've not heard of any, but they may exist. If so, keep the battery in the laptop and understand that — despite never using it — the battery eventually goes bad.

- ✔ If you remove the battery, consider plugging the laptop into a uninterruptible power supply (UPS). The laptop's battery acts as a UPS, by keeping the computer powered during brief outages and blackouts. If you remove the battery, consider a UPS as an alternative — just as you would for a desktop computer. Refer to my book *PCs For Dummies* (Wiley Publishing) for more information on using a UPS.

RIP, battery

Eventually, your laptop's battery will die. It's inevitable. Just as humans are subject to death and taxes, batteries are subject to death. (Fortunately, the government hasn't figured out how to plunder tax money from a battery. Yet.)

You can tell when your battery is about to die by observing one unique trait: It suddenly becomes useless. It no longer holds a charge, and the charge it does hold is quick and unreliable.

Don't mourn a dead battery! Toss it out!

Note that batteries are considered to be toxic waste in most communities. You must properly dispose of or recycle dead computer batteries according to the rules of your jurisdiction. Never just chuck an old computer battery in the trash.

And don't get all Viking on me and try to burn your battery, either. That's just a bad thing.

Managing Your Laptop's Power

The battery will drain. It's a matter of when. You may not have control over the physics, but you do have control over those things that go on in your laptop. By using the computer's power management software, plus a few deft moves that I'm about to share, you can squeeze every ion of electricity from your laptop's battery.

Power-saving tricks and tips

Your laptop was built to consume less power than a desktop computer. It uses a special CPU that draws less power and produces less heat. Everything inside the laptop case is geared toward battery savings. Even so, they do draw power.

Here's the short list of things that consume the most power in your laptop:

✔ The hard drive

✔ The optical drive

✔ The audio system (speakers)

✔ The modem

✔ The wireless network or Bluetooth adapter

✔ The network interface

✔ The display

Each of these devices consumes power when it's in use. I don't even mention the things you plug in that use power! Unless that external gizmo has its own batteries or plugs into the wall, it too adds to the battery drain.

By not using these devices, or by rationing their use, you can save power.

Some laptops come with the ability to quickly disable things you're not using. For example, on some laptops you can disable the optical drive when the laptop is battery-powered. Or, you can dim the display to save juice.

One common trick I use is to mute the speaker when I'm on the road. (And, no, using headphones still draws power and doesn't save battery life.)

Disabling the wireless networking adapter or Bluetooth connection saves the battery.

You can manually disable the modem by following these steps:

Device Manager

1. **Open the Control Panel.**

2. **From the Control Panel Home, choose System and Maintenance, and then click the link Device Manager; from Control Panel Classic view, open the Device Manager icon.**

3. **Click the Continue button if you're prompted by a User Account Control warning.**

   The Device Manager window appears. It lists all gizmos inside your laptop by category. You're going to hunt down the modem and disable it.

4. **Click the plus (+) sign next to the Modems item in the list.**

   The Modems branch of the computer's hardware tree expands. Your computer's modem is displayed by its name or the generic name Standard 56000 bps Modem.

5. **Double-click the modem's name to open its Properties dialog box.**

6. **Click the Driver tab in the modem's Properties dialog box.**

7. **Click the Disable button.**

8. **Click Yes to confirm.**

9. **Click the OK button to dismiss the Properties dialog box.**

   Notice that the list of gizmos in the Device Manager window is updated. The modem's icon now sports a downward-pointing arrow, indicating that it has been manually disabled.

10. **Close the Device Manager window.**

You can reenable the modem if you need it: Simply repeat the preceding steps, but in Step 7 click the Enable button. In the meantime, you might see some power savings from disabling the modem.

Further battery savings are possible by using your laptop's power management techniques, covered in the next section.

Using a power management plan

The real power-saving power comes not from the trivial crumbs you toss the battery, but rather from the power management hardware built into the laptop. To control that hardware, you visit the Power Options window, shown in Figure 9-3. Here's how you get there:

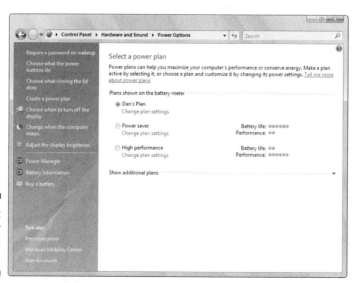

Figure 9-3:
The Power
Options
window.

1. **Open the Control Panel.**

2. **From the Control Panel Home, click the Change Battery link Settings, found below the Mobile PC heading; from Control Panel Classic View, open the Power Management icon.**

   The Power Options window appears (refer to Figure 9-3). Three general plans are listed.

3. **Choose a plan from the three.**

   Three plans are shown (they vary). You can view more plans by clicking the Show Additional Plans link

4. **Close the Power Options window when you're done.**

All plans control two things: when to turn off the display and when to put the computer to sleep. These two items have timeout values set separately for when the laptop is plugged in or when it's using battery power. You can examine a plan's details by clicking the Change Plan Setting link beneath the plan. Or, you can create your own plan, as covered in the next section.

Creating your own power management plan

Don't modify an existing power plan to suit your needs — create your own plan! That's what I did. (You can see Dan's Plan listed in Figure 9-3.) Here's how you can do it, too:

1. **Follow Steps 1 and 2 from the preceding section.**

   You need to open the Power Options window.

2. **From the list of links on the left side of the window, choose Create a Power Plan.**

3. **Type a name for your plan in the Plan Name text box.**

4. **Click the Next button.**

   In the next window, shown in Figure 9-4, you set the various timeouts and screen-brightness levels for your plan. The timeouts and brightness settings for my plan are shown in the figure.

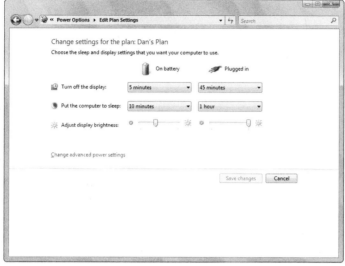

Figure 9-4:
Creating your own power management plan.

5. **Set a timeout for the display when the laptop is on battery power, and a timeout for when the laptop is plugged in.**

   Use the drop-down menus to choose the timeout values.

6. **Set a timeout value for putting the computer to sleep, one timeout for battery power, and another for when the laptop is plugged in.**

7. **Set the monitor's brightness level for when the laptop is on battery power, and set the brightness level again for when the laptop is plugged in.**

8. **Click the Create button to create your plan.**

   The plan you just created is selected and shown in the Power Options window.

9. **Close the Power Options window.**

You can follow these steps to update an existing plan: In Step 2, click the Change Plan Settings link beneath the plan you want to modify. Make the modifications, and then click the Save Changes button.

The screen may go blank before its time if you have a screen saver timeout set up that's less than the Turn Off Display timeout. Likewise, if you set your screen saver timeout to a value greater than the Turn Off Display timeout, you never see your screen saver kick in.

If you've modified the battery time-out values (see the section "Adjust low battery warnings" earlier in this chapter), then you must re-input that information for your new power management plan.

Chapter 10

Expanding Your Laptop's Universe

. . . .

In This Chapter

▶ Understanding USB

▶ Connecting a USB device

▶ Using a USB storage gizmo

▶ Removing USB storage media

▶ Working with PC Cards

▶ Adding an extra keyboard

▶ Connecting an external monitor

. . . .

Somehow, adding peripherals to a laptop doesn't really fit into the wild, untethered, on-the-road existence that's promised by portable comput-ing. "Sure, Ben, I have two laptop cases. One is this tiny one for the laptop, and the second holds all my favorite portable add-ons and their power bricks. Ah, life is swell. . . ."

I prefer to visit a cybercafé, grab my mocha-frappa-skinny-caramelatto, sit down, and whip out my laptop. Others, I suppose, don't mind the snickering because it takes them longer to set up, connect, and configure their so-called portable workstations. But, *dangit,* those people have a point: Your laptop comes with a bounty of expansion options. This chapter explores the many ways you can expand your laptop's universe — hopefully, without compro-mising its peripatetic nature.

USB Expansion Options

Once upon a time, expansion options on a laptop PC meant two serial, or COM, ports and a printer port. Those limiting days are, happily, over. Laptop expansion is now provided primarily by the versatile USB port. Only old farts such as myself truly appreciate the value, flexibility, and expansion potential that USB offers a typical laptop-toting human.

The miraculous expandability options of the USB port

USB stands for the University of Santa Barbara. *Go, Gauchos!*

Oh, wait. That's *UCSB*. Sorry, Gauchos.

On your laptop, USB stands for Universal Serial Bus. The key word is *Universal,* like the movie studio, but in this case it means that the USB standard supports a vast array of gizmos.

Table 10-1 lists many of the common USB gizmos you might use on a computer. Even better, Table 10-2 lists some uncommon USB gizmos that are beneficial to laptop computer owners.

Table 10-1	Typical, Plain, Boring Uses for the USB Port
Device	*Typical Boring Use*
External storage	Includes external hard drives, optical drives, thumb drives, and media card readers. See the section "Adding external USB storage," later in this chapter.
Printer	Prints stuff on paper. See Chapter 8 for printer information.
Scanner	Sucks images from flat surfaces and reproduces them as graphics inside the computer. (This topic isn't covered anywhere else in this book, mostly because scanners aren't portable.)
Network adapter	Provides another way to add networking to your laptop, such as WiFi or Bluetooth, which your laptop may not harbor natively.
Headphones	Allows you to listen to your laptop all by yourself. Headphones with a microphone let you use digital voice communications on your laptop.
Digital camera	Lets you grab photos from the camera's memory card and store them on your laptop. You can also do this directly, by removing the camera's digital storage media, which is covered in the section "Adding external USB storage," later in this chapter.

Table 10-2	More Unusual Ways to Use the USB Port
Device	*Unusual Thing It Does*
Legacy adapter	Allows you to connect antique *(legacy)* serial, parallel, joystick, and other ancient devices to your laptop. This adapter saves you from having to buy a port replicator and allows you to continue to use older hardware with your newer laptop.
Numeric keypad	Lets you (when numbers are your game) quickly enter values without having to toggle the main keyboard between numeric and alpha modes.
Sound hardware	Adds high-quality sound hardware to your laptop. For example, the Sound Blaster Audigy can be added by using the USB port to give your laptop full 5.1 Dolby surround sound. (No word on how best to lug around the five speakers and a subwoofer.)
Speakers	Lets you hear sound. To go along with the USB sound expansion, you can get some mini-USB-powered speakers for your laptop. Get the type with the handy tote-strap.
Video camera or Webcam	Handles all your on-the-road videoconferencing and self-voyeuristic needs.
Scanner	Lets lawyers and other people do their document scanning in a portable manner.
Little light	Imagine! Plugs in and is powered by the USB port. Furthermore, imagine it with a stiff-yet-twistable neck so that you can see the keyboard when you use your laptop in the dark.
Game controller	Controls your little man, pilots your spaceship, or wields that sword of truth.
Laptop cooler	Acts like a fancy pad on which to set your laptop. It contains a tiny, quiet fan that helps keep your laptop cool, and it runs from the power supplied by the USB port. (Also see Figure 23-1, over in Chapter 23.)
Mobile phone recharger	Lets you transfer some of the laptop's power to your mobile phone. Some may consider the use of this interesting USB gizmo to do that as robbing Peter to pay Paul, but I'm not really here to comment on the gizmos; I just list 'em.
Security device	Uses the USB port to power an alarm on a cable lock or plugs in to the USB port and unlocks (or unscrambles) the laptop's data.

That USB thing

Your laptop may have one or more USB ports on its sides or rear. Into those ports you plug a USB device. The gizmo attaches directly, or you use a USB cable to connect to the device. That's the gist of it.

For example, a memory card reader or Flash memory disk drive may plug directly into your laptop, as shown in Figure 10-1. A USB printer or external optical drive requires a USB cable in order to make the connection.

Figure 10-1:
A Jump Drive looks more like a diving board when it's attached to this laptop.

That's the essence of USB.

✔ The same USB ports and the same cables are used for all USB devices. As long as the devices are standard USB devices, you can add them to any laptop with USB ports.

✔ All USB devices, even the cables and the spot where the USB port lives on your laptop, sport the USB symbol.

The USB cable

Not every USB device requires a cable. When a USB gizmo needs a cable, you need to know a wee bit about the cable. No, this topic is nothing technical.

USB cables have *two* ends. Take a moment to absorb that knowledge, especially if you hail from a one-dimensional parallel universe or you grew up on a Möbius strip.

On one end of the cable is an A connector. The other end, most likely, has the B connector. The A connector is rectangular. It's what plugs into the computer. This connector is often called the *upstream* end. The B connector has a D shape. This type of hole and cable connector are fitted on USB devices. It's the *downstream* end.

For example, to connect a USB printer, you plug the A end of the cable into your laptop and the B end into the printer. That's it.

✔ Not every USB device comes with its own USB cable. USB printers are notorious for not including a USB cable in the box. You must buy a separate USB cable. Computer stores, as well as most office-supply stores, keep a variety of USB cables in stock.

✔ USB cables come in a variety of lengths, but they cannot be longer than about 16 feet. Any longer and the computer believes the USB device to have been disconnected.

✔ For your laptop, shorter cables are best.

✔ When you get a USB cable, you want a USB A-to-B cable.

✔ If you want a USB *extension* cable, you want a USB A-to-A cable, or one that's labeled as an extension.

✔ In addition to the standard A and B connectors are smaller connectors, dubbed *micro* and *mini*. Usually, when you have a device that requires these special types of connectors, that device comes with the proper USB cable. For example, my digital camera uses a cable with an A connector on one end and a micro B connector on the other.

Plug in that USB gizmo

USB devices are a snap to connect — literally. You don't need to turn off the computer, run a special program, or wave a magic wand. Just plug in the USB gadget, and you're ready to roll.

Given that I said that, please read the directions that came with your USB gizmo before just plugging the thing in. True, some USB devices are instantly recognized and configured when you attach them. But other USB devices require software to be installed on the laptop first.

- ✔ If the USB device has its own power switch, you must switch the thing on before the computer recognizes it.

- ✔ Be sure to read the manual that came with the device to determine whether you need to install special software before plugging in the device or turning it on.

- ✔ The ability to plug and unplug USB devices without having to turn the computer off or on is known as *hot swapping*. It sounds risqué, but it's not.

USB-powered devices

Quite a few USB doohickeys are powered by the USB cable itself. That is, they draw the electricity they need from the laptop's USB port. The good news is that you don't need an extra cable, power supply, wall socket, or battery for that device. The bad news is that it sucks up the laptop's precious power juice even faster.

I believe that the good news outweighs the bad on using USB-powered devices. For me, when I need the device, it's better not to lug around extra cables or to forget about including the power cables or batteries that are required by non-USB-powered doohickeys. Anything that lightens your load is good.

- ✔ Most flash memory devices are USB powered.

- ✔ Those cooling fan pads you can get for your laptop are also USB powered.

- ✔ Some laptops come with the option not to supply power to the USB ports, specifically when the laptop is running on battery power. Be sure to check your laptop's power management system, or use the Power Options icon in the Control Panel (see Chapter 6) to determine whether it's an option.

Here a hub, there a hub

Expandability is one key to the USB port's popularity. It may not seem practical, but your laptop can have as many as 127 USB devices attached to it at any given time. Yes, all at once. Imagine dragging that chain of goodies through the airport. You'd win a medal. Well, after making it through security.

A USB hub is nothing more than a USB doodad with more USB ports on it. You plug the hub into your laptop's USB port. Then you can plug anywhere from two to four to eight USB devices into the hub.

✔ Some devices cannot be run from hubs, such as certain high-speed hard drives. In that case, the device must be plugged directly into the computer's USB port. Don't fret: A warning message appears and instructs you what to do when such a thing happens.

✔ Keep your eye out for *pass-through* USB devices. This USB thingamabob sports an extra USB port somewhere on its body, so you can plug the USB device into your laptop and then plug another USB device into the first device. That way, you don't run out of USB ports.

✔ There are two types of hubs: *powered* and *unpowered.* The powered hub must have its own power source (it must be plugged into the wall). Powered hubs are necessary in order to supply more power to some USB devices.

✔ Note that smaller, more portable, laptop-size USB hubs are available. They're very quaint — and more portable than the desktop, or full-size, USB hubs.

✔ One of the best ways to add more USB ports to your laptop is to get them on a PC Card. See the section "Plugging in the PC Card," later in this chapter.

✔ Each USB port on your laptop is considered a *root port.* The 127-device limitation is per root port, so if your laptop has two USB root ports, it can access as many as 254 USB devices.

IEEE 1394, or FireWire, gizmos

USB was one of two standards that emerged to replace the morass of expansion options and ports that plagued computers for decades. Running neck-and-neck with USB is the IEEE 1394 standard, or IEEE, for short. On the Apple Macintosh computer, IEEE 1394 is referred to as the *FireWire* standard, which is a cool but frightening name.

At one time, both standards were considered necessary: USB was the expansion option of choice for connecting low-speed devices, and IEEE was preferred for external storage and video. At that time, IEEE was so much faster than USB. But the USB 2.0 standard improved USB's speed to match that of IEEE. That's why you seldom find IEEE ports on PC laptops.

Technically, IEEE works just like USB. You can plug and unplug cables, ports, hubs, and devices at your whim. Some devices — scanners and disk drives — may even support both USB and IEEE ports (although you can't use them both at the same time).

If your laptop didn't come with an IEEE port and you need one, you can add it by using a PC Card. Especially if you plan to transfer movies from a digital video camera, IEEE is your best option.

Adding external USB storage

One of the most common thingies to add to a laptop is a USB storage device, such as a flash memory card reader or an external optical drive. Both these devices meld into your computer system, just like any other disk drive does. Icons for external storage devices appear in the Computer window, along with your laptop's main hard drive and optical drive.

To add a USB storage device to your laptop, heed these steps:

1. **Insert the USB mass storage device into your laptop's USB port.**

   I am assuming that your computer is on and working.

   You may hear an audible alert, a signal letting you know that Windows has found and detected the device, and possibly installed software or drivers. That's normal.

2. **If a dialog box appears (see Figure 10-2), choose from the list what you want to do with the device.**

   The dialog box, shown in Figure 10-2, allows you to customize how you view or use the information stored on the USB drive. The displayed options depend on the drive's contents.

Figure 10-2: Options for reading a freshly inserted USB storage device.

3. **Use the drive.**

No matter what you choose to do with the removable drive (refer to Step 2), you still see it listed along with other storage media available to the laptop. An icon representing the storage device is found in the Computer window, as shown in Figure 10-3.

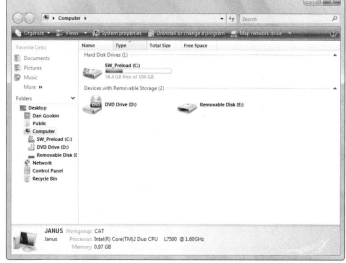

Figure 10-3:
The remov-
able drive,
showing
up as
Removable
Disk (E:).

You can leave the USB drive attached to your computer as long as you like. But be careful when you remove it! See the next section.

- *Mass storage* means that a gadget can store information just like a hard drive, optical drive, or silicon disk (flash memory, memory card, and that ilk).

- Be mindful of USB gizmos like thumb drives that stick out from your laptop. You could knock them off or maybe damage them when you put the laptop back into the case. It's best to always remove the drive when you're done using it; refer to the next section.

- Refer to Chapter 6 for information on using the Computer window.

Removing external USB storage

Lots of things are bad ideas: Angering a porcupine, buying a pair of jeans without trying them on, or visiting an all-night tattoo parlor while drunk after you just broke up. Add to that list yanking a USB storage device from your laptop without properly *unmounting* it first. Here's how:

1. **Open the Computer window.**

2. **Select the removable drive's icon.**

    For example, in Figure 10-3, the removable USB drive uses drive letter E. That's the icon to click and select.

3. **Click the Eject button on the toolbar.**

   You can now remove the media from the drive — for example, an optical disc from an optical drive or a media card from a media card reader.

   When the drive itself must be removed, you must also inform Windows of that decision. Continue.

4. **Right-click the drive's icon in the Computer window.**

5. **From the shortcut menu, choose the Safely Remove command.**

   In a few moments, the drive's icon disappears. A pop-up bubble appears from the notification area, telling you that you can safely remove the drive (hardware).

6. **Disconnect the device from your laptop's USB drive.**

7. **Click the Close button to make the annoying notification area bubble go thither.**

8. **Close the Computer window.**

Why bother with all this nonsense? Because the device may still be in use. You may have files open, or the computer may actively be reading data. How can you tell? You can't! That's why you must follow these steps to properly remove any USB storage device from your laptop.

   ✔ If you see a warning that the device cannot be removed, or "stopped," click the OK button. Locate whichever programs have open data files on the drive, save those files, and then close the programs. That should allow the drive to be removed.

   ✔ Refer to Chapter 6 for more information about the Computer window and the notification area.

Plugging in the PC Card

I'm honestly surprised that the PC Card is still around. For years it was the only convenient way to add gizmos to a laptop. You could use a PC Card to add a modem, network adapter, mini-hard drive, plus many other expansion options. Today, however, and thanks to the USB interface, the PC Card isn't as valued as it once was. Still, many PC Card options are available — including the often-necessary WiFi-anywhere connection.

Parking a PC Card in the PC garage

This is cinchy. Just stick the PC Card into the slot. It slides in only one way: The narrow edge with the holes goes in first. If the computer is on, Windows recognizes the card instantly, similar to what's shown in Figure 10-4. At that point, you can start using the card or whichever other features with which it just blessed your laptop.

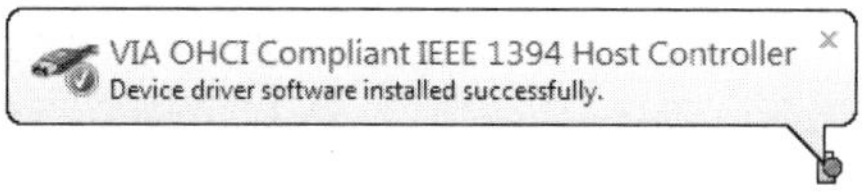

Figure 10-4:
You can't
hide new
hardware
from
Windows.

VIA OHCI Compliant IEEE 1394 Host Controller ×
Device driver software installed successfully.

✔ Some cards may require extra software to make them go. It says so in the card's manual. Other cards, like many USB devices, can just be plugged in, and they're off and running.

✔ The most common type of PC Card that's available is a wireless networking card. Installing the card is only half the battle; the rest involves properly configuring your laptop to connect to a wireless network. See Chapter 11 for the gory details.

✔ The device shown installed in Figure 10-4 is an IEEE 1394 port expansion card.

Using the PC Card

After the PC Card is inserted and properly set up, you can use its features. In fact, you can keep the card inside your PC for as long as you need those features. The only thing you need to be careful about is removing the card when you're done using it. Refer to the next section.

✔ Some cards jut out from the PC Card slots. Some may have pop-out connectors. Be careful with those! They can get caught on things, so you might consider removing the PC Card before you put the laptop back into its case and potentially break off an expensive gizmo.

✔ If you're adding USB or IEEE 1394 expansion with a PC Card, you can start using those ports right away. Refer to the sections on using USB devices, earlier in this chapter, for more information.

✔ Removable storage devices can be used after they're inserted and recognized by Windows. Be sure to properly remove the device, as covered in the following section.

✔ There are several types of PC Card: Type I, Type II, and Type III. Technical trivia aside, the main difference in card type is its thickness. Type III cards are twice as thick as Type II. The only caveat here is that you should avoid buying a Type III PC Card unless your laptop's PC Card garage can accommodate one.

Backing a PC Card out of the PC garage

To remove a PC card, you either pinch the card and pull it out or use the handy Eject button located to the side of the PC Card garage. Before doing so, ensure that you properly disable or unmount the card's hardware. Otherwise, you may anger Windows. And when Windows gets angry, Mr. Bigglesworth gets upset. And when Mr. Bigglesworth gets upset, people *die!*

Seriously. Follow these steps to properly remove a PC Card:

1. **Click the Safely Remove Hardware icon in the notification area.**

   Use Figure 10-5 to help you locate this icon. Clicking the Safely Remove icon displays a pop-up menu, shown in the figure, from which you select the PC Card to remove.

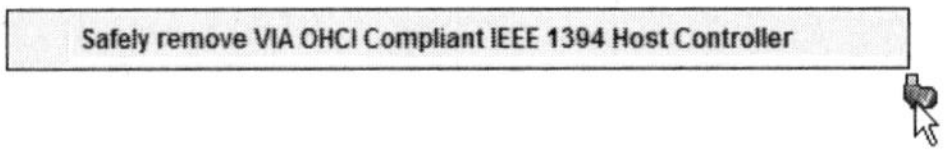

Figure 10-5:
Safely
removing a
PC Card.

> Safely remove VIA OHCI Compliant IEEE 1394 Host Controller

2. **Choose the device you want to remove.**

   A message appears, telling you that the device can be safely removed.

3. **Pull the PC Card from its slot.**

4. **Click OK to dismiss the message box, or close the message bubble that appears from the notification area.**

Store the PC Card in a proper place, such as in your laptop bag or in a drawer or cubbyhole with the rest of your laptop gear. The idea here is to keep the PC Card from being stepped on or crushed by a 20-ounce, ceramic coffee mug that says, "I really hate Mondays."

Reading Media Cards

A popular addition to a PC laptop is a media card reader. Media cards are the preferred storage device for digital cameras as well as for other popular, portable electronics. Your laptop may sport one or more media card readers, which means that you can easily transfer images from your digital camera to the laptop or use the media cards to ferry information back and forth between your laptop and other computers.

Various types of media cards are available. I use the generic term *media card;* another popular term are *flash drive* and *thumb drive.*

Specifically, each card type has a different size and slot type. Table 10-3 lists the common media card types and such.

Table 10-3	Media Card Types	
Card Name	*Abbreviation*	*Sample*
CompactFlash	CF	
Memory Stick/PRO	PRO	
Memory Stick Duo	Duo	
MutliMediaCard	MMC	
Secure Digital	SD	
SmartMedia	SM	
xD-Picture Card	xD	

Figure 10-6 illustrates typical media card reader slots. Note that some slots accommodate more than one type of media card. Also, the position of the slots relative to each other may vary on your laptop.

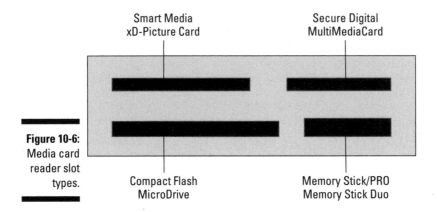

Smart Media
xD-Picture Card

Secure Digital
MultiMediaCard

Figure 10-6:
Media card
reader slot
types.

Compact Flash
MicroDrive

Memory Stick/PRO
Memory Stick Duo

✔ Your laptop may have no media card slots, one, or several.

✔ How can you tell whether your laptop has a media card reader? Look around! Refer to Chapter 5 for the Big Tour. (I'm embarrassed to admit that I owned my most recent laptop for almost half a year before I discovered its media card reader, tucked beneath the PC Card garage.)

✔ When your laptop lacks a media card reader, you can easily add one by plugging in a USB media card reader.

✔ Another name for the CompactFlash slot is *Microdrive.* It's not a different type of media card, but rather a miniature hard drive that fits snugly into a CompactFlash card's case.

✔ You must properly remove, or *eject,* a media card. Refer to the section "Removing external USB storage," earlier in this chapter.

Adding Some Big-Boy Toys

If you plan to park your laptop in one place all the time, you probably want to upgrade its teensy portable features with some more-robust desktop counterparts. Specifically, I speak of the keyboard, monitor, and mouse. Any of these desktop-size items can be added to and used with a laptop rather than with their feeble laptop counterparts. Use one. Use them all. It's quite easy.

"I want an external keyboard!"

If you miss the full size and action of a real PC keyboard, get one! Just plug it into your laptop's USB port. You can start using the keyboard the second it's plugged in.

Note that adding an external keyboard often doesn't disable the laptop's internal keyboard. You can use both! But you're probably not crazy enough to do that.

When you're done using the full-size USB keyboard, simply unplug it.

✔ If all you're yearning for is to have a separate numeric keypad, consider getting only that item. You can pick up a USB numeric keypad, which is just the keypad and not the entire keyboard, at most computer stores and office-supply stores.

✔ Sometimes, the only way you can add a non-USB keyboard to your laptop is by getting a port replicator or docking station.

✔ You can also add a wireless keyboard, either by using a USB wireless dongle or, if your laptop has it, Bluetooth.

 ✔ When using a traditional (non-USB) keyboard, do not plug in or unplug the keyboard unless the laptop is turned off. If you accidentally plug in or unplug a non-USB keyboard with the laptop's power on, you can fry the laptop's innards.

✔ The standard color for a PC's keyboard connector — the hole somewhere on your laptop for plugging in a non-USB keyboard — is purple.

Connecting a second monitor

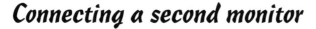

Your laptop is automatically equipped to handle two monitors: the laptop's own LCD and an external monitor. This is because many laptops are often used for storing and showing presentations, and it just makes sense to have the laptop all ready to go in that respect. But rather than attach a video project, you can just as easily plug in a second monitor.

To add the external monitor, locate the monitor connector on your PC's rump. Plug in the monitor, and you're ready to go. You can use that monitor in conjunction with your laptop's LCD or as your laptop's only display.

✔ On some laptops, the same image appears on both the LCD and the external monitor.

✔ If you want to use the external monitor exclusively, just close your laptop's lid. Most laptops are smart enough to see the external monitor and let you start using it, and also keep the laptop's power on while the lid is closed. When you open the laptop's lid, control returns to the laptop's LCD.

 ✔ Note that if you close the lid, it helps to have an external mouse or keyboard connected to the laptop so that you can still use your software.

✔ To activate the external monitor, you may have to press a special key or key combination on your laptop's keyboard.

✔ The monitor connector can also be an S-Video connector. It lets you connect your laptop to not only an external monitor but also many TV sets, VCRs, and DVD players. Refer to Table 5-1, in Chapter 5, for more information.

Gotta getta mouse

A computer mouse is perhaps the best companion you can buy for your laptop. Just grab your favorite desktop mouse and plug it into your laptop. It makes for a much more enjoyable laptop experience — even if you often have to use your thigh to roll the mouse around.

Mice makers are aware of laptop owners' fondness for "real" computer mice, so the makers have a whole line of options available to you. You don't have to buy a full-size desktop computer mouse. No, you can opt for one of those new mini-mice for laptops. Although they work just like desktop mice, they're about half the size. Some are even wireless. They're all better than using that silly touchpad.

Also see the section in Chapter 5 about getting a real mouse.

Part III
Your Laptop Talks to the World

The 5th Wave   By Rich Tennant

"He saw your laptop and wants to know if he can check his Gmail."

In this part . . .

Perhaps the simple description of a laptop computer
is that it *walks* and *talks*. For a computer, that's a
logical combination: portability and communications. It's
been the dream of computer scientists since the early
days (see Chapter 1). Laptops need to be on-the-go and
have the ability to chat up a storm in a variety of ways
with a variety of devices. It's kind of like a teenager on a
cell phone driving a car, minus the peril.

Laptops and communications make a happy duo. In fact,
communicating beyond your lap is such a vital part of the
portable computing experience that I've dedicated this
entire part of the book to the topic.

Chapter 11

Fear Not Networking

· ·

In This Chapter

▶ Understanding networking hardware

▶ Configuring your laptop for networking

▶ Connecting to the network

▶ Searching for computers on the network

▶ Sharing resources

▶ Understanding wireless networking standards

▶ Connecting to a wireless network

▶ Finding hidden wireless networks

▶ Disconnecting from the wireless network

· ·

I'm not a wagering man, but I'll bet that you didn't buy a laptop to become a computer networking expert. Nope. When you bought your laptop, there were probably some requirements you had in mind. But I doubt that they included "a basic understanding of TCP/IP and DHCP, and strong fundamentals in 802.11 protocol." So much for user-friendly.

Lucky for you, networking isn't that much of a hassle these days. Sure, you see some weird terms. Sure, you need to set up networking. But most of the difficult stuff is done for you. That doesn't mean that networking isn't an obnoxiously complex topic. It is! But with the gentle, supportive help offered in this chapter, you get to know some networking basics and get your computer connected and communicating in no time.

> ✔ Using your laptop's networking goodness to connect to the Internet is covered in Chapter 12.

> ✔ In an office setting, please ensure that your networking administrator, or one of his minions, assists in setting up your laptop for networking.

Basic Networking

Your basic networks include ABC, CBS, Fox, and NBC. Oh, there's that WB or whatever they call it. And, I suppose that HBO is a network too. But all that has to do with entertainment. On your computer, networking is about *communications*. Here's the technical definition from the *Mafia's Computer Dictionary:*

> It's not so much talk as it is action. There's both software and hardware, plus a protocol. The software is the message. I send. You receive. The hardware is the gun. The protocol is to use the gun when the message isn't properly sent or received.

Computer networking is about communications. There are hardware parts. There are software parts. This section covers networking basics with emphasis on wire-based networking. Specifics on wireless networking are covered later in this chapter, in the section "It's a Wireless Life."

Network hardware overview

The hardware side of networking consists of three parts:

✔ A network interface card, or NIC

✔ Cables and wires to carry the signal (for wire-based networking)

✔ A hub, switch, or router

Your laptop most likely came with a NIC. The thing is evident by the network hole, or RJ-45 *port,* found on the laptop's case. (See Chapter 5.) Each computer on the network must have a NIC.

The cables and wires are required in order to send the information from, and to get information into, your computer. The cables are how each computer on the network connects to the other computers. Of course, cables and wires aren't needed for a wireless networking setup.

Finally, all cables (or not) find themselves connected to a hub, switch, or router. Those devices, in various degrees of sophistication, manage and monitor the information as it flies over the wires, to and from the various networked computers.

Figure 11-1 illustrates the entire networking hardware concept. Each computer in the figure has its own NIC. The NIC is connected to the central router, which also hosts a USB printer.

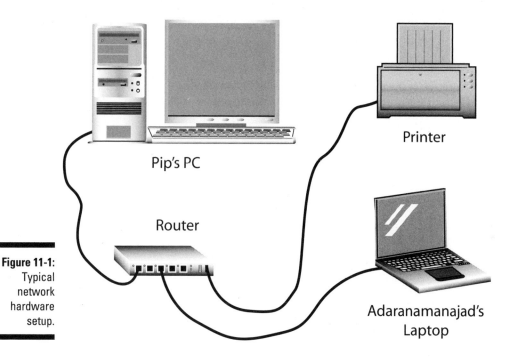

Pip's PC

Printer

Router

Adaranamanajad's Laptop

After the software side is set up, each computer on the network can access network *resources*. Those resources include any storage (disk drives) shared by other computers on the network as well as any shared network printers. The topic of shared and sharing network resources is covered later in this chapter.

- ✔ The cable you use to plug your laptop into the network is commonly called *Ethernet* cable. It's also known as Cat 5. You can buy it in assorted lengths, colors, and flavors. It's available at any computer- or office-supply store.

- ✔ *Ethernet* is the name of the computer networking hardware standard.

- ✔ A *hub* is simply a place where Ethernet cables from various computers (or printers or modems) plug in. It's the simplest way to network several computers.

- ✔ A *switch* is a faster version of a hub.

- ✔ A *router* is a faster, smarter version of a switch. Routers can handle large amounts of network traffic and manage connections between networks. This is why routers are most often used with broadband Internet connections.

✔ The basic network setup can include both wireless and wired networking. It all depends on the basic components involved. Wireless networking is covered later in this chapter.

✔ No, you don't really need a hub-switch-router thing. If you're just connecting two computers, plug an Ethernet, or Cat 5, cable into each computer's NIC, and then you can do peer-to-peer networking.

✔ You can also network computers by using an IEEE connection, though this book doesn't cover the specifics of doing that.

✔ If your laptop lacks a NIC or the RJ-45 hole, you can add one easily, by using either a PC Card or a USB–Ethernet adapter. See Chapter 10.

Network software overview

Blessed are ye for Windows cometh with all the networking software you need. That's the good news. The bad news is that, although most of the networking setup is painlessly automatic, you still to work through a few things to get your computer "on the network." First, here's a preview of necessary tidbits and where to find them.

Network names and such: All computers on the network have a unique identification, or network ID. You assign the network ID in the System window, shown in Figure 11-2. The Computer Name, Domain, and Workgroup Settings area lists various network nuggets.

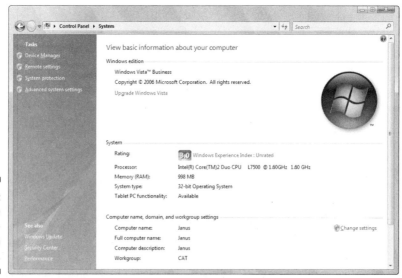

Figure 11-2:
Configure your network IDs in this place.

To display the System window and set or change your laptop's network ID, follow these steps:

1. **Open the Control Panel.**

2. **From the Control Panel Home, choose System and Maintenance and then choose System; from the Control Panel Classic View, open the System icon.**

   Behold! Or, simply refer to Figure 11-2.

   Four items are set with regard to networking your laptop:

   Computer Name: The name of the computer as it appears on the network. Other computers see this name when they "browse the network."

   Full Computer Name: The name given to the computer when you first set it up. It's probably your name or your company's name. It cannot be changed.

   Computer Description: Optional text to describe your computer or what it does or something rude and pithy.

   Workgroup: The name of the local peer-to-peer network to which your computer belongs.

3. **Click the Change Settings link.**

4. **If the User Account Control warning appears, click the Continue button or type the administrator's password to continue.**

   The System Properties dialog box appears.

5. **Ensure that the Computer Name tab is chosen.**

6. **You can type the laptop's description in the Computer Description text box.**

7. **To set a workgroup, or the computer's network name (Computer Name), click the Change button.**

   The Computer Name/Domain Changes dialog box appears.

8. **Type the computer's network name into the Computer Name text box.**

9. **Click to select the Workgroup radio button.**

10. **Type the workgroup name into the text box.**

11. **Click OK to confirm your changes.**

12. **Click OK to dismiss the System Properties dialog box.**

13. **(Optional) Close the Control Panel window.**

You can choose whichever network name or description suits you. The names and descriptions show up when you browse the network in the Network window or when network resources are shared.

The workgroup name is important when you join a local, peer-to-peer network. All computers in the same workgroup need to use the same workgroup name. Find more on that topic later in this chapter, in the section "Connecting to a peer-to-peer network."

Network Connections: The bulk of the network software configuration takes place in the Network and Sharing Center window, mentioned in Chapter 6. Figure 11-3 illustrates this window.

The Network and Sharing Center window instantly tells you how your laptop is connected to the network. In Figure 11-3, you can see that the laptop is connected to my home network (see the little house?) and the Internet (see the little planet?). Other information can be gathered from this window, but you also find important network settings there.

Making the Connection: Connecting to a network is mostly automatic for any laptop. After initial configuration, your laptop recognizes the networks you use most often and instantly connects.

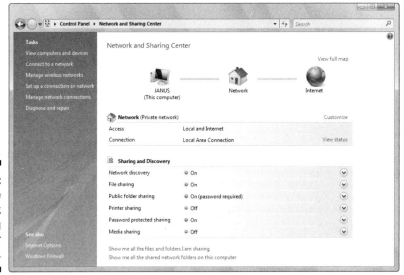

Figure 11-3:
The
Network
and Sharing
Center
window.

One key location for connecting to networks is the Start menu's Connect To command. It's on the right side of the menu, near the middle. Refer to Figure 6-1, over in Chapter 6, if you need help finding it.

✔ After the initial setup, connecting to any other network you've used works by simply plugging the network cable into your laptop. That's it.

✔ To disconnect from a network, simply unplug the network cable. You can do this when the laptop is on, sleeping, or off.

✔ Disconnecting the network cable while you're accessing the network, or while another computer is using your laptop, means that data will be lost. Try not to do that.

Connecting to a peer-to-peer network

The simplest form of network is a *peer-to-peer* network, where all computers on the network are considered equal; there's no main or bossy computer. Contrast this with other types of networks:

✔ **Client-server:** A main computer, the *server,* runs all the software, and drone-like PCs become mere clients that obey the server's dictates.

✔ **Pier to pier:** Maritime computers use this type of network to ensure that data doesn't sink between moorings.

✔ **Peerage to peerage:** An inherited aristocracy runs a network where all the computers sit upon the backs of peasants.

For your home or a small office, odds are good that you have a simple peer-to-peer network setup, like the one I attempted to illustrate in Figure 11-1. Adding your laptop to this type of network is cinchy.

First, discover the *workgroup name.* That's the name of the peer-to-peer network. Unless you change the name, it's most likely MSHome or Workgroup, depending on your version of Windows.

Second, use the Computer Name/Domain Changes window to set the workgroup name for your laptop. Follow the steps from the section "Network software overview," earlier in this chapter.

Finally, you may be required to restart your laptop. If so, you must restart it before it can easily access other computers and resources available to the workgroup.

To confirm that it all worked, see the following section. If it didn't work, either you mistyped the name or the other computers on the network aren't available (they're turned off or disconnected).

LAN party!

Thanks to the popularity of the film *Animal House,* toga parties were the rage on college campuses throughout the 1980s. Today's version of the toga party is just as popular but far more geeky: It's the *LAN party!*

LAN parties can be planned, but they're mostly spontaneous. A group of laptop computer users, many of the hip and most drinking coffee, suddenly find themselves together and create a small network, or LAN (local-area network). After working out the protocols and other network nonsense (don't worry — others will help you), the LAN partiers go at it. No, they don't sit around singing "Kumbaya" and sharing resources. They play games — violent, shoot-'em'-up, network games!

Normally, you need access to the Internet or contact with a remote game server to play online games. But, with a LAN party, you can have anywhere from half a dozen to hundreds of computer users networked together and playing games. The next time you're in a coffee shop or high-tech bistro and someone looking like John Belushi shouts out "LAN party!," don't throw your muffin! Instead, log in and play!

Finding other computers on the network

All computers on the same network can see each other. It's like being able to see all the houses on a single street. And, when the garage door is open, you can see all your neighbor's junk or perhaps marvel at how organized their garage is or wonder why they need such a huge meat freezer. Didn't their elderly aunt once live with them? What happened to that woman, anyway? Networking has various similarities.

In Windows, you can view other computers on the network by using the Network window. To see which window, choose the Network item from the Start menu. You see a list of icons. Those icons represent networked computers, shared devices, and potentially a router, similar to what's shown in Figure 11-4.

By opening icons in the Network window, you can peruse which resources other networked computers have to share. The resources include storage, printers, media players, and other stuff. The following sections cover resource sharing.

- The computers you see in the Network window are all on the same workgroup or domain, depending on how the network is set up.

- Seeing computers displayed in the workgroup window is a sure sign of success that the network is up, connected, and ready for action.

- When you don't see any computers in the workgroup window, you have a problem. The network cable either isn't connected or it's bad. The network interface is bad. Or, the computers don't share the same workgroup name.

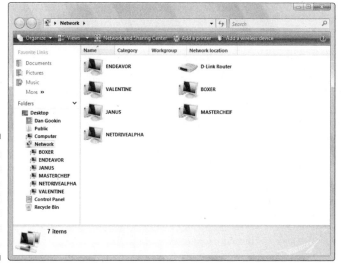

Figure 11-4:
Computers
sharing the
same local
network in
Windows
Vista.

Accessing network storage

Getting into a networked computer's disk storage is as easy as walking into a neighbor's open garage and, dammit, looking into that freezer. Of course, not every computer on the network has an open garage. Or, to put it in computer terms, not every computer is sharing part of its storage system.

To see access storage space shared by another network computer, open that computer's icon in the Network window (refer to Figure 11-4). Double-clicking the icon reveals which storage resources are being shared by that computer, as shown in Figure 11-5. Or, you may see a password dialog box prompting you for access.

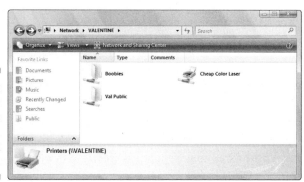

Figure 11-5:
Shared
resources
on a
network
computer.

In Figure 11-5 you can see resources being shared by the network computer named Valentine. Two folders are being shared, as well as a printer connected to the computer. If nothing is available, or nothing is being shared, the window is empty.

To access a shared folder, double-click to open the folder. If the folder isn't password protected, you see its contents displayed in a window, just as though it were a folder on your laptop's storage system. If the folder is password protected, you need to enter a username and password before you can access the folder's contents.

Using a network folder works just like using any folder in Windows: You can open files, copy files, rename, edit — within limitations. Some folders are *read-only,* which means that you can only view files or copy them from the folder. You cannot rename, modify, or delete files in a read-only folder.

Close the network folder when you're done using it.

✔ Folders are available for access on the network only when the computer owner volunteers to share the folders. This topic is covered later in this chapter, in the section "Sharing a folder from your laptop."

✔ When a computer or folder is password protected, you're asked to provide a password for access. If you have an account on the computer, type your account name and password; otherwise, type the name and password you were given for access. Click OK.

✔ The password may allow you to view the folder contents and to copy files from that folder, or it may allow you full access (read, write, modify, delete).

✔ Practice polite network etiquette: close a network folder when you're done using it. If you forget and don't close the folder, an error message appears when the other computer disconnects from the network or the network goes down.

Accessing network printers

If your computer network were the dating scene, the computers would be the homely-nerd boys and the printers would be the cute girls. You've got to make a little effort to get your laptop to talk with a network printer. The difficulty has to do with security, which I'm certain is what the cute girl is thinking about when the homely-nerd boy approaches.

Printers available to your laptop appear in the Printers window. These include any printers attached to your laptop directly, as well as network printers.

You can connect with and use a network printer in two ways:

Use a shared printer: To use a shared printer, such as the one shown in Figure 11-5, act upon these steps:

1. **Browse for the printer.**

   Refer to the earlier section "Finding other computers on the network." Opening a computer's icon in the Network window reveals its shared resources.

Cheap Color Laser

2. **Right-click the shared printer icon.**

   The printer's icon is found in the networked computer's window.

3. **Choose Connect from the pop-up menu.**

   Windows attempts to connect with the printer. If needed, drivers are installed. You may see a security warning when this happens; if so, proceed with installing the drivers.

4. **Close the networked computer's window.**

The printer is now ready to use.

Use a networked printer: Some printers dwell on the network directly, either because they're connected to the network just like a computer or because they're plugged into the network router using a USB cable. Either way, you have to do a little bit more work to find the printer.

First, when you can see the printer's icon directly in the Network window, just right-click the icon and choose Connect from the pop-up shortcut menu. (Refer to the preceding set of steps.) That's it.

Second, when the network printer's icon cannot be found in the Network window, you must make a manual connection. This isn't the easiest operation. Carefully follow these steps:

1. **Open the Printers window.**

   Refer to Chapter 8 for more information on getting to this window.

2. **Click the Add a Printer button on the toolbar.**

   The Add Printer Wizard steps forward. No, it's not wearing a pointy cap, and it doesn't have a wand. The *wizard* is a window where you make choices and fill in the blanks.

3. **Choose the option Add a Network, Wireless or Bluetooth Printer.**

   The next screen lists any printers that are readily available. Don't bother waiting on this screen; if the printer doesn't appear right away, it's not on the list.

4. When you find your printer in the list, select it and then skip to Step 6; otherwise, continue.

5. Click the button The Printer That I Want Isn't Listed.

You have two choices for adding a network printer at this point. If you know the printer's network name, you can add the printer by name. Otherwise, you have to add the printer by its IP address.

To add the printer by its name, follow these substeps:

A1. Choose the option Select a Shared Printer By Name.

A2. Type the printer's network name into the text box.

Or, you can use the Browse button to find the printer, though if that option didn't work in Step 4, it won't work here, either.

A3. Skip to Step 6.

To add the printer by its IP address, follow these substeps:

B1. Choose the option Add a Printer Using a TCP/IP Address or Hostname.

B2. Click the Next button.

B3. Type the printer's hostname or IP address into the Hostname or IP Address text box.

The hostname or IP address was set up when you installed the printer. For example, my HP LaserJet IV is configured to IP address 192.168.0.117.

B4. Type the port name into the Port Name text box.

Again, this information was provided when the printer was first configured on the network. For my printer, the port is named P1.

B5. Click the Next button.

When Windows cannot determine the network card, it requires you to select one.

B6. If you know the network card's name, choose it from the list. Otherwise, the Generic Network Card option works.

B7. Click the Next button.

When Windows cannot determine the printer type, you must select the printer's control software (its *driver*) manually.

B8. Choose the printer manufacturer and the make and model number from the lists that are presented.

Choose the manufacturer first.

B9. Continue with Step 6.

6. **Click the Next button.**

7. **Type the printer's name.**

   You may not be allowed to set the printer's name; it depends on which computer "owns" the printer.

8. **If you want to use the network printer as the laptop's main printer, keep the check mark next to the option Set As the Default Printer.**

   Refer to Chapter 8 for information on setting a default printer.

9. **Click the Next button.**

10. **If you desire, click the Print a Test Page button to ensure that the network printer works.**

11. **Click the Finish button, and you're done.**

The network printer now appears in the list of printers available in the Printers window. The printer is also available in any Print dialog box. As long as the printer is on and your laptop is connected to the network, you can use that printer.

Sharing a folder from your laptop

Yes, you too can sacrifice one of your laptop's precious folders to the network gods. It's not necessary, but it does make sharing files between computers easier.

You can share any folder on your laptop with everyone on the network. Rather than do that, which is a security risk, I recommend that you share only the laptop's Public folder. Here's how to go about that task:

1. **Open the Network and Sharing Center window.**

   Directions are found earlier in this chapter; the window is shown in Figure 11-3.

2. **Turn on Network Discovery, if it's not already on.**

   When Network Discovery isn't on, follow these substeps:

   A. **Click the down-pointing arrow on the right side of the Network Discovery bar.**

   B. **Choose the option Turn On Network Discovery.**

   C. **Click the Apply button.**

   D. **Type the administrator's password or click the Continue button to make the change.**

   Network discovery is necessary for other computers to see your laptop.

3. **Turn on file sharing.**

   Open the File Sharing area and choose the option Turn On File Sharing. Repeat the substeps from Step 2, if necessary.

   File sharing is needed so that others on the network can access your laptop's files.

4. **Open the Public Folder Sharing area.**

   Three options are available. The top two allow the Public folder to be shared. The top option is the read-only option, and the middle option is the full-access option.

5. **Choose the top option for read-only access or the middle option for full access.**

6. **Click the Apply button.**

7. **Type the administrator's password or click the Continue button.**

8. **Turn off password-protected sharing.**

   If password-protected sharing is on, only users with an account on your laptop can access files. To keep your laptop's Public folder "up for grabs," the Password Protected Sharing option must be off.

9. **(Optional) Close any Sharing and Discovery areas you opened.**

10. **Close the window.**

Folders shared from your laptop sport icons with a little *sharing-buddies* icon superimposed. That's your visual clue that a folder has been shared.

- ✔ The Public folder is a general-purpose folder designed for sharing files. It doesn't belong to any account. You copy into the Public folder the items you want to share or exchange with another computer, or with another user on the same computer.

- ✔ Other computers cannot access folders on your laptop when your laptop is turned off or in Sleep or Hibernation mode.

- ✔ Refer to my book *Find Gold in Windows Vista* (Wiley Publishing) for information on sharing other folders from your laptop.

It's a Wireless Life

I remember seeing an old film on the "triumph of electricity." In the film, the announcer boasted with pride about the thousands of miles of wires marching successfully across America. Truly, having 348 wires dangling above your head is the hallmark of progress. But not any more.

The latest craze in modern electronics is wireless *everything.* For your laptop, which is fairly wireless already, that refers to wireless networking. Yeah, verily, wireless networking has been heralded as the biggest boon to communications technology since the drum. This section explains what you need to know.

Wireless networking protocol

To put the *work* into a wireless network, there must be a protocol. A *protocol* provides the rules by which something operates. That makes sense. What often doesn't make sense are the acronyms, odd names, and strange numbers applied to protocols in the computer world. Allow game show host Pat Sajak to explain:

Pat: The puzzle is a protocol. Protocol.

Vanna turns parts of the big board to reveal `802.11` _

Pat: I need three consonants and a vowel.

You: I'll take a B *(ding)* G *(ding)* and an N *(ding)*.

Pat: And your vowel?

You: An A, please. *(Ding.)*

Congratulations! You solved the puzzle. The wireless networking protocol most commonly used on laptops is known as 802.11. It's pronounced "Eight-oh-two dot eleven" or, to save time, you can omit the *dot:* "Eight-oh-two eleven."

Just to make things more confusing, the number 802.11 is followed by one of four letters: A, B, G, or N. Those letters indicate the various flavors of the 802.11 protocol that are available. Here's the rundown:

802.11a: The first wireless networking standard. It's not used much now, though your laptop's wireless networking adapter, or NIC, may support it.

802.11b: The second standard, still widely supported, though fading fast. The B standard is also compatible with the A standard. It's also written as 802.11a/b.

802.11g: Perhaps the most popular standard now. The G standard can also work with A and B devices, though those devices don't recognize the G standard. This standard can also be written as 802.11a/b/g.

802.11n: The current standard, fully compatible with all the previous standards. And, naturally, none of the previous standards can work with the N standard. As you might suspect, the standard can also be written as 802.11a/b/g/n, though at this point that label is getting kind of ridiculous.

You laptop's wireless network adapter is most likely 802.11g or 802.11n, which means that your laptop can communicate with all wireless devices of a similar standard or with older A and B devices.

The newer standards offer more features and higher speeds than the older standards.

Wireless networking hardware

As with wired networking, wireless networking requires hardware in order to work. But, unlike wired networking, there are no cables (hence the clever name *wireless* networking).

For wireless networking hardware, you need two things:

✔ A wireless networking adapter, or NIC
✔ A wireless base station, which serves as the wireless hub or router

The basic setup is illustrated in Figure 11-6.

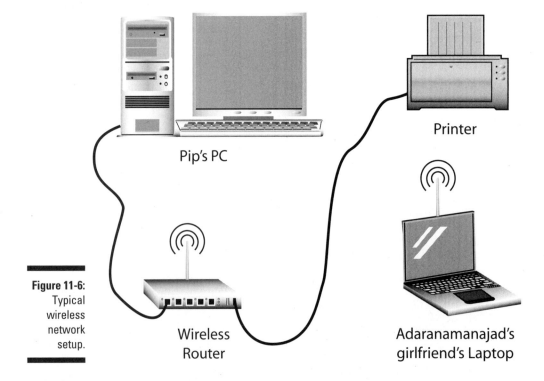

Figure 11-6: Typical wireless network setup.

Pip's PC

Printer

Wireless Router

Adaranamanajad's girlfriend's Laptop

That Bluetooth thing

Bluetooth refers to a wireless standard for connecting computer peripherals, as well as other noncomputer devices. As long as your laptop is equipped with Bluetooth technology, you can use various Bluetooth devices and gizmos with your laptop, including printers, keyboards, speakers, and input devices. As the theory goes, as long as the device is flagged as Bluetooth compatible, you can use it right away with your laptop. In practice, however, it may require a bit of setup and configuring to get things working — a process you should be used to by now if you've been using computers for any length of time.

Your laptop came with wireless networking hardware. It's built in. You may or may not see a little antenna. But it's an 802.11g or 802.11n wireless networking adapter.

To complete the network, you need a wireless base station. The base station receives, relays, and transmits the wireless signals between all wireless computers in the network. It may also sport wired-based networking options, such as a router. A typical base station is depicted in Figure 11-6.

For the network to work, all wireless devices must support the same standards. For example, if you have an 802.11n base station, both 802.11n and 802.11g wireless laptops can use it for networking.

✔ On the odd chance that your laptop lacks a wireless networking adapter, you can easily add one. Various USB and PC Card adapters are available for wireless networking convenience.

✔ Many laptops feature a switch (hardware or software) that turns off the wireless antenna. Locate that switch on your laptop, if it exists, and ensure that wireless networking is activated for those times when you need it.

✔ Yes, sometimes you need to turn off wireless networking, such as when you travel by air or work in a hospital. See Chapter 17.

Connecting to a wireless network

You don't actually "plug in" a wireless network. Instead, you must access the network. Three steps are involved:

1. Find the network.

2. Connect, which might involve typing a password.

3. Use the network just like you use any computer network.

Yep, it's that simple. But you'll probably use these nine steps instead:

1. **Choose the Connect To item from the Start menu.**

   The Connect to a Network window appears, as shown in Figure 11-7. The window lists the wireless networks broadcasting within range of your laptop's wireless networking gizmo.

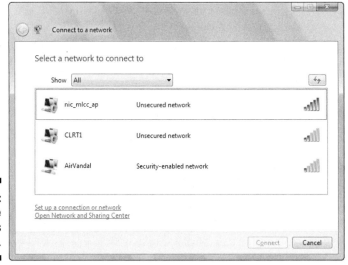

Figure 11-7:
Available
wireless
networks.

2. **Choose a network from the list.**

   The list shows the network name, *or SSID,* and its status and signal strength. When a padlock icon appears next to the signal strength, it indicates a password-protected, or secure, network.

3. **Click the Connect button.**

   Windows attempts to make friendly with the network.

   You may see a warning telling you that the network is unsecured. This message is common for certain free wireless networks that don't require a password for connection. Click the Connect Anyway option to proceed.

4. **Enter the network's password, if you're prompted to do so.**

5. **Choose whether the network is public or private, if prompted.**

   This question is vital. A public network is one that's out in public, one that others (strangers!) can also use. In that situation, you want to ensure that your laptop is locked down and not open to snooping.

A private network is one in your home or office, available only to safe computers or folks you know. This type of network is more open than the public network.

6. **Choose whether to save the network's connection information.**

   I recommend that you save the information if you plan to use that wireless connection again. That way, you don't have to reenter the password every time you connect (in theory, anyway).

7. **Choose whether to automatically connect in the future.**

   I recommend this setting for networks you plan on using often.

8. **Click the Close button.**

9. **If you're prompted by a User Account Control dialog box, type the administrator's password or click the Continue button.**

You're now connected and ready to use the network. A wireless networking icon appears in the notification area on the taskbar, showing that you're connected; point the mouse at that icon for more information.

✔ The password you enter may not be accepted. If so, you need to manually connect to the network. Refer to the section "'What if I don't know the SSID?'" later in this chapter.

✔ Sometimes it pays to wait a few moments for the wireless connection to sync up (or something). Don't take the lack of an immediate "Connection made, yee-ha!" message as a sign of failure.

✔ When given a choice, pick the wireless network with the strongest signal.

✔ Avoid connecting to unknown networks in a public location. It is a security risk when you do not know exactly which network you're using.

✔ The best way to hunt down wireless networks is to use a third-party wireless network browser. Such a program may have come with your laptop's wireless adapter, or it can be found on the Internet.

✔ There's a distance-and-interference issue with wireless networking, and the picture isn't as rosy as the brochures claim. Basically, the best way to connect with a wireless network is to be in the same room with the hub, switch, router, or other computer that's broadcasting the signal. Common items, such as walls, greatly reduce the potency of a wireless connection.

✔ To increase the signal of your home or office wireless network, buy more hubs! You'll have to configure the hubs to share the same network signal and create a Wireless Distribution System (WDS). Refer to the base station's manual for specific directions.

✔ A few wireless Internet locations offer their password-and-setup information on a USB flash drive. Simply insert the flash drive to connect to the network, or use the drive as indicated by the directions or when you're prompted to insert the drive when you connect to the network. Needless to say, a USB flash drive is a handy thing to have — much better than retyping those long password keys!

"What if I don't know the SSID?"

For security reasons, some wireless networks don't broadcast their SSIDs. Obviously, you cannot connect to a network if you don't know its SSID, just as you cannot call out to a fellow across the street when you don't know his name.

To get the SSID, you need to ask. The network manager or whichever human is in charge of the wireless network at your location should be able to divulge that information. After you know the SSID, follow these steps to connect to that network:

1. **Choose Connect To from the Start menu.**

   Yes, it's the same list of networks that appears in Figure 11-7. But it's too early in the game for you to give up.

2. **Choose the Set Up a Connection or Network link at the bottom of the window.**

   The Select a Connection Option window appears.

3. **Choose the option Manually Connect to a Wireless Network.**

4. **Click the Next button.**

   The next window that's displayed allows you to set up a manual connection, as shown in Figure 11-8.

5. **Type the SSID in the Network Name box.**

6. **Fill in the rest of the information as needed.**

   Check with the network administrator to see which other tidbits of information are required in order to complete the connection: security and encryption types and a password.

7. **My best advice: Put a check mark in the box labeled Start This Connection Automatically.**

   This step saves you some time by preventing you from having to repeat these steps later.

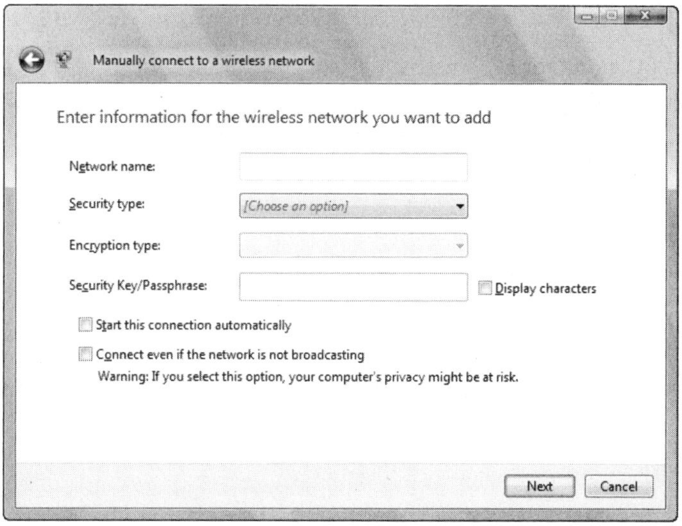

Figure 11-8:
Configuring
a manual
connection
in Windows
Vista.

8. **Click the Next button.**

   Hopefully, Windows goes out and finds the mystery wireless network. If not, you probably goofed something up; check with the network administrator or the settings on your wireless hub. Otherwise, you're ready to connect.

9. **Choose the Connect To option.**

   Surprise! You thought you were connecting to the network, but you were merely setting things up. Go to the section "Connecting to a wireless network," earlier in this chapter, to complete the connection.

"What's my computer's MAC address?"

Some wireless networks restrict access to only those computers they know. Not having eyeballs, a network needs some other piece of identification to distinguish between computers it knows and utter strangers. That piece of ID is the wireless networking hardware's MAC address.

A *MAC address* is a unique number assigned to every networking adapter on planet Earth. No two numbers are identical, and the MAC address is very difficult to fake. By using the MAC address, a wireless network can restrict access to only those computers that are known and registered.

To find your laptop's MAC address in Windows Vista, follow these simple steps:

1. **Open the Control Panel's Network and Sharing Center.**

   Directions for opening this window are found earlier in this chapter.

2. **Click the link labeled View Status next to the connection you want to examine.**

   A Network Connection Status dialog box appears.

3. **Click the Details button.**

   A Network Connection Details dialog box comes into view. Locate the item labeled Physical Address. That's the NIC's MAC address number.

4. **Copy that number.**

   Write it down on a sheet of paper.

5. **Close the various dialog boxes and windows.**

You can now use the MAC address or give it to a network administrator, who will help you set up things.

   ✔ Know that MAC stands for Media Access Control — like that will make your day any brighter.

   ✔ The MAC Address is 12 digits long, broken up into pairs, like this:

   `12:34:56:78:9A:BC`

   It's a base-16 value (also called *hexadecimal*), so the letters *A* through *F* are also considered numbers.

Renewing your lease

To keep goofballs out, some networks let you use their services for only a given amount of time. The time allotted is referred to as a *lease*.

What may happen, especially if you use a wireless network for a great length of time, is that your lease may expire. To renew it, you need to disconnect from the network and then reconnect.

The instructions for disconnecting from a wireless network are offered later in this chapter; for now, the simplest way to renew a lease is simply to restart Windows. Refer to Chapter 4.

Accessing a pay-service wireless network

Not everything is free. Some people out there have the gall to *charge* you for using their wireless services. Imagine! Darn those capitalists!

I've seen pay wireless access work two ways:

✔ You pay a cashier, and then he or she hands you a slip of paper with the SSID and a password to use. Then follow the steps in the earlier section "'What if I don't know the SSID?'" for instructions on connecting to the network.

✔ In the more devious way, the signal appears to be strong and available, and connection isn't a problem. But, when you go to the Internet, the only Web page you see is a sign-up page. Until you fork over your credit card number, you can't go anywhere else on the Internet or access any other service (such as e-mail).

Yep. If it's a pay service, you gotta pony up!

Disconnecting the wireless connection

The main way I disconnect from a wireless connection is to close my laptop's lid. By putting the laptop into Sleep or Hibernate mode, the wireless network connection is broken automatically. Opening the laptop's lid (assuming that it's within range of the wireless hub) reestablishes the connection.

Likewise, you can also turn off the laptop to disconnect from the wireless network.

To disconnect without turning off your laptop, follow these steps:

1. **Choose Connect To from the Start menu.**

   The Connect to a Network window appears (refer to Figure 11-7).

2. **If the network you're connected to isn't chosen, click to select it.**

   The network you're connected to appears, displaying the bold text *Connected.*

3. **Click the Disconnect button.**

   A confirmation screen appears.

4. **Click the big Disconnect button.**

5. **Click the Close button.**

If you preconfigured the network to automatically connect when it's available, after completing Step 5 you find your laptop instantly reconnected to the network.

✔ Some laptops have a handy On–Off button associated with their wireless networking connections. You can press the button to instantly disconnect from the network by turning off the wireless networking card.

✔ This technique was just suggested to me: You can start running in any direction. By the time you feel tired, you're probably far enough from the wireless hub that the connection is broken, although breaking a connection in this manner seems extraordinarily silly.

Chapter 12

Doing the Internet

· ·

In This Chapter

▶ Arming yourself for the mobile Internet

▶ Using broadband Internet

▶ Configuring for a public network

▶ Accessing the Internet through a dialup connection

▶ Configuring the dialup connection

▶ Disconnecting a modem connection

▶ Sharing a wireless Internet connection

· ·

*T*he *Internet* is the part of your computer that isn't inside your computer. It's no longer optional. So, as a mobile computer user, you need to — often and with the regularity of an addict — connect to and use the Internet. It's such a necessity that I don't even need to explain why any more. Good for me!

Using the Internet with your laptop works just like using it on a desktop. Good for you! With a laptop, of course, you can access the Internet from any-where — that is, from anywhere the Internet is. Though the Internet is every-where, it's not really *available* everywhere. So you must be flexible! To meet that flexibility, you have to be prepared to hop on the Internet in a variety of ways. This chapter covers those details.

Mobile Internet Tips

Like a quality rash, the Internet is something you can find everywhere. That's not really the issue. The issue for a portable PC person is whether you can access the Internet from wherever you are. That means getting the informa-tion you need from anywhere. It means being able to access your e-mail while you're on the road. And, for a dialup ISP, it means being able to access that ISP from a variety of locations.

- *ISP* stands for *Internet service provider,* or the outfit that provides you with Internet access. Your ISP can be your company or your school or any of a number of national and local Internet providers.

- Just because you use dialup ISP access at home doesn't mean that you're limited to dialup access on the road.

- With wireless networking, you can access the Internet for free if you find an open wireless connection. My local coffeehouse offers free wireless Internet access for the price of a cup of joe. (Well, I suppose I'm paying for the joe, but I view the Internet access as free anyway.)

- Free Internet access is available in most community libraries.

- Many national ISPs — such as AOL, EarthLink, and NetZero — have access points all over. Before you leave, check to see whether your ISP has any local-access numbers for your destination. That way, you can use your laptop's modem to connect with your ISP just as you do at home.

- In addition to local access, a dialup ISP might offer a toll-free phone number to connect. Note that you may have to pay a surcharge for accessing this feature.

- Some dialup ISPs offer a form of Web-based e-mail. This system allows you to access your e-mail from any computer connected to the Internet. Just navigate to your ISP's Web e-mail page and log in as you normally would. You can then read your e-mail on the Web rather than use an e-mail program.

- See Chapter 15 for more e-mail tips and such.

- Also see Chapter 17, which covers using the Internet while you're on the road.

Ask Professor Dan: What is the Internet?

Billy: What is the Internet?

Prof. Dan: Glad you asked, Billy. The Internet isn't a computer program. Nor is the Internet a single large computer somewhere. And, no, the Internet isn't owned by Bill Gates.

Billy: But I hear that it's one of his most secret desires.

Prof. Dan: Indeed.

Jane: So where is the Internet located?

Prof. Dan: Don't be goofy, Jane. The Internet isn't one computer; it's thousands upon thousands of computers, all connected. Information is stored on many of those computers, and the protocols and methods of the Internet allow your computer, or any other computer connected to the Internet, to access and use that information. Indeed, any computer connected to the Internet is "on" the Internet.

Billy: Cool! Now can we test the effects of sulfuric acid on optical discs?

Prof. Dan: Sure! Billy, you grab the flask of acid. Jane, will you hold this disc?

Broadband Internet Access

Getting on the Internet in the high-speed way is simple: Just connect your laptop to any existing wired or wireless network already attached to the Internet. Because most networks are already on the Internet, so is your laptop when it's connected to the Internet. Cinchy.

Broadband access overview

The Internet is based on the same type of networking used to create a local-area network (LAN), such as the peer-to-peer, workgroup networking discussed in Chapter 11. Having that type of network setup, even when your laptop is the only computer on the network, is how you get broadband Internet access. Use Figure 12-1 as a guide for basic broadband Internet access setup.

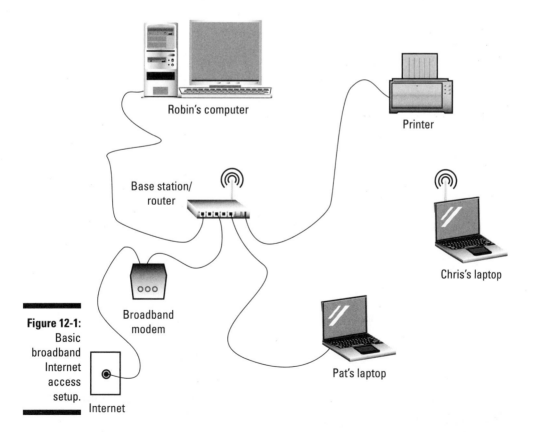

Robin's computer

Printer

Base station/
router

Chris's laptop

Broadband
modem

Figure 12-1:
Basic
broadband
Internet
access
setup.

Pat's laptop

Internet

Yes, the broadband Internet setup looks just like the basic network setup. In fact, they're nearly identical. That's not just because I recycle illustrations in this book. It shows that any time you're connected to a network, you're probably connected to the Internet. The key is the broadband modem, shown in Figure 12-1.

The broadband modem connects to the Internet by using cable, DSL, or satellite Internet service. The broadband modem also connects to a router. The *router* provides the bridge between the local network and the Internet. It does all the magic for you.

The router can be wire-based or wireless. In Figure 12-1, Chris is connected to the Internet using a wireless connection. Pat is using a wired connection. Both laptops have the same access to the Internet, thanks to the combination wired/wireless router.

✔ Broadband means *high speed.*

✔ Router rhymes with *chowder.* Do not pronounce it "ROO-ter."

✔ Broadband Internet access works the same no matter where you are. Even for a public network, such as in a hotel or café, the access works the same.

✔ When your laptop is connected to the network, you're "on" the Internet. Just start your Web browser, check e-mail — the whole nine yards.

✔ The number of computers on your network can be anything from one up to as many computers as the router can handle. That's usually dozens of computers for a good router. By the way, if you have dozens of laptops, note that your laptop warranty requires you to buy one copy of this book for each laptop. Thank you.

✔ When you set up broadband access for yourself, you must configure the router. That's done by logging in to the router using your Web browser. The router has an IP address, and you use Web browser software, such as Internet Explorer, to connect to the router, log in, and configure the settings. Instructions for doing this come with the router. (For public networks, the router is configured by whichever outfit is hosting the network.)

Watch out! That network is public

After making the network connection, you should be prompted by the Set Network Location window, as shown in Figure 12-2. Anytime you use a network in public — in a hotel, cybercafé, public library, or similar location — always choose the Public option.

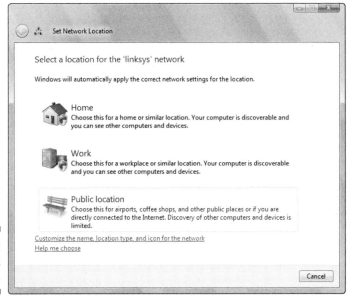

By designating a network as Public, you're ensuring that Windows kicks in a few extra protections for your laptop.

When you're unsure about the network's location, you can confirm it by visiting the Network and Sharing Center window. (Directions for opening this window are in Chapter 11; a beautiful depiction can be found in Figure 11-3, over in Chapter 11.) The network you're using appears in the window, followed by the text *Public* or *Private.* There you go!

To change the network type, follow these steps:

1. **Open the Network and Sharing Center window, if it's not open already.**

2. **Click the Customize link just to the right of the network name.**

   The Set Network Location Wizard appears.

3. **Choose Public from the list.**

   (Optional) You can change the network name as well. This is useful when you use one too many networks named `Network` or `Linksys`.

4. **Click the Next button.**

5. **Click the Close button.**

Whew!

Disconnecting from broadband access

There's no formal requirement for disconnecting from the broadband Internet. Unlike when you use a dialup modem (covered later in this chapter), you don't need to worry about disconnecting officially or hanging up a modem. Like Robin Williams, a broadband connection is always on.

To disconnect from a wired network, simply unplug the network cable. You can also turn your laptop off, put it to sleep, or hibernate it.

To disconnect from a wireless network, turn off your laptop, sleep it, or hibernate it. Sometimes, just closing the lid works. (See Chapter 4 to determine what happens when you close the laptop's lid.)

To disconnect from a wireless network while still using the laptop, follow these steps:

1. **Choose Connect To from the Start menu.**

   The Connect to a Network window appears.

2. **If the wireless network you're using isn't highlighted in the window, click to select it.**

   The network you're using has the word *Connected* by its name.

3. **Click the Disconnect button.**

   Another screen appears because Windows really doesn't believe that you seriously want to disconnect from the network.

4. **Click the larger, more determined Disconnect button.**

5. **Click the Close button.**

You're free!

If your laptop sports a power switch for the wireless networking adapter, you can also disconnect from the network by turning the adapter's power off. That has a bonus of saving battery power.

Dialup Internet Access

Nothing beats the 1990s! Ho-boy! We were younger then. Had a booming economy. A lovable but morally questionable guy in the White House. And dialup Internet access as far as the eye could see. Welcome to the slow days.

Even if you prefer broadband, have it at home, and use it all over the world, there may still be those few times when you need to play E.T. and phone home to the Internet using one of those annoying things developed by Antonio Meucci and properly stolen by Alexander Graham Bell. The telephone. Antique. Sluggish. Unreliable. Annoying. Your last hope. Good luck.

For general information on using your laptop's modem, refer to Chapter 13.

Configuring a dialup connection

Setting up your laptop for a dialup Internet connection is something you have to do manually. Unlike with the Ethernet thing, you cannot just plug and go. Instead, you need to know some basic information:

✔ The ISP's name (used to identify the dialup connection)

✔ The connection's phone number

✔ The username for your ISP account

✔ The password for your ISP account

Your ISP, or whichever outfit is giving you Internet access, provides this information for you. You then use the tidbits to configure the dialup connection:

1. **Choose Connect To from the Start button menu.**

    The Connect to a Network window appears.

    If you see your dialup connection listed in the window, you're ready to connect. Refer to the later section "Making the dialup connection."

2. **Choose the item Set Up a Connection or Network.**

    A list of various items you can set up appears.

3. **Select the item in the list labeled Set Up a Dial-Up Connection.**

4. **Click the Next button.**

    If you disabled your laptop's modem to save power, no modem is found at this point. Refer to Chapter 9 for directions on how to reenable the modem.

5. **Fill in the information as given to you by your ISP: the phone number, your account name, and your password.**

    The username and password here are used to get into your ISP's account. They may be different from the username and password used to access your e-mail inbox, and definitely not the same as the logon and password you use for Windows.

6. **Place a check mark by the option Remember This Password.**

7. **Type a name for the connection.**

   My ISP is named *CompuSoft*, so I type **CompuSoft** in the box.

8. **Ensure that your laptop is plugged into a phone cord and that the phone cord is plugged into a telephone jack.**

9. **Click the Connect button.**

   Windows uses your modem to test-dial the phone number you entered.

If all goes well, you should be connected to the Internet. To dial up the Internet by using the modem in the future, see the later section "Making the dialup connection."

✔ Connect the laptop's modem to a phone jack before you dial the Internet!

✔ There are more options for dialing a phone number with a modem than most people would dare to dream of. Don't fuss over the options now; wait to read about the details in Chapter 13.

✔ When you're using more than one ISP, you need one dialup connection icon for each one.

✔ If your ISP requires special software to connect, use it to connect to the Internet.

Making the dialup connection

Dialup Internet works just like making a phone call. A nice, slow phone call. You're connected to the Internet only when the modem is using the phone. And, most importantly, you need to "hang up" the modem when you're done. You'll probably forget that advice more than once.

Before you do anything, ensure that your laptop is properly wired to the phone jack. The cord must plug into the modem hole on your laptop and into a phone jack on the wall or else piggyback on another telephonic device.

The easiest way to connect to the Internet is to simply open or use an Internet program. For example, start up Internet Explorer to browse the Web, or tell your e-mail program to fetch new mail. Either action forces the laptop to look for an Internet connection, by either connecting automatically or presenting a list of connections for you to choose.

If starting up an Internet program doesn't work, try these steps:

1. **From the Start menu, choose the Connect To item.**

   The Connect to a Network window appears, listing the various and potential ways for your laptop to find the Internet or any other network.

2. **Choose the dialup connection.**

   Its name was chosen when you set things up.

3. **Click the Connect button.**

   Windows dials the modem and attempts to make the connection.

After the connection has been made, the little modem buddies appear in the notification area. They're your clue that you're connected to the Internet. You can now use any Internet software.

   ✔ Yes, the connection speed you see may be much lower than the speed your modem is capable of. The speed depends on the quality of the connection and the phone lines connecting your laptop to the ISP.

   ✔ Rarely, if ever, have I connected at any speed higher than 49 Kbps.

   ✔ Rumor has it that the phone company guarantees connection speeds of only 14.4 Kbps. In some areas, that's as good as it gets.

   ✔ Do not plug your modem into a digital phone system! It will fry your modem's gizzard! Digital phone systems are common in hotels and medium- to large-size businesses. When in doubt, ask!

Don't forget to disconnect the dialup connection!

Just as you said "Hello," you must always say "Goodbye," and often such action requires a restraining order. For your laptop, a dialup connection must officially be disconnected when you're done using the Internet. You may forget this statement, especially when you use dialup on the road and have broadband at home.

Disconnecting works like connecting does: Choose the Connect To command from the Start menu. When the Connect to a Network window appears, choose your dialup connection from the window and then click the Disconnect button.

You can also disconnect the modem from the Internet by right-clicking the little modem guys in the notification area. Choose the Disconnect command from the context menu that pops up.

Shared Internet Access

Say that you're at a trendy wireless location, *Café du Nerds*. You're settling in with your lattè and scone (blackberry, overpriced), and along comes your friend Phil. He's ecstatic because he just discovered MySpace.

Now you're on the Internet. You bought this book. You're set up with wireless access. You're looking cool with your lattè, laptop, and half-eaten scone. But Phil has only a wired connection on his laptop. He cannot use the *Café du Nerds* wireless connection. Yet you graciously offer to help.

First, you connect your laptop with Phil's laptop by using a standard Ethernet cable. Phil doesn't have one of these items, but you do because you read Chapter 24.

Second, you share your Internet connection like this:

1. **Open the Network and Sharing Center window.**

2. **On the left side of the window, click the link that says Manage Network Connections.**

3. **Right-click your laptop's Wireless Network Connection icon, the one you're using presently to get on the Internet.**

4. **Choose Properties from the pop-up menu.**

5. **Type the administrator's password or click the Continue button if you're faced with a User Account Control warning.**

6. **In the network connection's Properties dialog box, click the Sharing tab.**

7. **Put a check mark by the box that says Allow Other Network Users to Connect through This Computer's Internet Connection.**

8. **Click OK, and close the Network and Sharing Center window.**

Phil should now be on the Internet. He can test it by opening his Web browser and navigating to MySpace (or any other Web page). After he thanks you profusely, simply recommend that he buy this book — not *borrow* your copy, but buy his own! And, he can buy you another scone.

Chapter 13

That Modem Thing

In This Chapter

▶ Understanding the dialup modem

▶ Setting the modem's volume

▶ Configuring the dialing and area code rules

▶ Setting modem and connection timeouts

▶ Sending and receiving faxes

Originally, modems were oddball, expensive, technical peripherals. Only a few of the most diehard computer hobbyists bothered to have them installed. With the boom of the Internet, modems suddenly became a must-have part of every computer. Now, in the era of fast, broadband Internet connections, the dialup modem is once again relegated to the margins. That is, unless you have a laptop computer.

You can use your laptop's modem to connect to the Internet when a broadband connection isn't available. You can also use the modem to send and receive faxes. Both topics are covered in this chapter.

Introducing Mr. Modem

When it comes to computers, the word *modem* applies to a variety of communications thingies. Basically, there are broadband modems — cable, DSL, and satellite — and there are dialup modems. Unlike broadband modems, dialup modems don't use an Ethernet network connection. Instead, they plug directly into the phone system, sending audio signals over the phone lines.

On your laptop, the modem is included as part of the main circuitry. In fact, the only evident part of the modem is the hole into which you plug the phone cable. That's about as technical as it gets.

✔ Not every laptop has a dialup modem. Apple dropped the dialup modem from the Macintosh laptop line years ago. (A dialup modem is available as a USB peripheral.)

Cellular modems

Another type of modem is the *cellular modem.* It works like a dial-up modem, but for a laptop it allows you to access online services anywhere you can get a cell-phone signal. That allows you more freedom than a land line.

Cellular modems connect to your laptop using the USB interface, though some PC Card variations exist. Just like a cell phone, you must subscribe to the cellular modem service to access the Internet. For folks always on the go, especially where wireless Internet access isn't available, the cellular modem makes a wonderful alternative.

✔ Modems are gauged by their speed in bits per second (bps). That speed determines how much information can be sent and received by the modem. All modems today are capable of 56 Kbps, or 56,000 bits per second. That's about $1/8$ the speed of a low-end broadband modem.

✔ The only part of the modem you're likely to see is the hole, or *jack,* into which the phone cord plugs. Refer to Chapter 5 for information on locating the thing.

✔ Some laptops may have two modem holes or jacks. One is used to connect the laptop to the phone jack on the wall. That's the *line* jack. The second hole can be used to connect a phone. That's the *phone* jack. That way, you can still use the phone without having to unplug the modem.

✔ No, you cannot use the phone while the modem is online.

✔ The computer makes phone calls just like a human does: It dials a number, and then it screeches its unmelodic tones at the other computer, which also screeches back.

✔ Long-distance charges apply to modem calls just as they do to regular phone calls. Hotel surcharges apply as well.

✔ Some countries charge extra for modem-made phone calls. When you're traveling overseas, be sure to inquire about any extra fees before you use the phone.

✔ On the rare chance that your laptop lacks a modem, you can readily find a modem PC Card.

✔ *Modem* is a contraction of *mo*dulator-*dem*odulator. The electronic (digital) signal from the modem is modulated into an audio (analog) signal for the phone line. Likewise, a modulated analog signal is demodulated by the modem back into digital information for the computer. Or something like that.

Modem Setup

Your laptop's modem is one of the last computer devices you'll ever use that must be configured before you can use it. Yes, there's a certain amount of "dumb" in a modem. Because the modem dials the phone just like a human, that basic setup operation includes telling the modem how to dial the phone, which numbers are long-distance, and how to dial long-distance numbers.

You'll find the modem deep in the Control Panel jungle

To do the initial modem setup, pay attention to these steps:

1. **Open the Control Panel.**

Phone and Modem Options

2. **From the Control Panel Home, choose Hardware and Sound, and then choose Phone and Modem Options; from the Control Panel Classic view, open the Phone and Modem Options icon.**

   If you see the Location Information dialog box, as shown in Figure 13-1, you need to continue setting up your modem. Otherwise, carry on with the later section "Setting modem properties."

Figure 13-1: Windows demands to know where your laptop dwells most of the time.

Location Information
Before you can make any phone or modem connections, Windows needs the following information about your current location.
What country/region are you in now?
United States
What area code (or city code) are you in now?
If you need to specify a carrier code, what is it?
If you dial a number to access an outside line, what is it?
The phone system at this location uses:
⦿ Tone dialing ○ Pulse dialing
OK   Cancel

All the questions that follow relate to the location where you use your laptop the most, such as your home or office or the labor camp where you're being reeducated.

3. **Choose your country or region from the drop-down list.**

For example, if you're in Canada, you choose the United States because everyone knows that the U.S. secretly desires domination of our northern frontier. (Though my editor tells me that if you're in Canada, you can choose Canada. For now.)

4. **Enter your home location's area or city code.**

I'm in area code 208, so if you're pretending to be me, you type **208**.

5. **Enter a carrier code, if one is required.**

I have no idea what a *carrier code* is, so I left it blank. No doubt it's something Canadians worry about.

6. **Enter the number you need in order to access an outside line, if necessary.**

For example, if you need to dial an 8 or a 9 to escape the local PBX, enter that number; otherwise, leave the box empty.

To insert a pause in dialing, use the comma. For example, if you have to dial 9 and then pause, type **9,** in the box.

7. **Choose whether you need to use tone or pulse dialing.**

8. **Click OK to continue.**

After you complete these steps, the laptop is now satisfied that you know where you are and that the modem knows how to dial the phone from that location. The next thing you see is the Phone and Modem Options dialog box (see Figure 13-2), which is covered in the next section.

You can customize, at any time, the location information you enter. This includes adding information or disabling call waiting as well as doing other fine tuning. You can also create a new location for places you visit often and are required to use a dialup connection. The remaining sections in this chapter describe how that's done.

Setting modem properties

After betraying your location to the computer (see the preceding section), you can proceed with using the Phone and Modem Options dialog box, shown in Figure 13-2. That's the dialog box you see when you open the Phone and Modem Options link or icon in the Control Panel — well, after you use the initial Location Information dialog box (refer to Figure 13-1).

Chapter 13: That Modem Thing **201**

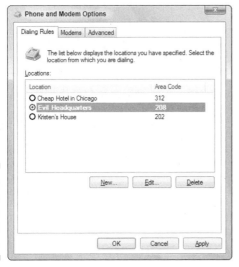

Figure 13-2:
The Phone
and Modem
Options
dialog box.

The Phone and Modem Options dialog box is where you configure new locations for using the laptop's modem. You can also use the dialog box to control the modem's behavior.

One key way to control the modem's behavior is to use the modem's Properties dialog box. As you've come to expect from Windows, this is *another* dialog box you must open and fool with from time to time.

To open your laptop's modem's Properties dialog box form the Phone and Modem Options dialog box, pursue these steps:

1. **Open the Phone and Modem Options dialog box.**

   Refer to Steps 1 and 2 from the preceding section.

2. **Click the Modems tab.**

   A list of any modem (or modems) installed in your computer is shown.

3. **Select your laptop's modem from the list.**

   Yeah, it's probably the only one in the list.

4. **Click the Properties button.**

   The Properties dialog box for your modem appears, as shown in Figure 13-3.

Figure 13-3:
The
modem's
Properties
dialog box.

Adjustments to the modem are made according to the sections that follow.

Silencing the modem

Most people enjoy hearing the modem make its hideous noise as an online connection is being made. If you don't, you can mute the modem. Quietly follow these steps:

1. **Open the modem's Properties dialog box.**

   Refer to the preceding section.

2. **Click the Modem tab.**

3. **Use the volume slider control to set the modem's volume.**

   Loud is on the right. Soft is toward the left. Off is all the way over on the left.

4. **Keep clicking the various OK buttons to close the various dialog boxes.**

You can put away those noise-reducing headphones now.

Adding special modem-command settings

Some ISPs require you to give the modem special commands. This is done to improve the connection or, often, to troubleshoot a bad connection. The settings are entered into a text box labeled Enter Initialization Commands, on the Advanced tab of the modem's Properties dialog box.

Suppose that you're told to use the modem command ATS58=33 to help set up the laptop's modem. If so, type that text into the box *exactly* as written. Click the OK button to close the dialog box and make this change permanent.

Dialing Out of Strange Places

You'll take your laptop with you everywhere, even to the Twilight Zone someday. Maybe you'll stop in Willoughby, or visit a roadside café where a little box tells your fortune, or perchance arrive at some post apocalyptic wasteland library. If you plan to come back, it makes sense to set up your laptop so that you can dial up into what remains of the Internet — or at least get e-mail sent before everyone turns into a monster.

Location, location, location

When you first set up the modem, you told it how to dial the phone. You entered information for the laptop's primary location. But consider that you visit other locations where you use your laptop. If you plan to return to those locations, it pays to set them up permanently. That way, you can quickly configure the modem to dial from any of your favorite haunts.

To create a new location, tread these steps:

1. **Open the Phone and Modem Options dialog box.**

   Directions for accessing this dialog box (refer to Figure 13-2) are found earlier in this chapter.

2. **Ensure that the Dialing Rules tab is selected.**

   The Dialing Rules tab lists the locations where you use your laptop. *My Location* is your home base (unless you already renamed it).

3. **Click the New button.**

   The New Location dialog box appears, as shown in Figure 13-4. Use it to customize the way the modem dials the phone from any location.

4. **Enter a name for the location.**

   For example, type **Cliffordville**.

5. **Select whichever country where the location is found.**

6. **Enter the area code.**

New Location

General | Area Code Rules | Calling Card

Location name: Maple Street

Specify the location from which you will be dialing.

Country/region:
United States

Area code:
310

Dialing rules

When dialing from this location, use the following rules:

To access an outside line for local calls, dial:

To access an outside line for long-distance calls, dial:

Use this carrier code to make long-distance calls:

Use this carrier code to make international calls:

☑ To disable call waiting, dial: *70,

Dial using: ◉ Tone   ○ Pulse

OK | Cancel | Apply

Figure 13-4:
Phone stuff
for any
location.

7. **Fill in the Dialing Rules area.**

   You can leave these items blank if none is required.

   If you're creating a location for a hotel and it requires you to dial an 8 before making a local call or a 9 for making a long-distance call, put those numbers into the appropriate boxes.

8. **To disable call waiting while the modem is online, select the To Disable Call Waiting Dial check box. Then select the proper code sequence from the drop-down list.**

   The call-waiting signal disconnects an active modem connection. You select this box to disable call waiting on a per-phone-call basis.

9. **Finally, select whether your connection requires tone or pulse dialing.**

   Select the Pulse option only if your area is limited to pulse dialing. You'll be painfully aware of this annoyance; otherwise, you can choose Tone.

10. **Click OK to save the settings.**

Windows uses this information whenever you use the modem. It may seem silly to enter this information now, but eventually you'll have a whole collection of locations. You can save time by using that information rather than have to enter it over and over again when you travel.

   ✔ You can use these steps to rename your home location from My Location. Just select the My Location item and click the Edit button. Type a new name using the Edit Location window, which looks similar to Figure 13-4. Click OK.

✔ You don't need to disable call waiting if you don't want to. Various software programs and hardware gizmos are available that monitor incoming calls and alert you to them without disconnecting the modem. Check out www.buzme.com

✔ If you use AOL dial-up, check out AOL Call Alert.

✔ Also refer to the next section to find out how and when you can direct the modem to automatically dial an area code for you.

Area code madness! To dial or not to dial

There are rules about dialing area codes. You may not know them all, but you certainly know the frustration when the automated voice says, "You do not need to dial a 1 . . ." or equally as often, "You must first dial a 1 or 0 . . ." Who really knows what to dial? And why, if they know whether you need to dial a 1, doesn't the phone company do it for you automatically?

When you set up a location for your laptop's modem, you also have the opportunity to explain to the computer all about dialing long distance numbers, or just how and when to use an area code. Here's what you do:

1. **Choose your current location in the Phone and Modem Options dialog box.**

   The directions for opening the Phone and Modem Options dialog box are concealed earlier in this chapter.

2. **Click the Edit button.**

3. **In the Edit Location dialog box, click the Area Code Rules tab.**

4. **Click the New button to create a new rule.**

   The New Area Code Rule dialog box appears, as shown in Figure 13-5.

   Here's how this works:

   If you're calling into your own or another area code and you must always dial 1 plus that area code, fill in the dialog box like this:

   a. Enter the area code.

   b. Click the Include All the Prefixes within This Area Code radio button.

   *c. Select the Dial check box and enter **1** into the box.*

   This step assumes that you dial 1 before dialing into another area code.

   d. Select the Include the Area Code check box.

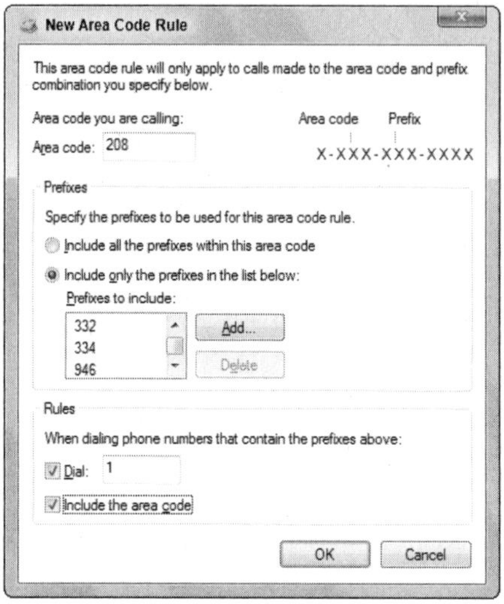

New Area Code Rule

This area code rule will only apply to calls made to the area code and prefix combination you specify below.

Area code you are calling: Area code   Prefix

Area code: 208   X - XXX - XXX - XXXX

Prefixes

Specify the prefixes to be used for this area code rule.

○ Include all the prefixes within this area code

◉ Include only the prefixes in the list below:

Prefixes to include:

332		Add...
334		
946		Delete

Rules

When dialing phone numbers that contain the prefixes above:

☑ Dial: 1

☑ Include the area code

[OK]   [Cancel]

Figure 13-5:
Making up
a new area
code rule.

If you're calling locally and you need to enter the area code for only certain prefixes — the so-called local long-distance prefixes, or when you live in a large area covered by one area code and certain prefixes are long distance, fill in the dialog box like this:

   a. Enter your own area code.

   b. Click the Include Only the Prefixes in the List Below radio button.

      Don't open the phone book and enter all the prefixes! Enter only those you have to dial. For example, in my area code, prefix 334 is local long distance, and I have to dial the area code.

   c. Click the Add button.

   d. Type one or more prefixes into the box and click OK.

      You have to enter only those prefixes that the modem will be dialing.

   *e. Select the Dial check box and enter **1** into the text box.*

   f. Select the Include the Area Code check box.

Finally, if you have to always dial the area code, do this:

   a. Enter your own area code.

   b. Click the Include All the Prefixes within This Area Code radio button.

   *c. Select the Dial check box and enter **1** into the text box.*

   d. Select the Include the Area Code check box.

Every time you dial any local number, the modem automatically prefixes 1 and your area code to the number.

5. **Click OK to add the new rule.**

6. **Repeat Steps 4 and 5 to create as many rules as necessary.**

To put these dialing rules into effect, you need to select the Use Dialing Rules check box whenever you enter a new phone number for the modem to dial.

Yes, you can ignore and forget about all these things! Rather than create rules all the time, simply type the full number to dial every time you set up a new modem connection. But, if you're dialing a lot of numbers in different locations, setting up the rules can make things far easier.

Calling card info

The far right tab in the Edit Location dialog box is for entering calling card information. This tab allows Windows to automatically blast out the calling card information as the modem connects, allowing you to charge, for example, a specific call at a business center to your company's credit card.

To enter calling card information, edit the Location information as described in the previous sections. Click the Calling Card tab, and you see a buncha options. Fill them in with the information you need in order to use the calling card, and leave irrelevant items blank.

✔ If your card isn't listed in the Card Types list, click the New button. Then you can use the quite detailed dialog box that appears to enter information about your credit or calling card.

✔ Yes, this information is obviously sensitive. See Chapter 18 for information on laptop security.

The Various Disconnect Timeouts

Just like when you're hanging up a phone, you should always remember to manually disconnect the modem when you're done using it. Even if you forget, the modem eventually hangs up by itself. That's because Windows runs a timeout clock on the modem. After a period of inactivity, the modem eventually hangs up itself.

Yes, it's a good thing that the modem can time-out and hang up. That may save you money on some pricey calls. But it's also a bad thing when the timeout hits unexpectedly. To ensure that the modem doesn't time-out on you when you don't want it to, consider checking two separate places in Windows.

The general timeout

The general modem-timeout value is set in the modem's Properties dialog box. Refer to the directions earlier in this chapter for displaying that dialog box. After you're there, heed these steps:

1. **Click the Change Settings button on the General tab.**

2. **Type the administrator's password or click the Continue button when you see the User Account Control warning.**

   You must have administrator privileges to change the modem's timeout. A second, more productive modem Properties dialog box appears.

3. **Click the Advanced tab.**

4. **Click the Change Default Preferences button.**

5. **Select the Disconnect a Call If Idle for More Than check box, and then enter a timeout value into the text box.**

   Yes, if you leave this item deselected, no general timeout takes place.

6. **Click OK and close the various open dialog boxes.**

Timeouts for each session

Timeouts are also set for each connection you make with the modem. These connections are discussed in Chapter 12; refer to that chapter for details beyond what's mentioned here. Follow these steps:

1. **Choose Connect To from the Start menu.**

2. **Right-click the dialup connection you want to modify.**

3. **Choose Properties from the pop-up menu.**

4. **Click the Options tab in the Properties dialog box.**

5. **Set the timeout value next to the item Idle Time before Hanging Up.**

   To disable the timeout, choose Never from the menu.

6. **Click OK and close the various open dialog boxes and windows.**

Putting the Fax in Fax/Modem

Your modem sports a secret identity. It may be a mere *modem* by day, but at night it dawns a mask and cape and it becomes . . . *fax/modem.* Yes, you can use your laptop's modem to send and receive faxes. Damn that on-the-road business center and the $4 fax fee! You can fax with only a phone cable.

✔ There's no need to confirm anything! Trust me: Your laptop's modem can send and receive faxes.

✔ The following sections describe how to use the faxing facility inside Windows. Other faxing programs are available that you might find easier to use and manage than the one Windows offers. Visit your local Software-o-Rama to see the variety. You can also use various Web-based fax services.

✔ Not every edition of Windows Vista comes with faxing software.

✔ The faxing facility described in this chapter might be available only if the Microsoft Office suite of programs has been installed on your laptop. I'm not really sure about this, seeing as how I can't find a laptop without Office installed to verify it.

✔ Faxes are a bit antique when you think about it. The e-mail attachment has supplanted the fax as the standard way documents are sent these days. Even so, I recognize that the legal and medical communities continue to use faxes. So, it's obvious that I can't just wiggle out of writing about this stuff.

✔ See Chapter 15 for more information on e-mail.

✔ Fax technology was merged with the standard computer modem in the early 1990s.

Finding the fax modem

From a computer user's standpoint, it helps to think of a fax machine as nothing more than a remote printer. Although it's the modem's hardware that carries out the faxing, you need to look for your computer's fax machine in the list of printers in the Printers window.

The fax modem is represented by a fax icon, shown in the margin. The icon is found in the Printers window, along with any printers available to your laptop, directly connected or on the network. When you see a fax machine or anything named Fax in the list of printers, you're all ready to go.

Refer to Chapter 8 for more information on how to open the Printers window.

✔ Note that although the fax machine appears as an icon in the list of printers, you don't use that icon to send a fax. Sending faxes is covered in the next section.

✔ If you don't see a fax machine in Windows Vista, your copy of Windows Vista may not come with faxing abilities; get a third-party fax program for your modem.

Sending a fax

Faxing works just like printing. So, sending a fax starts with the standard printing operation. Do this:

1. **Prepare the document you want to fax.**

   You can fax from any application that has a Print command on its File menu.

2. **Choose File⇨Print, or use whichever command prints a document in your application.**

   Do not click the Print button on the toolbar! That often just prints the document on whatever "default" printer you selected. If the default printer is the fax machine, fine. Otherwise, beware!

3. **Choose the fax modem as your printer.**

4. **Make any other selections as needed in the Print dialog box.**

   For example, specify which pages to print, the number of copies, and other options as they're available in the dialog box.

5. **Click the Print button.**

   The Fax Setup window appears if you haven't ever sent a fax. Set things up by following these substeps:

   a. *Choose Connect to a Fax Modem.*

   b. *Click the Next button.*

   c. *Choose the option I'll Choose Later; I Want to Create a Fax Now.*

   d. *If prompted by a firewall warning, unblock access for Fax and Scan.*

   The New Fax window appears, which looks a lot like a new e-mail message window, as shown in Figure 13-6.

6. **(Optional) Choose a cover page.**

   When you choose a cover page, you detour here and work for a while to configure that page.

7. **Use the To button to select a recipient from the Windows Contacts folder, or just type a phone number for the receiving fax.**

8. **(Optional) Fill in the rest of the fields.**

9. **Click the Send button.**

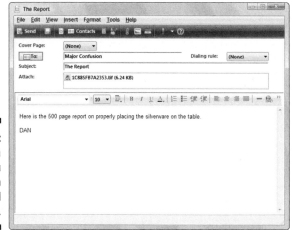

Figure 13-6:
Sending a
fax like you
send an
e-mail
message.

At this point, the fax goes into the queue, which means that it sits and waits for the fax modem to do its job and send the fax. A fax status window holds you in suspenseful agony while the modem does its thing.

To confirm that the fax has been sent, you must visit a place I call Fax Central. Refer to the next section.

Visiting Fax Central

To observe all the fast-paced, thrilling fax action as it happens (or even after the fact), visit Fax Central in Windows. Because faxing in Windows works like sending an e-mail, the Fax Central window greatly resembles an e-mail program. Know e-mail, and you can work the Fax Central window.

To get to Fax Central, open the Fax icon in the Printers window. Yes, the real name of the place is Windows Fax and Scan. I call it Fax Central.

Fax Central is also where you can cancel a fax, if you have a modem or connection problem. Simply locate the fax by opening the Outbox folder. Click to select the fax, and press the Delete key on your laptop's keyboard. This action is necessary because simply unplugging the phone cord from the fax modem merely delays sending the fax.

Receiving a fax

When you're aware of a thundering fax speeding your way, summon the Windows Fax and Scan window (I call it Fax Central), as described in the previous section. Then follow these steps:

1. **Ensure that the modem is connected.**
2. **Wait for the ring (if you have another phone attached to the incoming line).**

3. **From the window's toolbar, click the Receive a Fax Now button.**
4. **Sit and wait.**

   Doh-dee-doh-do.

After the fax has been received, a pop-up bubble may appear, or you may notice the little Pending Fax Guy in the notification area. That's your clue that a fax has come in.

Any fax that's received appears in the window's Inbox — just like e-mail. To view the fax, double-click its icon or select the fax and then click the View button on the toolbar. The fax is displayed in a special window, from which you can print, save, or mess with the fax.

Faxes are received as *image* files. Specifically, they're TIFF images. You cannot edit the files as text documents. Faxes are *images*.

Chapter 14

Internet Security

In This Chapter

▶ Recognizing malware

▶ Using Windows Firewall

▶ Protecting your laptop from viruses

▶ Avoiding virus risks

▶ Understanding spyware

▶ Thwarting a hijack or phishing scam

*N*o technology is perfect. There are unintended consequences for everything. Consider the *Star Trek* transporter: It works great on television, of course, providing the immediate teleportation of people and goods. Who wouldn't want such a thing? But they never mention acceptable quantum divergence, random molecular reorientation, missing-limb syndrome, or a variety of chance side effects that would come with any new revolutionary tool.

Consider the Internet: It was designed for communications, with the bonus of being able to withstand a nuclear attack. Its communications ability and vast storage of information make the Internet a desirable thing. But the unintended consequences are gross: The Internet is also a spring of unwanted advertising and malicious programs and a purveyor of pornography. To best use the Internet, you must be prepared to deal with Internet security — especially with a device so closely linked with communications as a laptop computer.

✔ General laptop security is the domain of Chapter 18.

✔ Also refer to my book *Troubleshooting Your PC For Dummies* (Wiley Publishing) for more Internet security information and tips.

The Four Horsemen of the Internet Apocalypse

There are four things you need in order to best protect yourself from vile on the Internet:

- ✔ A firewall
- ✔ Antivirus software
- ✔ Anti-spyware software
- ✔ Anti-hijacking software

A *firewall* is used to filter Internet traffic coming into and going out of your laptop. The firewall helps to protect you from nasty programs that can take over your computer and carry out evil or flood your laptop with unwanted junk.

Antivirus software protects your laptop against special programs called *viruses* or *worms.* These programs take over your computer, often destroying data and erasing files. Some worms scour the hard drive for passwords and credit card numbers and then send off that information to be used by the bad guys. Some viruses use your e-mail address list to mail copies of themselves to all your friends. O! It's nastiness in the worst form!

Anti-spyware software helps protect your computer against programs that quite literally spy on your Internet activity. The Web sites you visit are monitored, and as a result, specific advertising is flooded into your computer. Spyware is also the number-one reason that a computer becomes slow.

Hijacking software is used to take control over your Web browsing adventures. What happens is that you may want to visit one Web page but instead are hijacked and taken to another Web page. Often, you cannot visit anywhere you want to go and are always taken back to some advertising-infested Web page. It can be very frustrating.

The sections in this chapter tell you more about these nasty programs on the Internet, and specifically what you can do on your laptop to fight them.

Behind the Firewall

In the real world, a firewall is a specially constructed part of a building designed to impede the progress of a blazing inferno. Firewalls are rated by how long it takes the fire to burn through the wall. Most importantly, it acts as protection for whatever lies on the other side of the firewall.

On the Internet, a *firewall* keeps nasty things from either coming into or escaping from your laptop. It does that by monitoring the Internet's virtual doors, called ports. Each *port* is an individual connection used by some Internet program. The reason the firewall is necessary is that many of the Internet's ports are left open. Just like leaving a window open, an open port invites unwanted guests. The firewall software not only helps close those ports but also alerts you when anything unexpected knocks on the port's door and wants in or out.

- ✔ Without a firewall in place, your computer is wide open to attack from any number of nasties on the Internet.

- ✔ The best firewall is a *hardware firewall.* Most network routers come with this feature installed and are more than capable of defending your Internet connection, as well as all computers on the router's network, from incoming attacks.

- ✔ When you have a hardware firewall on a router, there's no need to run a redundant software firewall in Windows.

- ✔ If you don't have a hardware firewall, note that you need only one firewall program on your computer. Running multiple firewalls merely clogs up the system.

- ✔ The survival time of an unprotected, nonfirewalled Windows computer on the Internet averages just 13 minutes. After that length of time passes, your laptop *will be* infected and overrun by nasty programs sent from the Internet.

Using Windows Firewall

Windows comes with firewall software that provides a modest level of protection for your laptop. Third-party firewall software is also available. Remember that using a hardware firewall is often the best solution.

Access Windows Firewall as follows:

1. **Open the Control Panel window.**

2. **From the Control Panel Home, choose Security and then choose Windows Firewall; from the Control Panel Classic View, open the Windows Firewall icon.**

   The Windows Firewall window appears, as shown in Figure 14-1. It provides a quick summary of the Firewall's status.

3. **To change the Firewall's status (turn it off or on), click the Change Settings link.**

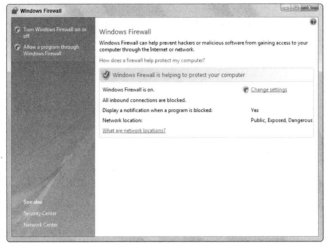

Figure 14-1:
The Firewall window.

4. **In the User Account Control warning dialog box, either click the Continue button or type the administrator's password to continue.**

   The Windows Firewall Settings dialog box appears, as shown in Figure 14-2.

5. **Enable Windows Firewall by clicking the On button, or disable Windows Firewall by clicking the Off button.**

6. **Click OK to confirm your choice.**

7. **Close the Windows Firewall window.**

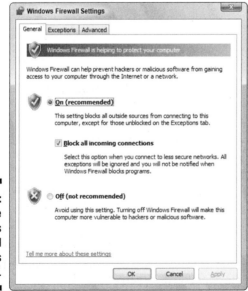

Figure 14-2:
The Windows Firewall Settings dialog box.

It's okay to disable the firewall when you know that you're on a local network behind a hardware firewall. When you do this, however, an annoying warning is displayed each time you start Windows, to alert you to the missing firewall. You have to live with it.

Monitoring Windows Firewall

Windows Firewall lets you know when suspicious Internet access is taking place. A pop-up message appears, alerting you that a program is attempting to access your computer from the Internet or from your computer to the Internet. But be careful to note that this isn't always a panic situation.

When the warning appears, *read it.* The name of the program is listed. In Figure 14-3, the name of the program trying to access the Internet is provided. It's Microsoft Windows Fax and Scan. Because at the time the message appeared I was trying to send a fax, the access is okay.

Figure 14-3: Is it okay for this program to access the Internet?

- ✔ Take those firewall warnings seriously! Do not get in the habit of automatically clicking the Unblock button.

- ✔ When you're in doubt about a program, you can click the Ask Me Later button. Doing so blocks access, but not permanently. To permanently forbid the program from accessing the Internet (or your laptop), click the Keep Blocking button.

- ✔ No, the firewall doesn't warn you incessantly. As you tell it what's allowed and what's denied, it learns. After you trained it awhile, the firewall stops alerting you as much.

- ✔ You train the firewall by clicking the Keep Blocking and Unblock buttons.

- ✔ Some firewall programs use the terms Allow and Deny rather than Unblock and Keep Blocking, respectively.

Which programs are okay to allow, and which ones should be blocked?

The best rule about blocking programs with the firewall is "When in doubt, keep blocking." That's the best advice I can offer you. The other option is to become a computer nerd, and I don't recommend that.

A good way to tell whether a program is okay is to simply know which programs you're using on the computer. For example, I play games on the Internet program Steam. When Steam accesses the Internet, I know that it's okay. As a general rule, however, when you're surprised to see a firewall warning (seemingly out of the blue), *block, block, block.*

Antivirus Software

The oldest Internet threat is the computer virus, which existed long before the Internet. Early computer viruses were exchanged by using floppy disks, usually disks containing pirated programs or pornography. Some doof would start his computer by using the infected floppy disk, and then the computer was infected. Computer viruses are spread far more efficiently these days.

Odds are best that a computer virus will fly into your laptop through the Internet, most probably through some program you download or e-mail file attachment. The bad guys use something called *social engineering*. Say that you get an e-mail from your old pal Guy. The message says, "This file is hilarious! Please open the attachment!" So, you open the attached file, which is a program that runs and may in fact do something cute. But the program is a virus, and it has infected your computer.

To protect yourself against this scourge, you need to run antivirus software on your laptop. This section explains the details.

✔ Don't blame your e-mail buddy! That virus you got by e-mail may or may not have come from the person indicated. Most nasty viruses try to cover their tracks, so although you see Guy's or Wilma's name listed in the message, he or she most likely didn't send you the virus.

✔ Viruses have many names. The term *worm* is also used to describe a computer virus, and some nerds weave tales of how a worm is different from a virus. Many white papers have been written. Yadda-yadda-yadda. Worm. Virus. Same thing.

✔ A *Trojan horse* is a type of virus where the nasty program masquerades as something else. The program may really do the advertised task, but secretly, inside, the Trojan horse program does something malevolent.

✔ A general catch-all term for all bad computer programs — viruses, worms, Trojan horses, and even spyware and hijacking programs — is *malware* (*mal* comes from *mal*evolent, and *ware* comes from soft*ware*).

✔ A firewall cannot protect your computer from a virus. It may prevent the virus from replicating itself on other computers, but it doesn't stop the virus from coming in. You should use *both* antivirus software and a firewall.

Checking for an antivirus program

Windows doesn't come with antivirus software installed. You must use a third-party antivirus program. The good news is that your laptop most likely came with such software installed. The popular programs Norton AntiVirus and McAfee VirusScan come as popular, preinstalled programs on most laptops.

As far as Windows is concerned, you should visit the Windows Security Center to determine the status of any antivirus software installed on your laptop. Follow these steps:

1. **Open the Control Panel window.**

Security Center

2. **From the Control Panel Home, choose the link Check This Computer's Security Status; from the Control Panel Classic View, open the Security Center icon.**

   The Windows Security Center window appears, as shown in Figure 14-4. The window is a center for all the key issues surrounding your laptop's Internet security. Antivirus software status is shown in the third area, Malware Protection. In Figure 14-4, the laptop lacks or is unaware of any antivirus software.

3. **Close the Windows Security Center window when you're done.**

If you don't have antivirus software for your laptop, get some! In addition to Norton and McAfee, I recommend that you consider the following antivirus programs:

✔ Avast! Antivirus: `www.avast.com`

✔ AVG Anti-Virus: `www.grisoft.com`

✔ Kaspersky antivirus protection: `www.kaspersky.com`

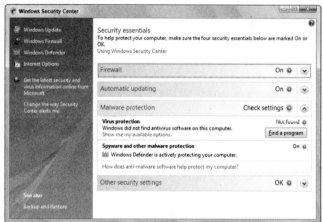

Figure 14-4:
The
Windows
Security
Center.

Scanning for viruses

You can scan for viruses on your laptop in two ways: actively and passively.

To actively scan for viruses, the antivirus program does a complete scan of memory, the laptop's storage system, and, finally, individual files. Everything is checked against a database of known viruses.

The passive virus scan is done as files are received into your computer. Each file coming in is individually scanned and then checked against the virus database. Most virus programs are configured to do this automatically. For example, when you receive an e-mail message with a virus attachment, your antivirus software alerts you and immediately destroys or "quarantines" the bad program.

✔ Obviously, each antivirus program does things differently. You have to refer to the documentation that came with your antivirus software program to see how things work.

✔ Generally speaking, I recommend turning off the active virus scan after it finishes scanning once. Try to configure your antivirus software so that it scans incoming e-mail, e-mail file attachments, and downloads you collect from the Internet. That should keep you safe.

✔ Another tip: Sometimes it helps to have and run *two* antivirus programs — not at the same time, but perhaps run one first, and then shut it down and run a second antivirus program. The second one may catch some things that the first one misses.

✔ Yes, some antivirus programs require a paid subscription. You don't pay for the program, but rather for accessing and updating the antivirus database, or *signature*, files. Believe me, the cost of the subscription is *worth it!* Don't delay in updating your antivirus database!

Disabling the antivirus program

Sometimes, you're asked to turn off the antivirus software. For example, when you install a new program, the directions may suggest turning off any antivirus software. Doing so helps the installation go smoothly and doesn't distress the antivirus program, which may believe that a new virus, and not a new program, is being installed.

To temporarily disable your antivirus software, locate its icon in the notification area. Right-click the icon and choose the Disable, Exit, or Quit option. That temporarily shuts down the antivirus software, allowing your new software to be installed.

After the software installation is done, restart your computer. That also restarts the antivirus software.

Protecting your laptop from the viral scourge

Viruses happen to good people, but they also happen to fools who don't heed good advice, such as:

- ✔ Don't open unexpected e-mail file attachments, even if they appear to be from someone you know and trust. If you weren't expecting anything, don't open it!

- ✔ When I send something that someone isn't expecting, I first send a heads-up message. That first message lets the person know that the second e-mail has a legitimate file attached.

- ✔ Especially avoid any file attachment that can be run as a program. These include files ending in the following letters: BAT, COM, EXE, HTM, HTML, PIF, SCR, or VBS.

- ✔ Avoid opening compressed zip files, or Compressed Folder attachments, specifically when they require a password to open them.

- ✔ A plain-text e-mail message cannot contain a virus. But a virus may be in an e-mail signature or attachment!

- ✔ Odds are good that if you don't open the attachment and just delete the message, your computer will not be infected.

- ✔ Disable the feature that makes your e-mail program automatically save e-mail file attachments. Only save attachments manually.

- ✔ The best protection against nasty programs in e-mail is to use antivirus software.

Sneaky Spyware

Spyware is a specific category of evil computer software, or *malware*. It sounds innocent: Software monitors your activities on the Internet in order to target you with better, more appropriate advertising. In fact, many people willingly sign up for such services. The fools!

The problem is that spyware is often installed without your permission or knowledge. Often, the spyware is disguised as some other program, computer utility, or cute little game. It purports to do one thing, but it's secretly monitoring your Internet activity.

To help fight spyware, Windows Vista comes with *Windows Defender*. It works automatically to stop spyware, but it also can be run manually.

To view the Windows Defender window, choose Windows Defender from the All Programs menu on the Start button's menu. When your computer is behaving well, the message says "Your computer is running normally," as shown in Figure 14-5.

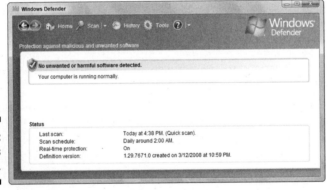

Figure 14-5:
Windows
Defender.

To manually scan for spyware, click the Scan link at the top of the Windows Defender window. Or, you can click the triangle button next to Scan and choose Full Scan from the pop-up menu to do a thorough scrubbing of your laptop for spyware. If spyware is found, you're alerted and given directions on the screen.

Close the Windows Defender Window when you're done.

✔ Windows Defender works automatically, so there's no real reason to scan for spyware unless you suspect something or your laptop is sluggish.

✔ Other anti-spyware tools are available in Windows Defender. For more details on using them, see my book *Troubleshooting Your PC For Dummies* (Wiley Publishing).

✔ Your antivirus software may not check for or remove spyware programs. You may need specific, anti-spyware software.

✔ As a bonus, try to find and use anti-spyware software that also provides protection against hijacking and phishing. See the later section "More Malware: Hijacking and Phishing."

✔ Your firewall cannot protect against spyware. That's because you typically invite spyware into your computer (whether you're aware of it or not). The firewall does, however, detect when the spyware uploads its vital information back to its mothership; a good firewall stops such activity from taking place.

✔ Windows Defender is just one of many anti-spyware solutions available. Some free and nearly free programs are

- Ad-Aware, from www.lavasoft.de

- Spybot Search & Destroy, from www.safer-networking.org

- SpywareBlaster, from www.javacoolsoftware.com

More Malware: Hijacking and Phishing

Two relatively new Internet scourges are *hijacking* and *phishing*. They both work by redirecting your Web browsing from the site you think you're going to, directly to another Web site, usually someplace obnoxious or offensive.

A *hijack* happens inside your computer by resetting where the Web browser takes you. For example, rather than go to your page or to Google, you go to an advertising page or a porn page. That's a hijack.

Phishing (say "fishing") happens in a Web browser and in e-mail. You believe that you're clicking a link to go to your bank or another official Web site, but the Web site is really run by the bad guys. Often, you're asked sensitive questions; requested to submit credit card numbers, PINs, or your Social Security number; or asked to give other information that you should never tell anyone. Because the fake Web page looks official, many people fall prey to this scam.

Antivirus and anti-spyware software can help avoid a hijack. You can also get some help from the User Account Control (UAC) dialog boxes, which appear unexpectedly whenever a hijack is occurring. If you suspect a hijack, click the Cancel button in the UAC dialog box.

To help fight phishing in Internet Explorer, ensure that the phishing filter is active. Follow these directions:

1. **Open Internet Explorer.**

2. **Click the Tools toolbar button.**

3. **From the menu choose Phishing Filter⇨Turn On Automatic Website Checking.**

Of course, you don't have to choose the menu item when it says Turn Off Automatic Website Checking; that means that the phishing filter is on and running.

If you suspect that a Web page is phishing, from the Tools menu choose Phishing Filter⇨Check This Website. That command ensures that the Web page is really what it claims to be. Even if it doesn't, and you still doubt the Web page's credibility, don't input personal information on the Internet!

The government, banks, and other official organizations never require you to provide sensitive information on the Web or through e-mail. If it appears that they are doing that, pick up the phone and call them. Always be on your guard.

Chapter 15

Portable Internet Stuff

· ·

In This Chapter

▶ Saving Web pages to your hard drive

▶ Reading e-mail on the road

▶ Using Web-based e-mail

▶ Forwarding e-mail to another account

▶ Disabling automatic connections

▶ Skipping large messages

· ·

This isn't a book on psychology, and I only practice psychology on barstools (they're really messed up), yet I often find myself asking whether there's such a thing as *Internet separation anxiety.* You know what I'm talking about. It may or may not exist, but it's certainly evident in the ubiquity of the Internet. When Apple's iPhone advertisements question how you could ever live without being separated from the Internet, you have to wonder. Are people truly cyber-needy or just rejecting mankind's traditional methods of diversion? Like, say, reading a book?

Regardless of whether you're enmeshed with the Internet, there are ways to read Web pages and access e-mail when an Internet connection isn't readily available. That might happen quite often with your laptop. Therefore, this chapter presents some tips and tricks for reading Web pages and accessing e-mail when your laptop can't make a connection.

> ✔ A side effect of not using the Internet connection is that it does save a scrap of battery power.

> ✔ Eventually, few locations will remain worldwide where Internet access isn't available. Even in the hallowed tube of a jet airliner, wireless Internet access will soon be available. Separation anxiety, indeed!

Web Browsing When You're Out and About

I have only one suggestion for Web browsing on the road, especially if you're away from an Internet connection for some time (such as on an airplane): *Save your Web pages!*

For example, before you wander from your beloved high-speed Internet connection, go to a few of your favorite Web pages and quickly browse around. As you do, save those Web pages to the laptop's mass storage medium for offline reading while you're away. Here's how that works:

1. **Click the Page button on the Internet Explorer toolbar.**

2. **From the menu, choose the Save As command.**

   A typical Save As dialog box appears, though it's titled Save Webpage.

3. **Use the gizmos in the dialog box to find a location for the Web page.**

   Unless you specifically specify a folder, the Web page is saved in the Documents folder for your user account. That's fine.

   Note that the name given to the Web page is the same as the Web page's title.

   You can click the Browse Folders part of the Save Webpage dialog box to see a more traditional type of Save As dialog box.

4. **Carefully choose a format option for saving the Web page.**

   Four options are on the Save As Type drop-down list. These options determine the format for the Web page file you're saving. Choosing the right one is important:

   - *Web Page, Complete (*.htm, *.html):* Saves everything on the Web page, including graphics, sounds, and fun stuff like that. It takes up quite a bit of storage space, creating a special folder to hold all the graphics and nontext items referenced by the Web page.

   - *Web Archive, Single File (*.mht):* Saves the Web page itself, but uses the Internet storage cache to supply the images. This method takes up the least amount of hard drive space, and I recommend it, especially for reading.

   - *Web Page, HTML Only (*.htm, *.html):* Saves only the bare-bones Web page; that is, just the text — no graphics or multimedia. It's okay for offline reading, but not the best option.

- *Text File (*.txt):* Saves the Web page for editing purposes that don't apply here.

My advice: Choose the Web Archive, Single File option for reading. Only if the Web page has graphics that you want to peruse later should you choose Web Page, Complete.

5. **Click the Save button to save the Web page.**

Continue browsing to other Web pages you want to save for reading later. I often stock up on my favorite opinion writers and bloggers before I leave on a trip. That gives me plenty of reading material on the plane.

To view the Web pages later, open the Documents folder for your account. Then click the icon representing the Web pages you saved. Those pages are opened and displayed in Internet Explorer, where you can read them just as though you're connected to the Internet.

- ✔ Continue your regular Web-page-perusing schedule. Don't stop to read! Just collect and save those Web pages on your hard drive for offline reading.

- ✔ You can open any saved Web page just as you open any other file on your hard drive. The Web page opens in your Web browser, and you can read it just as you would read on the Web.

- ✔ None of the links on the Web page you save are active. Only when you reconnect to the Internet does clicking the links lead somewhere.

- ✔ If you keep seeing a prompt to connect to the Internet, click the Tools button and choose Work Offline from the menu.

- ✔ If you use the Web Page, Complete option, some of the images may not appear on the Web page.

E-Mail Tips Galore

Things are as bad on the road as they were in the old days. I remember staying at one hotel in San Francisco in the early 1990s. To get my e-mail, I had to disassemble the phone jack in the wall. Using alligator clips, I manually connected my laptop's modem to the hotel's phone system. That was fun in a nerdy way, but those days are long over.

With the Internet everywhere, getting your e-mail on the road is no longer a major hassle. It definitely doesn't require a CIA-type of hardware kit to access e-mail from even the skeeziest hotel rooms. Even so, this section contains a bunch of e-mail tips and suggestions you may find handy during your laptop journeys.

✔ If you have a broadband (high-speed) connection at home, using the Internet on the road with a broadband connection works exactly the same. See Chapter 12.

✔ Refer to Chapter 13 for information on using a modem in strange and wonderful places away from home. Though, when broadband is available, your laptop can use it instead of the dialup modem.

Read your e-mail on the Web

Your e-mail program should work from any remote location. There's no need to change anything. That is, unless you use dialup. In that case, you can either incur the long-distance phone charges, follow my advice from Chapter 12 and see whether local or toll-free access points are available for your ISP, or use a Web-based version of the ISP's e-mail system.

In Figure 15-1, you see my own ISP's preview and pickup page. After logging in to this Web page, I can see all e-mail pending for me. (It's all spam in Figure 15-1.) I can click a message to read it, click a link to view an attachment, or just delete the messages.

✔ Be sure to check with your ISP to see whether this type of service is available.

✔ Some national ISPs, such as AOL, offer a Web-page system for picking up and previewing e-mail.

✔ Wow! Cialis pills that dissolve under your tongue! What an amazing world we live in.

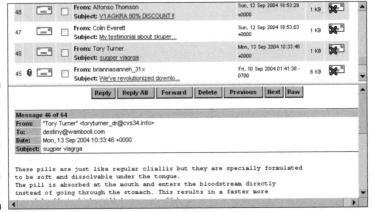

Figure 15-1:
An ISP's
Web-based
e-mail
preview-
and-pickup
page.

Get a Web-based e-mail account

A free Web-based e-mail service makes e-mail available to you anywhere you can find Internet access. Using these services is easy and, best of all, free. With Web-based e-mail, you never have to worry about connecting to your ISP's e-mail account. Your e-mail is available anywhere there's Web access — even if you don't have your own computer with you.

Here are some of the more popular Web-based e-mail services you might consider:

- ✔ **Yahoo! Mail:** `http://mail.yahoo.com`
- ✔ **Hotmail:** `http://mail.live.com`
- ✔ **MyWay Mail:** `http://mail.myway.com`
- ✔ **Gmail:** `http://gmail.google.com`

Just because you have a Web-based e-mail account doesn't mean that you need to abandon your ISP's e-mail account. Many people often juggle more than one e-mal account. For example, you can get a free account on Yahoo! Mail and either tell everyone to send your mail to that account when you're on the road or have your regular mail forwarded to that account. (Forwarding e-mail is covered later in this chapter.)

Some people even use their Web-based e-mail accounts as their main accounts and keep their main accounts secret or reserved for private e-mail. That way, the main account remains relatively spam-free. And, when the public, Web-based e-mail account becomes overwhelmed with spam, it can be discarded and a new, free, Web-based e-mail service used.

Access your e-mail from a friend's computer

I don't believe that Miss Manners covers this topic: What do you do when you're visiting friends or relatives and the urge to check your e-mail hits you?

If you have a laptop and your friends or relatives have their own network, it's easy to hook into their network and use your laptop that way (assuming that they're open to the idea; always ask and be prepared for a "no" answer).

They may offer to set up an account for you on their computer. That's nice, and it's a good thing to do for security reasons. But all you really need in order to pick up your e-mail is a computer with Internet access. Then you can use your ISP's Web-based e-mail system to peruse your mail or visit any mail waiting for you on a Web-based e-mail system (Hotmail or Yahoo!, for example).

- ✔ I don't recommend setting up your own e-mail account on a friend's or relative's computer. It's just too much of a security risk.

- ✔ The best option is to pray that your friends or relatives have a wireless connection and then use your laptop's wireless network adapter to hook into their network for full Internet access.

- ✔ Yes, I've taken a wireless router with me when I visit with relatives. By plugging the router into their broadband connection, I give myself wireless access throughout their home without having to trouble them with permission.

- ✔ If Internet access is disallowed, keep in mind that you still have the library as an option. Cybercafés and wireless hotspots also have Internet access that you can consider.

Forward your e-mail

E-mail servers have the option of forwarding all incoming e-mail if you know that you're going to be away for a while and want to pick up your e-mail at another address. This service is known as *e-mail forwarding,* and your ISP may offer it for free, or your company or business may have it available as a feature.

For example, if you know that you're going to be out for three weeks, you can have your e-mail forwarded to your Web-based e-mail account for that length of time. Any e-mail coming into your regular account is immediately redirected to the other account. That way, you don't miss a thing.

There is, sadly, a problem with forwarding your e-mail, which is why you may not find it available as an option. Occasionally, e-mail gets stuck in the space-time continuum, in what's scientifically referred to as an *endlessly forwarding loop.* Your mail gets forwarded to you, which then reforwards the mail back to you, which then repeats the process. Eventually the system becomes clogged with e-mail, and when the IT guys figure things out, they just delete your e-mail account to fix the situation. That's a bad thing.

So, if e-mail forwarding is an option, look into it. But be careful to ensure that your e-mail is being forwarded to a real account and isn't just lost in a loop. In, fact, test the system by forwarding all your e-mail a day or so before you're set to leave so that you can ensure that everything works.

✔ Refer to your ISP for more information on e-mail forwarding. Sometimes it's something you can set up for yourself, such as an option to choose on the ISP's e-mail Web site. Sometimes it's something that someone there may have to configure for you. Sometimes it's just not available.

✔ Don't forget to stop forwarding your e-mail when you return.

Disconnect after picking up e-mail

When you're using a dialup account, keep in mind that you don't need to be connected to the Internet while you read your e-mail. Especially given how much battery power the modem draws, I recommend having your e-mail program immediately hang up (or disconnect) after sending or receiving e-mail. Here's where to check those settings in Windows Mail:

1. **Choose Tools⇨Options.**

   The Options dialog box duly appears.

2. **Click the Connection tab in the Options dialog box.**

3. **Put a check mark by Hang Up after Sending and Receiving.**

4. **Click OK.**

You may also want to disable automatic checking, as covered in the next section.

✔ This setting isn't needed for broadband access.

✔ Similar settings are available for other e-mail programs. Search the program's Help index for the term **hang up**.

Disable automatic checking

On a laptop with a dialup connection, you probably don't want the battery being systematically drained every ten minutes when Windows Mail attempts to collect new messages. To fix that situation, you can direct the laptop not to automatically pick up your e-mail. Here's how it goes:

1. **Start Windows Mail.**

   These steps are specific to Windows Mail. Other e-mail programs doubtless have similar options.

2. **Choose Tools⇨Options.**

3. **In the Options dialog box, click the General tab (if needed).**

4. **Deselect the Check for New Messages Every [blank] Minutes check box.**

5. **(Optional) From the If My Computer Is Not Connected at This Time drop-down list, choose Do Not Connect.**

   Setting this option ensures that merely starting your e-mail program doesn't cause it to try to dial in to the Internet.

6. **Deselect the check box next to the option Send and Receive Messages at Startup.**

   This step is optional but recommended. The setting prevents Windows Mail from immediately contacting the Internet when you first start the program. That way, you can read pending messages and then connect with the Internet when you're ready.

7. **Click OK.**

To connect to the Internet and then send or receive messages, click the Send/Receive button, or use the keyboard shortcut Ctrl+M.

Making these settings only saves time and battery power when you use the dialup modem to retrieve your e-mail.

Send everything in one batch

As you peruse your e-mail, you read messages and reply to messages and then click the Send button to send those messages. On a broadband connection, that's fine. But when you're not connected to the Internet or you're using a dialup connection, that send-as-you-go option isn't practical. Instead, you should configure your e-mail program to send everything in one batch.

Here are the directions for setting up Windows Mail to send messages all at once:

1. **Choose Tools➪Options.**

2. **In the Options dialog box, click the Send tab.**

3. **Deselect the Send Messages Immediately check box.**

4. **Click OK.**

The messages now sit in the outbox and wait until you choose the Send option. In Windows Mail, the Send All command is found on the Send/Receive toolbar button's menu. You can also use the Ctrl+M keyboard shortcut.

Skip messages over a given size

I originally created this section with dialup modems in mind. After all, there's no point in wasting battery power and long-distance fees downloading some silly 3MB video that your in-laws have sent. But even over a broadband connection, a certain amount of time is wasted downloading anything big.

Some e-mail programs, such as Eudora, have an option that lets you skip e-mail of a given size. In Microsoft Mail, you must create a mail rule to specifically skip messages of a certain size. Here are the steps to take:

1. **Choose Tools⇨Message Rules⇨Mail.**

   The New Message Rule window appears, as shown in Figure 15-2.

2. **In Area 1, scroll through the list to find the option labeled Where the Message Size Is More Than Size; put a check mark in that box.**

3. **In Area 3, click the word *Size*.**

4. **Enter a size in kilobytes (K).**

   Short files seem to be okay, and I often expect files in the 70K-to-120K range, so I set the value at 200KB on my laptop. (On the desktop, I use the value 500KB.)

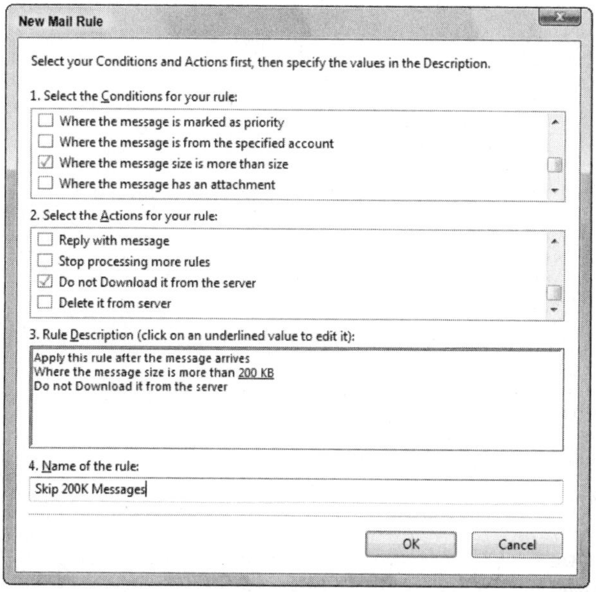

New Mail Rule

Select your Conditions and Actions first, then specify the values in the Description.

1. Select the Conditions for your rule:

- ☐ Where the message is marked as priority
- ☐ Where the message is from the specified account
- ☑ Where the message size is more than size
- ☐ Where the message has an attachment

2. Select the Actions for your rule:

- ☐ Reply with message
- ☐ Stop processing more rules
- ☑ Do not Download it from the server
- ☐ Delete it from server

3. Rule Description (click on an underlined value to edit it):

Apply this rule after the message arrives
Where the message size is more than 200 KB
Do not Download it from the server

4. Name of the rule:

Skip 200K Messages

OK   Cancel

Figure 15-2:
A message rule to skip large e-mail attachments.

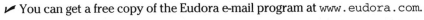

5. **Click OK.**

6. **In Area 2, choose the option labeled Do Not Download It from the Server.**

7. **In Area 4, give the rule a descriptive name.**

   On my laptop, the rule is named Skip 200K Messages (refer to Figure 15-2).

8. **Click OK to create the rule.**

9. **Click OK to close the other dialog box.**

The sad part about this approach is that you never know that any huge messages are pending for you. When you return to the desktop, or any e-mail system that lacks the "Skip 200KB messages" (or similar) rule, you discover and download the big messages. (Unlike Eudora, Outlook Express doesn't let you know that the big message is pending and offer you the option of downloading it.)

✔ You can get a free copy of the Eudora e-mail program at www.eudora.com.

✔ If you're one of those people who sends your friends large video files by e-mail, do what I do instead: Send a link. Just link to the YouTube Web page or file online. Ditto for large image files: Consider reducing the image size and using a compressed format, such as PNG or JPEG. Others will admire your thoughtfulness.

Chapter 16

The Desktop–Laptop Connection

In This Chapter

▶ Getting your laptop and desktop connected

▶ Exchanging files

▶ Using Sync Center

▶ Setting up a sync partnership

▶ Synchronizing files

▶ Accessing the desktop remotely

*Y*ou have a laptop PC. You have a desktop PC. Both computers run Windows. They have similar software programs. You are both computers' lord and master. Yet getting them to talk with each other is like having two surly children. It's not that they're unwilling to cooperate, or that your computers, like children, harbor an innate desire to make your life miserable. Nope, you just need to know the proper way to cajole them into harmonious cooperation.

If your only computer is your laptop, bless you: You'll probably never have to worry about any of the information presented in this chapter. Otherwise, as the user of two different PCs, one of your primary concerns is how to get information between your laptop and desktop computers. Beyond that, you probably want to know how to coordinate or synchronize your information when you leave or come back from the road.

Can We Talk?

Computers are all about input and output, called *I/O*. Information is input, processed or stored (or both), and some type of output is produced. That's basic computer science.

The whole I/O thing works well for a single computer. When you have more than one computer, however, the I/O thing becomes a wee bit more complex.

Ever since the first proto-nerds of the pre-digital age developed two different and utterly incompatible computers, exchanging information has been an issue. The question is, how do you get information from one computer into another? The solutions are various, some simple, some complex, some fast, some slow. This section covers the gamut.

Sneakernet

The traditional way of getting information from one computer to another is to place that information on some type of media that can be read by both computers. In the early days, the media was magnetic or paper tape. Then came floppy disks, optical discs, and now, media cards and drives. The information exchange works like this:

1. You save or copy information from one computer to removeable media.

2. You walk (in your sneakers) to the other computer.

3. You plug the media into the second computer.

4. You open the media (assuming that the second computer can read it in the first place).

In four steps, that's the process of *sneakernet,* or the physical, human-powered moving of data from one computer to another.

Sneakernet exists today, even when the laptop and desktop are sitting next to each other and footwear isn't an issue. To exchange information between your desktop and laptop, copy the information to a recordable optical disc or media card. Remove the card from one PC and plug it into another. Copy the files from the media card to the other PC's hard drive. It works, but it's not the easiest, fastest, or bestest way to exchange information.

Ugly octopus net

Before a networking standard appeared, computer users could connect their desktop and laptop computers by using both systems' serial or printer ports. To accomplish this feat, an ugly cable octopus was used, similar to the one shown in Figure 16-1.

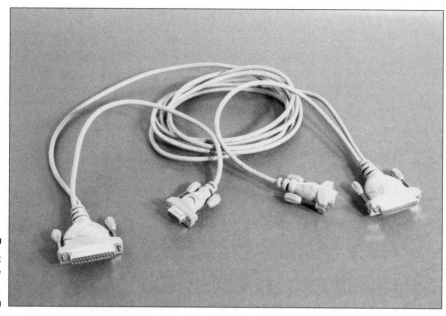

Figure 16-1:
The ugly
cable thing.

The ugly cable octopus connects the desktop system and laptop systems. Then special software is used to connect the computers and exchange information. Although this method was more automatic than sneakernet, the complex setup and software requirements meant that using such a thing was a major pain in the butt.

Ethernet

The simplest way to send files between laptop and desktop is to place them both on the same network. When they're configured and connected properly, you can share and access folders on both the desktop or laptop's storage system to easily exchange files.

After the network connection is made, copying files works just like copying files on a single computer. In fact, Windows Vista comes with something called the Sync Center, which makes the process easy. (Refer to the next section, "The Bliss of Synchronization.")

✔ Networking is the preferred way to connect two computers. Even if all you have is a desktop and a laptop, I highly recommend getting networking hardware to make connecting the two a snap.

✔ Refer to Chapter 11 for more information on networking your desktop and laptop, both with and without wires.

The Bliss of Synchronization

Aren't computers supposed to make life easier? Yeah, I thought so. I mean, I read the brochure. It said, "Make your life easier. Organize your recipes. Trade stocks online. Easily transfer information between your laptop and desktop computers." I don't believe that the computer marketing people would intentionally lie.

Your computer should make things easier for you. One of those tasks, repetitive and boring, is to synchronize files between your desktop and laptop. Thanks to the Sync Center, the operation is painless and easy.

✔ Earlier versions of Windows used the Briefcase for synchronizing files. Windows Vista doesn't come with the Briefcase.

✔ Only one of the computers needs to be running Windows Vista. You merely need to access the other computer (which can be a Mac or Linux computer) over the network.

✔ The ability to sync network files as described in this section isn't available with computers running Windows Vista Starter, Windows Vista Home Basic, and Windows Vista Home Premium.

✔ The Sync Center works on computers that are networked with each other, either wired or wirelessly. Refer to Chapter 11 for information on networking as well as information on sharing the Public folder between two Windows Vista computers.

✔ When you become frustrated with the Sync Center (because it's not the dream you expected it to be), consider reading the later section "Your PC from Afar" for another way to access your desktop PC's files.

✔ The Sync Center is really designed for mobile devices, such as MP3 players, personal information managers (PIMs), or other portable USB gizmos. It can, however, be used to help manage files between a desktop and laptop computer, which is what I concentrate on here.

Visiting the Sync Center

Synchronizing files between two computers is done in the everything-but-the-kitchen Sync Center. To visit the Sync Center, follow these simple steps:

1. **Pop up the Start menu.**

2. **Choose All Programs⇨Accessories⇨Sync Center.**

The Sync Center window opens, looking similar to the one shown in Figure 16-2. Links on the left side of the window help you configure and use the Sync Center. Details are covered in the sections that follow.

✔ When syncs have been set up in the Sync Center, you see a weensy Sync Center icon in the notification area, similar to what's shown in the margin. Double-clicking that icon also opens the Sync Center window.

✔ You can also open the Sync Center from the Control Panel Home by choosing Network and Internet and then choosing Sync Center. From the Control Panel Classic View, open the Sync Center icon.

✔ The Sync Center can be accessed from the Windows Mobility Center; press Win+X to quickly summon the Mobility Center window.

Figure 16-2:
The Sync
Center.

The Sync Center works by comparing files from two locations. For a laptop user, that means a folder on your laptop computer as well as a folder on the desktop PC. When you sync the folders, newer files from one folder are updated on the other folder.

For example, when you leave on a trip, you can sync your desktop and laptop so that important files are up-to-date on both computers. Ditto for when you return: Sync the computers so that your files are always current.

The following steps describe setting up a sync between a laptop and desktop computer. It is assumed that the folder being synced on the desktop is shared and available for access on the network. After doing so, follow these steps:

1. Open the Network window.

Specific directions can be found in Chapter 6.

2. **Browse to the computer that has the folder you want to sync to.**

3. **Open the computer's icon.**

   The Network window displays a list of folders being shared by that computer.

4. **Right-click the folder you want to sync with.**

5. **From the shortcut menu, choose Always Available Offline.**

   Windows dawdles, impressing you with a busy-looking dialog box while it does lord-knows-what. Just wait a few. (When Windows is done, the Cancel button becomes dimmed.)

6. **Click the Close button.**

7. **Close the network computer's window.**

You can confirm that the sync is ready by reviewing the sync partnership in the Sync Center window. This topic is covered in the next section.

✔ Out on the network, you see folders and files that you're syncing with flagged by a tiny Sync Center icon, as shown in the margin.

✔ The steps in this section merely set up the sync partnership. Before you flee down the road, you must first sync your files. That's covered in the section "Synchronizing files," later in this chapter.

✔ You can find general networking information in this book's Chapter 11. More information on networking and folder sharing can be found in my book *Find Gold in Windows Vista* (Wiley Publishing).

Reviewing your syncs

No, it's not called a *sync*. If you say "sync," people hear "sink," and that has too much potential for humor to be a computer topic. So, instead, say *sync partnership*. There.

The Sync Center window displays devices and folders that your laptop is partnered with when it first opens, as shown in Figure 16-2. But what you see, Offline Files, is merely an overview. To see the details, double-click the Offline Files folder. You see a list of all network folders your laptop is synced with, as shown in Figure 16-3, plus the time and date of the last sync and its status.

Sync errors are shown in the Offline Files window, as shown in Figure 16-3. Click an error link to review that folder's specific issues, or choose the View Sync Results link from the left side of the window to peruse all problems.

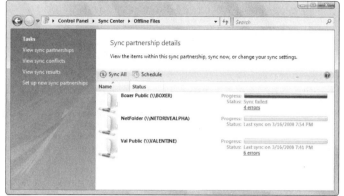

Figure 16-3:
Synchro-
nized
network
folders.

Not to spoil your fun, but most of the problems have to do with denied access to folders on the network computer. Only when you share a folder plus all its subfolders do you not get the armada of Accessed Denied errors.

Synchronizing files

To synchronize files, and coordinate files on your laptop with files on the net-work, follow these steps:

1. **Open the Sync Center window.**

2. **Choose the View Sync Partnerships task from the left side of the window (if necessary).**

3. **Click the Sync All button.**

   The Sync All button transmogrifies into the Stop All button. You can wait and watch (get some popcorn and a beverage) or go off and do some-thing else.

4. **Close the Sync Center window when you're done.**

You can review the results of the operation by choosing View Sync Results from the task list on the left. Any problems are most likely unavailable files and folders, or Access Denied errors.

Your laptop must be connected to the network and the shared folders acces-sible for a sync operation to be successful.

As a shortcut, when you want to sync only a specific folder, open the Offline Files folder in Step 3 (in the preceding set of steps). Then select only the folder you want to synchronize; click the Sync button on the toolbar.

Accessing synced files

You're gone. You're on the road. You're away. Now comes the time to access those files you synchronized with the desktop computer. Here's what you do:

1. **Open the Sync Center window.**

2. **Choose View Sync Partnerships from the left side of the window (if necessary).**

3. **Open the Offline Files folder.**

4. **Open the folder for the files you need to access.**

5. **Open a file.**

   The file opens on your computer, ready for you to use it.

If the file isn't available, the computers didn't completely sync their information. Refer to the preceding section.

   ✔ Unavailable files appear with a ghost-like, dimmed icon.

   ✔ Yes, you can copy the file from the synced folder to another folder of your hard drive. But it doesn't stay synced unless you copy it back when you're done.

Syncing a new file

If you're on the road and you create a new file you want to sync, you should follow these steps:

1. **Save the file as you normally would.**

   For example, save it in the Documents folder in your user account area.

2. **Open the folder in which you saved the file, such as the Documents folder.**

3. **Open the Sync Center.**

4. **Open the Offline Files folder.**

5. **Open the sync partnership folder in which to save the file.**

6. **Copy the file into the sync partnership folder.**

I use the mouse to drag the file's icon from one folder to the other, but you can also employ any of the zillions of ways to copy a file in Windows.

Only with the file in the sync partnership folder is it properly synchronized with your desktop computer.

Scheduling automatic synchronization

 The Sync Center can be set up to synchronize files between your laptop and desktop on a regular schedule. To make that happen, click the Schedule button on the Sync Center toolbar. Work through the Offline Files Sync Schedule Wizard to set up a time or an event schedule.

Ending a sync

If the need ever arises to stop syncing with a network resource, follow these steps:

1. **Open the Network window.**

2. **Browse to the network location where you have sync partnerships.**

3. **Right-click a sync partnership folder.**

    Remember that those folders sport the little green Sync Center flag on their icon.

4. **Choose Always Available Offline to remove the check mark.**

5. **Click the Close button to dismiss the Always Available Offline dialog box.**

   The partnership terminates regardless of whether you sit and gape at the box.

6. **Close the Sync Center window when you're done.**

There may be a chance that these steps don't work and the sync partnership still shows up. That's probably your old friend the Access Denied error. Ensure that the network resource has full permissions (Read, Write, Own) for your account, and then try again.

Your PC from Afar

A truly amazing feat that your laptop is capable of is accessing your desktop computer for serious remote-control action. It's amazing. From any location where the Internet is available, you can *phone home* and use your desktop PC just as though you were sitting in front of it and not having a *verre de vin rouge* in *Le Café Connexion à Distance*. If there were ever a reason to give a random nerd a hug, this would be it.

Although remote access is truly something, it's also a security risk. Do you really want every creep on the Internet using your desktop PC? It can happen! Therefore, I strongly advise that you try the following tricks only with a well-established firewall in place — specifically, one designed to let in only your laptop and not any other computer system. (This may take the abilities of a computer security expert to set up, but that's good. This isn't something to try casually.)

Setting up for Remote Desktop

The tool to use for accessing one computer from another, on either the local network or the Internet, is Remote Desktop. It's available on every version of Windows Vista, but you cannot use it to connect to a PC running Windows Vista Starter, Windows Vista Home Basic (N), or Windows Vista Home Premium.

Follow these steps to configure your desktop computer for remote access from a laptop; start by performing these steps on the desktop PC:

1. **Open the Control Panel window.**

   System

2. **From the Control Panel Home, choose System and Maintenance, and then System; from Control Panel Classic View, open the System icon.**

   You can also press the comical Win+Break key combination to summon the System window.

   To make this connection easier, take note of the computer's name. You need to use that name when connecting to the computer on the network.

3. **In the list of tasks on the left side of the window, choose Remote Settings.**

4. **Click the Continue button or enter the administrator's password to dismiss the User Account Control dialog box warning.**

   The System Properties dialog box appears, with the Remote tab up front.

5. **Choose the item labeled Allow Connections Only from Computers Running Remote Desktop with Network Level Authentication (More Secure).**

6. **If a warning dialog box appears, click OK to dismiss the warning.**

7. **Click OK to close the System Properties dialog box.**

8. **Close the Control Panel window.**

The computer is now open to sharing its desktop remotely with another computer on the network.

If you're using Windows Firewall, you have to set up an exception for the Remote Desktop connection. Follow these additional steps to ensure that Windows Firewall is okay with the Remote Desktop connection:

1. **Open the Control Panel window.**

Windows Firewall

2. **From the Control Panel Home, choose Security and then choose Windows Firewall; from Control Panel Classic View, open the Windows Firewall icon.**

3. **In the Windows Firewall window, click the link that says Change Settings.**

4. **Click the Continue button or type the administrator's password if you're prompted by a User Account Control warning.**

5. **In the Windows Firewall Settings dialog box, click the Exceptions tab.**

6. **Scroll through the list to find the Remote Desktop item, and place a check mark by it.**

   If a check mark already appears by the Remote Desktop item, you're ready to go.

7. **Click the OK button, and then close the Windows Firewall and Control Panel windows.**

Accessing Remote Desktop on the network

After you coerce a computer into the idea of a remote connection, the next step is to use a second computer, such as your laptop, to access the first computer and use it remotely on the network. Yes, this sounds like mind control, but I'm avoiding the temptation to make references to any religion or the book _The Puppet Masters._

To access the other computer's desktop, heed these directions:

1. **From the Start menu, choose All Programs⇨Accessories⇨ Remote Desktop Connection.**

   The Remote Desktop Connection dialog box appears. (It's really boring, so I won't put an illustration in here.)

2. **If the computer you want to connect to is available from the drop-down list, choose it. Otherwise, type the computer's name that you remembered to write down from the preceding section.**

   The computer must already have been configured to accept a remote desktop connection; refer to the previous section.

3. Click the Connect button.

You must log in to the remote computer by using your user account name and password on that computer.

4. In the security window, type your User Name and Password, just as though you were logging in to the other computer.

5. Click OK.

Wait a few seconds.

Eventually, the laptop's screen changes. What you see displayed is the other computer's desktop. In Figure 16-4, my laptop's screen is displaying the desktop PC's desktop.

Your clue that you're using another computer comes from the banner at the top of the screen. In Figure 16-4, it says VALENTINE, which is the network name of my desktop computer.

6. Use the remote computer

When the remote desktop is set up and connected, what you see on your computer's screen is the display of another computer on the network. Moving the mouse on your computer moves the mouse on the other computer, and ditto for the keyboard. It's just as though you're sitting at that computer, when you're actually working things from a remote location.

7. To break the connection, click the X button in the strip at the top of the screen.

Refer to Figure 16-4 to see where to click.

8. Click OK to confirm the disconnection.

The connection is broken, and you're using only your own PC again.

Note that any programs you started or any activities you run on the remote desktop continue to run after you disconnect. You must specifically stop them before you disconnect, if that's what you want.

✔ After the connection is made, the remote computer might log off any user and display the Welcome screen.

✔ The remote desktop can be displayed in full screen mode or in a window. In full screen mode, a strip appears across the top of the screen and acts as a sort of window control. In window mode, the remote desktop appears in a window on your computer's screen.

✔ Sadly, you cannot copy files and folders between the remote system and your own computer by dragging items into and out of the remote desktop's window. The Remote Desktop Connection is more of a control-and-access feature than a file exchange utility.

✔ Remote Desktop Connection works best on the network. When you need to access your desktop PC from the Internet, I recommend using the program Real Virtual Network Computing, or VNC. This product was once free, but now costs money, so I don't write about it in any detail. For more information, visit

```
www.realvnc.com
```

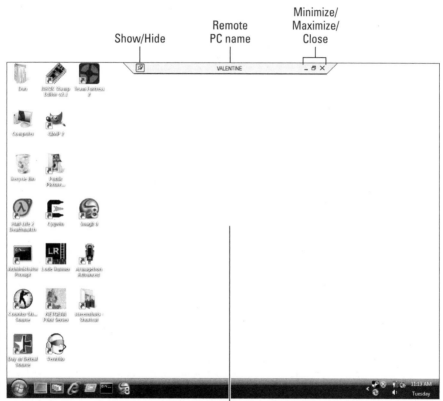

Show/Hide   Remote PC name   Minimize/ Maximize/ Close

Figure 16-4: Remote Desktop in action.

Remote computer's desktop

Part IV
Hit the Road, Jack

In this part . . .

A laptop computer is a mobile device, no doubt about it. It's not a question of where you can take your laptop. The more curious question is "Where are the unusual places that you've taken your laptop?" Mere mortals can attest to using a laptop on a plane, in a library, at the Café à un Autre Endroit, or just shuttling between home and the office. But what about taking your laptop deep into the woods of the Pacific Northwest? How about the south of France? And how many people take their laptops to bed with them? I know that I'd never admit to that.

If you haven't yet hit the road with your laptop, it's high time that you do! This part of the book covers lots of on-the-road topics in several nifty little chapters. Read them. Enjoy them. Then take your laptop on the road!

Chapter 17

On the Road Again . . .

In This Chapter

▶ Selecting a laptop case

▶ Preparing your laptop for the airport

▶ Dealing with airport security

▶ Using your laptop on an airplane

▶ Disabling the wireless network adapter

▶ Finding power on an airplane

▶ Setting up the laptop in a café or bistro

▶ Using your laptop in a hotel room

▶ Keeping the laptop cool

My grandmother amazed me. She would be scheduled to leave for a trip in two weeks, yet she was already packed. My father (her son), on the other hand, traveled quite a bit. For him, packing was done in the morning, mere minutes before leaving. Both approaches worked. With more experience in traveling, however, my dad was able to make packing decisions quickly and with less worry over making a mistake.

If you've never taken a laptop on the road, whether to your local Starbucks or overseas, you might spend some time wondering what to take with you. But, why bother? Rather than go through the agony, just read this chapter, where I offer suggestions on what to take with you and how to prepare for the trip before you go. The idea is to make your pending road-warrior laptopping experience fully enjoyable, without fussing for two weeks over what to pack and what not to pack.

Nancy Drew and the Case of the Laptop Case

Your laptop needs a laptop case, not because carrying a laptop computer by itself makes you look like a nerd, but rather because the laptop is only one part of a larger collection of stuff you take on the road. Furthermore, the laptop needs a comfy storage place to protect it from damage and disguise it from thieves. Getting the proper laptop case is just a darn good idea.

- ✔ Your laptop needs a case.
- ✔ Suggestions about the stuff you should pack into your case are covered in Chapter 24.

Avoid the manufacturer's case

Many laptop manufacturers provide cases for their laptop systems as bonus or extra items — perks for being such wise customers as to purchase that particular brand of laptop. Generally speaking, getting such a case is probably the worst choice you can make.

Manufacturers generally give you a case in either of two extremes.

First, they provide you with something that they call a "case," but it's really little more than a zippered pouch. That's cheap and shameful.

Second, manufacturers provide you with too much case. They go overboard on size and give you something hulking and unwieldy. The case shown in Figure 17-1 is from a manufacturer. It's made with genuine, luxurious leather. It's sassy! But it's too boxy. The case is mostly padding to keep the laptop from sliding around. Who wants to tote around padding in a laptop case?

Figure 17-1:
A computer manufac-turer's bulky yet luxuri-ous leather case.

The bottom line with manufacturer laptop cases is that they just don't give you any choice. Unless you've researched laptop cases and the manufacturer happens to offer one of the brand-name cases that agrees with you, just set aside any notion of getting a brand-name computer manufacturer's case.

Things to look for in a case

I always look in a new case to see whether there's any money in it. That's one thing to look for in a case. But, seriously, the title of this section deals with features to look for when you're buying a laptop case. Here's a list:

- ✔ Does your laptop fit? This question doesn't imply that the case needs a compartment designed to fit your specific laptop. Instead, you want to ensure that your laptop fits comfortably inside the case and that the case can zip up or close easily with the laptop inside.

- ✔ Actually, you _don't_ want a case with a compartment designed to fit your specific laptop. You may not be using the same laptop years from now, but it's nice to keep using the same case.

- ✔ Get a soft case, not something hard, like the traditional briefcase. I think that a soft case holds the laptop more securely, whereas a laptop tends to jostle around inside a hard case.

- ✔ Does the case have plenty of pouches? You need pouches for storing accessories, office supplies, discs, manuals, Altoids, year-old receipts, and other things you plan on carrying around with you. The pouches can also be used for smuggling.

- ✔ I recommend a case that opens to display two large and separate areas. You can slide your laptop into one and put paper, notepads, or computer accessories into the other area.

- ✔ Zippers are preferred over snaps, buckles, or latches. Be sure, however, that the bag isn't so snug that the zipper can damage the laptop. In that case, look for those Velcro or "touchless" zippers.

- ✔ Having an easy-access pouch on the case's outside helps with storing important documents and other information that you need to grab quickly.

- ✔ A carrying handle is a must, but a shoulder strap is better.

- ✔ A backpack can also make a great laptop carrying case. The bonus here is that shouldering the backpack keeps both your arms and hands free. That way, you can hold your boarding pass in one hand and coffee in the other and still carry the laptop with you.

- ✔ If you know that you have to carry lots of stuff (extra material for your job or perhaps something heavy, like a printer or video projector), consider getting a laptop case with wheels and a retractable handle.

✔ As far as size goes, keep in mind that the bag needs to fit beneath the seat in front of you on an airplane. Don't get something too big.

✔ Avoid a laptop case that's too tiny! Some trendy cases hug the laptop like a thong on a stripper. That's ineffective! (Well, for the laptop, not for the stripper.) You need a laptop case with some extra room in it. Think sweat pants, not hot pants.

✔ The idea behind your laptop bag is to safely carry and protect the laptop while you're traveling; plus, it needs to carry all your laptop toys and other, related goodies. Go nuts on the extra features if you must. But, honestly, if you can find a solidly made case, bag, or backpack that does what you need, you're set.

Recommended brands

I've used an Eddie Bauer soft briefcase as my laptop bag for 15 years. You can see a picture of this handy nylon bag in Figure 17-2. It has plenty of pouches, zippers, and storage compartments, plus room left over for me to toss in magazines and books or even a box of chocolates to take home. That bag has been all over the world with me.

Figure 17-2:
My trusty
old Eddie
Bauer soft
case.

For longer trips, I instead use a backpack, primarily because it's roomier but also because thieves don't suspect backpacks to contain laptops as much as they do briefcases. If you choose a backpack, ensure that it's well put together, with reinforced seams on heavy-duty material.

The following is a list of brand-name bags that I can recommend or that have been recommended to me. If you have an outlet mall or retail location near you, pay the place a visit and peruse the stock. Don't forget to take your laptop with you for a test fitting!

- ✔ www.ebags.com
- ✔ www.eddiebauer.com
- ✔ www.targus.com
- ✔ www.thenorthface.com
- ✔ http://oakley.com

- ✔ If you can find one, get a CIA bag. They're built, designed with a locking zipper so that spooks can carry secret stuff around the world. But no one in the CIA uses them because they're so dang obvious. If you can pick up one on eBay or from a retired Federal worker, do so at once!

I'm Leaving on a Jet Plane Checklist

You may not be jetting across the country. Perhaps you're just walking over to the neighborhood coffee bistro. Either way, consider this section your laptop checklist.

Things to do before you go

Here are some things you should consider doing before you toddle off with your laptop:

- ✔ Charge the battery! In fact, this is probably something you want to do well before you leave. For example, I typically charge my laptop batteries the night before I leave on a trip.
- ✔ If you're lucky enough to have a spare battery, charge it as well.
- ✔ Synchronize your laptop with your desktop. Refer to Chapter 16 for more information.
- ✔ Back up your important files. See Chapter 18.

✔ Remove any discs from the optical drive. This action avoids having the drive spin into action when you start up on battery power. It also helps to put that disc with your other discs so that you don't forget about it or neglect it.

✔ Go online and save a few Web pages to your hard drive for offline reading while you're away. (Refer to Chapter 15.)

Things to pack in your laptop bag

A good laptop case is useful for holding more than just the laptop. Otherwise, it would be called a laptop *cozy* and not a case. When you're at a loss about what to put into your laptop case, consider this list for inspiration:

✔ Two words: office supplies. Pens. Paper. Sticky notes. Paper clips. Rubber bands. Highlighter. And so on.

✔ Pack the power cord and AC adapter!

✔ Bring any extra batteries you should have.

✔ Bring along your cell phone, although many people prefer to keep their phones clipped to their belts or stuffed in purses.

✔ When you're traveling overseas, remember to bring along a power conversion kit or overseas power adapter.

✔ Bring a phone cord if you plan on using the laptop's modem.

✔ Bring a 6-foot Ethernet cable — even if you don't plan on using a network.

✔ Bring headphones if you plan on listening to music or watching a DVD. It's more polite than sharing the noise with those sitting next to you.

✔ If you're making a presentation, don't forget the presentation! If you need your own video projector, pack it too!

✔ Pack any necessary peripherals: mouse, keyboard, PC cards, and external storage, for example.

✔ Ensure that you have some screen wipes.

✔ Bring a deck of cards. (You need something to play with after the battery drains.)

✔ If you're taking along a digital camera, don't forget the camera's computer cable or a memory card reader. It's nice to be able to save those digital images directly to the laptop when you're away.

Also take a look at Chapter 24 for more goodies you may want to take with you.

Looming Questions at the Airport

Taking a laptop onboard a commercial airliner today is about as normal as bringing onboard a paperback book and a sack lunch. That's good news. It means that bringing your laptop with you on a commercial airline flight isn't unusual and that the airlines are willing to accommodate your needs and not consider you as some oddball exception.

Is your laptop case one carry-on bag or half a carry-on bag?

Sadly, your laptop's case is often your only carry-on luggage. Some airlines let you carry the laptop case plus the typical overnight bag — the same kind of bag many folks try to jam into the overhead bins. Other airlines are less forgiving.

 Do not check your laptop as luggage! You don't want to subject the laptop to the kind of torture that most checked bags suffer. You don't want your laptop to be in the subzero cargo hold, and you don't want to risk your laptop being stolen. Do not check your laptop!

When the plane is full and you've tried to sneak on too much carry-on luggage, check the luggage, not the laptop.

If you absolutely must check the laptop case, keep the laptop with you; just check the case.

Laptop inspection

Thanks to the takeover of airport inspections by the Transportation Security Administration, the security-screening procedures for laptop computers are standard all over the United States. Here's what you need to do:

1. **Before you get into the inspection line, remove your laptop from its carrying case.**

   Yes, you're burdened with *stuff* for a few moments. You have to carry your boarding pass, picture ID, laptop case, coat, and carry-on bag — plus any small children, coffee cups, croissants, and whatnot. But it's only for a few moments.

2. **When you get to the X-ray machine, place your laptop in its own container and put the container on the conveyer belt.**

3. **Mind your laptop through the X-ray machine.**

4. **Pick up your laptop on the other end of the X-ray machine.**

After the ordeal, you can put everything away, replacing the laptop in its case and storing all the other stuff that was disassembled or removed during the screening process. Then you're on your way to the gate.

✔ Watch your laptop! The X-ray machine is a popular spot for thieves! Refer to Chapter 18.

✔ The X-ray machine doesn't harm the laptop.

✔ You may be asked to turn the laptop on. That's a good reason to have the batteries fully charged. If they're not, be sure to pack the power cord; most X-ray stations have a wall socket you can use.

All aboard!

When you get into the plane, find your seat. Try to store the laptop under the seat in front of you. It's okay to put it in the overhead storage, but I recommend the underseat storage, which is easier to get to and avoids the peril of having latecomers jamming their steamer trunks and body bags into the overhead bins and crushing your laptop.

Keep the laptop in its carrying case! Wait until you hear the announcement that it's okay to turn on your electronic devices before you whip out your laptop.

✔ Obviously, it helps to avoid the bulkhead seats, which lack underseat storage.

✔ I prefer window seats for computing aloft. That way, I can control the window blind, to shield my laptop's screen from the sun. Plus, it's easier to angle the laptop toward me and away from prying eyes in other seats.

✔ When the airline offers an extended legroom class, such as United's Economy Plus, take it! More room for legs means more room on the tray table for your laptop.

✔ 3M makes a special laptop display cover, the 3M Laptop Privacy Filter. It prevents peering eyes from seeing what's on your laptop screen, which is a problem on airplanes. The 3M Laptop Privacy Filter can be found at office-supply and computer stores all over the place.

Airplane mode

Before the airplane takes off, and just before it lands, you'll doubtless be reminded by the crew to turn off all electronic devices. That includes laptop computers. Further, you're asked to disable any wireless transmission emitting from your electronic gizmos should you turn them on again.

For your wireless laptop, computing aloft means turning off the wireless network adapter. The simple way to do that is with a hardware switch; many laptops come with a wireless On–Off switch. If your laptop has such a switch, be sure to turn off the wireless network adapter when you use your laptop in the air.

When a wireless network adapter switch isn't evident, follow these steps to disable the thing:

1. **Open the Network and Sharing Center window.**

   Refer to Chapter 11 for more information on opening this window.

2. **From the list of tasks on the left side of the window, choose Manage Network Connections.**

   The Network Connections window appears, as shown in Figure 17-3.

Figure 17-3: Disable the wireless network adapter here.

3. **Right-click your Wireless Networking Connection icon.**

4. **Choose Disable from the shortcut menu.**

5. **Click the Continue button or type the administrator's password if you see a User Account Control dialog box.**

6. **Close any open windows.**

You can now use your laptop in the air without fear of its wireless network adapter interfering with the cockpit's instrumentation and the plane crashing into the ground in a smoldering heap.

> ✔ Don't forget to reenable the wireless network adapter when you need it again. Repeat the preceding steps, but in Step 4 choose the Enable command.
>
> ✔ If your laptop sports *airplane mode,* use that mode of operation when you compute at 30,000 feet.
>
> ✔ Some laptops feature a keyboard combination to turn the wireless networking off or on. On my Lenovo laptop, the key combination is Fn+F5.

Up, up in the air

After the announcement allowing you to use your electronic devices in the plane is made, and ensuring that the laptop's wireless network adapter doesn't pose any peril to your fellow passengers, you can whip out your laptop and . . . do whatever with it.

Of course, the real conundrum is trying to find a place for the thing. Some seats are so close together that it's nearly impossible to open the laptop while it's sitting on your tray table. And, when the jerk in front of you lowers his seat, computer time is over! Well, unless you have a Tablet PC, in which case you flip over the display and keep computing.

When you can get the laptop open and running, the real choice becomes this: Do you get work done or play games, or perhaps watch a DVD movie? Hmmm.

How long you have to use the laptop depends primarily on the battery life, but also on the flight duration. When the announcement comes to shut down electronic devices, shut down Windows and turn off (or hibernate) your laptop.

Air power

The airlines have heard your cries for help, or at least those cries for in-flight power. Many of them now offer AC power for use with your laptop on many flights. Three power plans are might be available:

AC power: This is the power you're used to, provided with a standard U.S. or European power outlet. Sometimes it's a two-prong outlet, and sometimes there's a grounding plug.

DC "cigarette lighter" power: This kind of power is the same as the kind offered in your car, with what is still curiously called the cigarette lighter. You need a cigarette lighter power adapter to use this type of power with your laptop.

EmPower DC power: The most common type of laptop electricity available on airlines is *EmPower*. You need a special EmPower adapter to use this system, or you can use a cigarette power adapter / EmPower adapter — an adapter adapter.

Note that the power adapters aren't universal. You need to ask the airlines whether your flight has a power adapter you can use, and, furthermore, to ensure that your seat is near a power adapter. An extra fee may also be involved, although most of these adapters are in the business or first-class section, so my guess is that you already paid the extra fee when you overpaid for your ticket.

Remember that your laptop comes with batteries. Use them whenever power isn't available. Just because the airplane lacks something to plug into for power doesn't spell doom for your laptop computing abilities aloft.

- ✔ Cigarette and EmPower adapters are available wherever laptop goodies are sold. Also check the iGo Web site: www.igo.com.

- ✔ AC means *a*lternating *c*urrent. It's the same type of power that comes out of the wall in your home or office.

- ✔ DC means *d*irect *c*urrent, which is the type of power you get from a battery.

- ✔ Shhhh! Apparently, the 747 aircraft has a standard U.S. wall socket located near one of the exit doors. It's used to plug in the vacuum for cleaning the plane, but you can probably sneak your laptop into that socket during a flight. Don't tell anyone I told you.

Café Computing

It used to be that you'd go into a coffeehouse, order a cappuccino, sit around with artsy folks dressed in black, and discuss Marxism. Today, you go to the coffeehouse, order your double-tall decaf machiatto, sit around with frustrated people dressed in "Friday casual," and discuss how to connect to the café's WiFi. The gal sitting next to you may still be a Marxist. But so what? If she knows the SSID and WEP, you can have a conversation.

This section mulls over a few of my observations while café computing:

- ✔ It doesn't have to be a café. In fact, a park in a major U.S. city soon became a hub of wireless activity with all sorts of people using their laptop computers. The reason? The new business next to the park set up a wireless network *without security*. So, laptop users were "borrowing" the free Internet access.

- ✔ You see one other difference between the cafés of yesterday and today: Whereas a Marxist could sit in a café all day, laptop users eventually get up and leave when the battery runs dry.

Where to sit?

Before visiting the counter to order your beverage and hard-as-fiberboard cookie, scout out the entire café for a good place to sit.

You want a table, unless you think that it's fun to balance a laptop on your knees while you sit on a sofa or an old sack of Columbian coffee beans.

Grab a table that's either away from the windows or facing the windows. You want to avoid having that bright light from the windows reflecting on your laptop screen and washing everything out. (You can tilt the screen to avoid the glare when there's nowhere else to sit.)

Another suggestion: Be mindful of high windows and skylights. As a sunny day grows long, the sun sweeps a slow swath of bright light across some tables. You don't want to be sitting at a table that's in the path of that moving shaft of light. (The voice of experience is speaking here.)

When you really want to get work done, find a spot away from the door and away from the sales counter. Do the opposite if you prefer to be social.

Be a socket sleuth

Another important factor in determining where to sit in a café is the presence of wall sockets. Without trying to look like you're searching for bombs, duck down and look under some tables or up against walls for a helpful AC power source.

When you find a power source, great! Grab that table.

If you want to be honest about things, inquire at the counter whether it's okay to plug in. Otherwise, just sneak a cord over the socket as nonchalantly as possible.

Note that not all the power sockets are on. My favorite coffeehouse in my hometown has a row of very obvious wall sockets next to some nice tables. Those wall sockets, sadly, are usually turned off. You can tell when you plug in: Your laptop doesn't alert you to the AC power presence and continues sucking down battery juice.

When you do manage to plug in, try to arrange the power cord so that no one trips over it. If someone does trip over your cord, expect expulsion.

Other tips 'n' stuff

It's always good to buy what they're selling when you're computing in a coffeehouse, diner, or café. Get a cup of coffee. Have a biscotti. Get a snack. The management at some places may enjoy having you there because it adds to the atmosphere, but these places are also in the business of making money. It has already been established in court that they can throw you out for using their wireless networking if you don't buy something, so buy something!

In my book *PCs For Dummies* (Wiley Publishing, Inc.), the rule is simple: No beverages near your computer! That goes double for the laptop, where the keyboard and computer are in the same box. But who am I to deny you a nice, delicious, warm cup of joe? If you want to drink and compute, get your beverage in a heavy, hard-to-topple, ceramic mug. Also grab yourself a nice thick wad of napkins, Just In Case.

Never leave your laptop unattended! If you have to go potty, take the laptop with you. *Never* leave your laptop all alone at the table. It will be stolen. (Also see Chapter 18.)

Don't forget to pack a mouse in your laptop bag! When I work on the road, especially in a spot where I'm setting up shop for a few hours, the external mouse is a blessing.

Sometimes you may be asked to leave or relocate, especially when you're taking up an entire booth all by yourself. Be knowledgeable about this situation in advance. If you see the place filling up, try to move to a smaller table or just pack up and leave.

Laptopping in Your Hotel Room

These days the hotel industry honestly expects you to have a laptop with you. The phone jack for the dialup modem is obvious. The directions for the wireless Internet are on the same table where you will, predictably, set your laptop. Now, there isn't yet a Nerd section on the room service menu, but I expect that change coming soon. Until then, peruse these hotel room laptop tips:

- If you're using a dialup modem, be sure to create a location and a set of dialing rules for the hotel. Especially if you plan on returning, creating the location and rule set now saves you time in future visits. See Chapter 13.

- Many hotels have broadband, or high-speed, Internet access. If it's not free, you're staying at a discount hotel or motel. In that case, you probably have to pay for broadband access, usually in 24-hour increments. After connecting to the network, open your Web browser and follow the instructions on the screen to set things up.

- I recommend staggering the 24-hour periods that cheap hotels grant for Internet access. Start your 24-hour session at 6 p.m. That way, you can use the connection that evening, and then the following morning, and all through the next day's afternoon.

- If you're planning on staying a week or more, see about negotiating a lower Internet connection rate. Also check to see whether any of your credit cards or the auto club offers free Internet access at that hotel.

- Some hotels provide an Ethernet cable; look for it either in the desk drawer or (oddly) hanging in the closet.

- Beware of digital phone lines! Do not plug your modem into anything other than a hole properly labeled Modem.

- Use the inexpensive printer: Send a fax to the hotel's fax machine. Refer to Chapter 13.

- It's a security risk to leave your laptop set up in the hotel room. It's not that the housekeeping staff will steal it; they probably won't. It's more likely that an information thief will get hold of your laptop to cull out passwords and credit card numbers. See Chapter 18 about security issues while in a hotel.

- Another security risk is the hotel's wireless network. Be very careful when you're sending sensitive data — passwords, account numbers, credit card information, and so on — over the wireless (or even wired) network. Who knows how secure that network is or whether hackers are lying in wait nearby?

✔ Occasionally, I find the rare hotel room that lacks enough power sockets by the desk. Note that if you unplug a lamp or TV in some hotels, it activates the security system. So, if the hotel dick comes knocking at the door, be prepared to tell him that he can keep the lamp — you just want to use the wall socket. (And, consider a more trustworthy hotel for your next trip.)

✔ Nerd food: Pizza. Hot Pockets. M&Ms. Doritos. Pringles. Tacos. Skittles. Beef jerky. Beer. Red Bull. Diet Coke. Cigarettes. Popcorn (butter and salt). Chinese anything. Cookies. Cool Whip. Potato chips and dip, coffee.

Mind the Laptop's Temperature

One reason that your laptop doesn't have the latest, fastest microprocessor is heat. Even in a desktop PC, cutting-edge technology generates lots of heat. Managing that heat in a desktop is a huge chore, so you can imagine the things your laptop has to do to keep cool.

So many electronics are packed into the laptop's case that, when coupled with the battery, which heats as it discharges, there be a whole lot of heatin' goin' on. The laptop comes with a wee li'l cooling fan, one that may even have two speeds for when the temperature gets too hot. But that may not be enough! It's important not to let your laptop get too hot.

✔ Avoid putting your laptop anywhere that it will be in direct sunlight.

✔ Do not store the laptop in your car's trunk.

✔ Don't let the laptop run in a closet or any closed environment where air cannot circulate.

✔ Do not block the little vents on the laptop that help it inhale cool air and expel hot air.

✔ When the laptop continually runs too hot, especially when the battery compartment becomes too hot to touch, phone your laptop dealer for service.

✔ As a suggestion, consider buying your laptop a cooling pad. Chapter 23 covers this and other gizmos.

Chapter 18

Laptop Security

In This Chapter

▶ Preventing a theft ahead of time

▶ Marking your laptop

▶ Watching for crooks

▶ Attaching a security cable

▶ Using passwords

▶ Making a lost laptop phone home

▶ Using a thumbprint reader

▶ Backing up your stuff

▶ Restoring from a backup

Laptops are hot! I don't mean that they're hot as in they're the best new technology or they're selling extremely well or they physically generate enough heat to toast bread. No, I mean that laptops are one of the favorite things that the bad guys like to steal — and not only for their resale value; often, the data stored inside a laptop is worth more to the crook than the laptop itself.

This chapter is about laptop security. It covers not only the things you can do to help prevent your laptop from becoming yet another statistic but also those things you can do to protect your sensitive data.

Laptops Are Easy to Steal

Unless you stole this book, you probably don't have the mind of a thief. This is good news for humanity. In fact, most people aren't thieves and tend to be fairly trusting. Sadly, it's our trusting nature that the bad guys take advantage of.

First, the good news: Most laptops are forgotten and not stolen. As silly as that sounds, people leave their expensive laptops sitting around unattended more often than someone sneaks off with them. But don't let that trivial tidbit lull you into a false sense of security. Many laptops are stolen right out from under the eyes of their owners.

Think of the laptop as a sack of cash sitting around. To a crook, that's exactly what it is. Treat the laptop as a bag full o' money, and chances are that you'll never forget it or have it stolen.

The best way to protect your laptop is to label it. Specific instructions are offered later in this chapter. Keep in mind this statistic: 97 percent of unmarked computers are never recovered. Mark your laptop! (See the next section.)

Other interesting and potentially troublesome statistics:

- ✔ The chance of your laptop being stolen is 1 in 10.
- ✔ Most laptop theft occurs in the office. That includes both coworkers and Well-Dressed Intruders, or thieves in business suits.
- ✔ Laptop theft on college campuses (from dorm rooms) is up 37 percent.
- ✔ A thief who steals a $2,000 laptop typically gets about $50 for it on the street.
- ✔ According to law enforcement, 90 percent of laptop thefts are easily avoidable by using common sense.

What to Do before Your Laptop Is Stolen

Any law enforcement official will tell you that a few extra steps of caution can avoid a disastrous theft. Like any shopper, a thief enjoys convenience; if your laptop is more difficult to pinch than the next guy's, it's the next guy who loses.

Mark your laptop

It helps with the recovery of a stolen laptop if you marked your laptop by either engraving it or affixing a tamper-resistant asset tag. After all, the best proof that something is yours is your name on the item in question.

- ✔ You can use an engraving tool to literally carve your name and contact information on your laptop.

✔ I know some folks who are clever and merely write their names inside their laptops, either on the back of some removable door, inside the battery compartment, or in other places a thief wouldn't check. Use a Sharpie or other indelible marker.

✔ Asset tags are available from most print shops. The tags peel and stick like any stickers do, but cannot be easily removed or damaged. For an investment of about $100, you can get a few hundred custom tags, for not only your computers but also other valuable items (cameras, bicycles, and TVs, for example).

✔ The STOP program offers bar-code asset tags that leave a special tattoo if they're removed. The program also offers a recovery system that automatically returns stolen (or lost) property directly to your door. STOP stands for Security Tracking of *Office* Property, although home users and (especially) college students can take advantage of the service. Visit www.stoptheft.com for more information.

Avoid using an obvious laptop carrying case

That carrying case with the emblazoned Dell logo, or one that stylishly says *LAPTOP* diagonally, isn't just a proud buyer-appreciation and marketing gimmick. That label provides a sure clue to the casual thief that something valuable lurks inside the bag. This is why I recommend, in Chapter 17, against getting a manufacturer's laptop case.

✔ A nondescript, soft laptop case works best.

✔ Backpacks are also good places to store laptops.

Register the laptop and its software

Be sure to register your laptop; send in the registration card or register online. Do the same for any software you're using. If the laptop is then stolen, alert the manufacturer and software vendors. Hopefully, if someone using your stolen laptop ever tries to get the system fixed or upgraded, the company cares enough to help you locate the purloined laptop.

Be sure to keep with you a copy of the laptop's serial number and other vital statistics — specifically, in a place other than in the laptop's carrying case. That way, you know which number to report to the police as well as to the manufacturer.

Be mindful of your environment

They say that gambling casinos are a purse-snatcher's paradise. That's because most women are too wrapped up in gambling to notice that their purses are being pilfered. The purse can be on the floor, at their feet, or even in their laps. Thieves know the power of distraction.

When you're out and about with your laptop, you must always be mindful of where it is and who could have access to it. Watch your laptop!

For example, when you're dining out, put the laptop in its case beneath the table. If you need to leave the table, either take the laptop with you or ask your friends to keep an eye on it for you.

Take your laptop with you when you go to make a phone call.

Keep your laptop with you when you go to the restroom.

Secure your laptop in your hotel room's safe. If the hotel lacks a room safe, leave it in the hotel's main safe at the front desk.

Be especially mindful of distractions! A commotion in front of you means that the thief about to take your laptop is behind you. A commotion behind you means that the thief is in front of you. Thieves work in pairs or groups that way, using the commotion to distract you while your stuff is being stolen.

Here's one place to watch out for a group of thieves pulling the distraction ploy: At the airport screening station! Just one raised voice or "the woman in the red dress" can divert your attention long enough for your laptop to be gone. Also be aware of distractions on crowded escalators, where the movement of the crowd can knock you down and someone can easily grab the laptop bag and take off.

Attach the old ball-and-chain

In Chapter 5, this book takes you on a tour around your laptop's externals. One thing I point out over there is the place for the old ball and chain: a hole or slot into which you can connect a security cable. That hole has an official name: the *universal security slot,* or *USS.*

The USS is designed to be part of the laptop's case. Any cable or security device threaded through the USS cannot be removed from the laptop; the cable itself must be cut (or unlocked) to free the laptop.

Obviously, the USS works best when the laptop is in a stationary place. Like using a bicycle lock, you have to park the laptop by something big and stable and then thread the cable through that big thing and the USS for the lock to work.

- The best place to find a security cable for your laptop is in a computer- or office-supply store.

- Some cables come with alarms. You can find alarms that sound when the cable is cut, plus alarms that sound when the laptop is moved.

Protecting Your Data

Passwords protect only your laptop's data, not the laptop itself. Most thieves are looking to make a quick buck; generally, for drugs. They don't care about the contents of your laptop; they just want the quick cash it brings. But, a data thief wants more.

Data thieves feast on information. They want your passwords. They want credit card numbers, which are valuable to sell. Furthermore, they can use your own computer to order stuff on the Internet or make transfers from your online bank account to their own.

The sad news is that password protection really doesn't stand in the way of most clever data thieves. They know all the tricks. They have all the tools. At best, you merely slow them down.

This section offers various ways to protect the data on your laptop. These methods may not prevent a theft, but they help keep the information on your computer away from the weirdoes who want it.

Avoid the Setup password

Your laptop's Setup program allows you to specify a password that's required well before the operating system loads. Although this is the first line in data defense, I cannot recommend it because of two issues.

First, if you forget your password, you're screwed. Many people march forward with this Setup password scheme and then end up leaving the laptop on 24 hours a day and, over time, forgetting the password. That's bad.

Strong passwords

Too many passwords are easy to figure out. Do you know what the most common password is? It's *password*—believe it or not! People use as passwords their own first names, simple words, single letters — all sorts of utterly unsecure things.

If you're serious about protecting your computer's data, create a serious password. The computer jockeys like to call it a *strong* password. That usually involves a mixture of letters and numbers using both upper- and lowercase letters. The password should contain more than eight characters.

Try to avoid using symbols other than numbers in your passwords. They may not be accepted in some instances.

When you have trouble remembering your password, write it down! Just don't keep the password list near your computer. I know folks who write their passwords on their kitchen calendars or in their address books. Random words and numbers there may not mean anything to a casual onlooker, but they're helpful when you forget the password.

Second, the Startup password can be circumvented because too many people forget it. Just about every manufacturer has some method of overriding the password, which essentially nullifies the reason for having it in the first place.

- ✔ If your laptop manufacturer has assured you that the Setup password cannot be circumvented, corrupted, erased, or overpowered, feel free to use it. But, do not forget that password!

- ✔ You're prompted for the password every dang doodle time you start your laptop. That means turning on the laptop or waking it up after hibernation.

- ✔ Some data crooks just yank the hard drive from the laptop so that they can steal the information from your hard drive by using their own, special equipment. Information can also be stolen directly from the laptop's memory chips. In either instance, the Startup password doesn't protect you.

- ✔ Refer to Chapter 4 for more information on the Setup program, which is how you can access and change the system's password.

Use a password on your account

Another method of providing reasonable protection is to ensure that your account on Windows has a password. True, you can use Windows without a password-protected account. Don't, especially on a laptop. You *need* a password on your user account, and a *strong* password as well. (See the nearby sidebar, "Strong passwords.")

- ✔ Passwords are set and changed in the User Accounts window. For details, see the section in Chapter 8 about configuring your user account.

- ✔ Computer security nabobs say that you should change your password every few months or so, and more often in a high-security area.

- ✔ Never use the word *password* as your password. It's too easy to figure out.

- ✔ If you forget your password, you're screwed. It's possible to recover Windows, but all your account information may be utterly lost and not retrievable. Keep that in mind when you're choosing a password.

Tell Windows not to memorize Internet passwords

Even with a password locking up your user account, you may still want to take extra security precautions with other passwords you may use. For example, when a Web page asks for your password, *do not* check the box to automatically remember the password later.

When Internet Explorer asks whether you want to remember a password, answer in the negative.

In Windows Mail, I recommend not having your e-mail password entered automatically. Here's how to set up that option:

1. **In Microsoft Mail, choose Tools⇨Accounts.**

    The Accounts dialog box reports for duty.

2. **Click to select your e-mail account from the list.**

3. **Click the Properties button.**

    Your ISP's e-mail connection Properties dialog box appears.

4. **Click the Servers tab.**

5. **Erase your password from the Password text box and deselect the Remember Password check box.**

    See Figure 18-1.

6. **Click OK to make the change.**

    Repeat Steps 2 through 7 for each e-mail account listed.

7. **Click the Close button when you're done, and (optional) quit Windows Mail.**

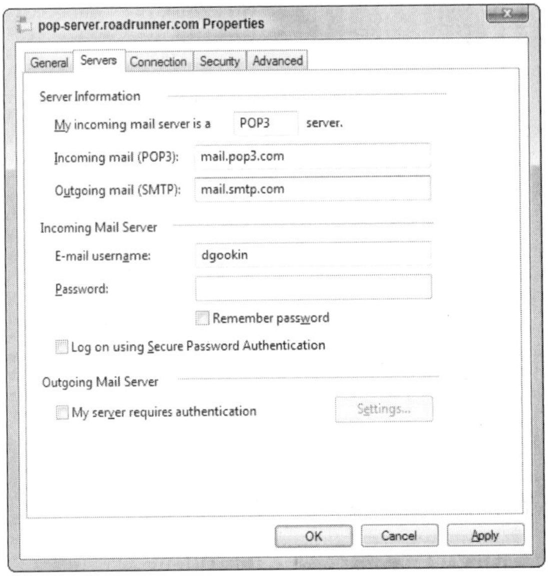

Figure 18-1: Removing your password from an Internet e-mail account.

From now on, you're prompted for your e-mail password each time you go to pick up e-mail. A dialog box appears. Just enter your password, and then you can pick up your mail.

Disable the Guest account

The Windows Guest account allows anyone to enter your computer. Even considering that the Guest account is highly limited, that's just enough for a data thief to establish a foothold and start hacking away.

To remove the Guest account, follow these steps:

1. **Open the User Accounts window.**

   The easiest way to do this step is to click on your account picture, located in the upper-right area of the Start menu.

2. **Choose the link Manage Another Account.**

3. **Click the Continue button or type the administrator's password to proceed.**

   If the Guest account is already turned off, you're done; go to Step 6.

4. **Click the Guest Account icon.**

5. **Choose the link Turn Off the Guest Account.**

6. **Close the Manage Accounts window.**

Lock Windows

Windows has a unique locking command. By pressing the Windows key (Win) and then the L key, you can quickly lock the computer, temporarily logging yourself off Windows. Only by logging in again — which requires you to type your password — can you regain access.

If you plan to leave your laptop for a moment, consider locking it: Just press Win+L. That way, even if you trust the other folks with you, they're prevented from doing even the most harmless mischief.

 You can also lock the laptop by clicking on the padlock icon on the Start button's menu.

Having the Laptop Phone Home

The reason that you've never lost your spouse or large child is that they have the unique ability to phone home when they're lost. Even a young child or the most intoxicated spouse can relate location information and then sit and wait for a speedy pickup. Believe it or not, your laptop can be just as smart.

The ability of a laptop to *phone home* was supposedly discovered by accident: A programmer set up his laptop to phone his home computer every night at about 8:00. The two computers then exchanged data and updated each other.

One day, the laptop was stolen from work. But then a few days later, the home phone suddenly rang at 8:00 p.m. The programmer picked up the phone and heard the sound of his laptop's modem making the call. He immediately grabbed the incoming Caller ID and, long story short, the police nabbed the thief, and the laptop was returned.

That laptop was recovered because it was programmed to phone home at a specific time every day. The program ran automatically, so when the thief began using the laptop, the program continued to run.

You don't need to be a programmer to set up a similar system for your own laptop. Many such programs do basically the same thing: They make the laptop phone home, or often they alert a tracking service over the Internet. The result is the same: A stolen laptop's cry for help is heard, and the laptop is quickly recovered.

For more information, refer to the following Web sites of companies that offer these phone-home services:

- ✔ www.ztrace.com
- ✔ www.computrace.com
- ✔ www.xtool.com
- ✔ www.lojackforlaptops.com

Your Fingerprint, Please

A popular craze in security devices is the fingerprint reader. It requires that you either slide or press a finger or thumb on a special gizmo as a form of identification. When the correct digit is present, the reader's software unlocks the laptop and lets you proceed.

If your laptop doesn't have a fingerprint reader on the case, you can buy an external USB device or, often, find a combination mouse/fingerprint reader. Of the two types, I prefer the fingerprint reader on the laptop's case and use it all the time to log in. The USB fingerprint reader I messed with was awkward; the cord was too long and the process to slow to be effective.

Obviously, a fingerprint reader is a far more secure method of identification than a password. I mean, who ever forgets their hand?

Backing Up Your Data

When you lose your laptop, you lose two things: the laptop's hardware and, more important, your stuff — the important data stored on the laptop. If that data means something to you, I highly recommend that you keep a *backup copy* of that data.

There are many ways to make a backup copy of data. I often copy information from my laptop to a network hard drive. Sometimes I use a media card to back up important files. It's simple: Just drag the folders I use from the laptop's hard drive to the media card. There are, however, more sophisticated ways to back up your stuff. One of the best is to use a first-rate backup program.

Windows Vista comes with its own backup program. Call it *backup*. I think the official name is *Windows Backup,* but whatever. It's used to copy your files, and potentially all the information stored on your laptop's hard drive, to external media. The reason: It's safe to have a second copy. Not a second copy on the same hard drive, which can be stolen, but a separate copy on a removeable disc or external hard drive.

This section covers backing up in Windows Vista.

Preparing for backup

To make a backup operation work, you need a few things:

✔ Software, such as Windows Backup

✔ A schedule

✔ External backup media

Your laptop comes with Windows Backup. You can also find a third-party backup program, though I don't cover using that program in this book.

The schedule helps keep the backup operation automatically updated. Windows Backup provides for scheduling. As long as your laptop is on and attached to the external backup media, backups can happen automatically.

For external media, you need a storage device that's separate from the laptop. Although you could use your laptop's recordable optical drive, those discs just don't hold enough information. Therefore, to make the process effortless, I recommend getting an external, USB hard drive for your laptop's backups.

✔ Each edition of Windows Vista has a subtly different version of Windows Backup: The Starter version has no backup; the Home Basic version has backup, but without scheduling ability. Only Windows Vista Business, Ultimate, and Enterprise versions sport the Windows Complete PC Backup program.

✔ For more information on Windows Complete PC Backup, refer to my book *Troubleshooting Your PC For Dummies* (Wiley Publishing).

✔ Western Digital makes some inexpensive, external USB hard drives called *My Book*. You can also get USB-powered drives, such as the Western Digital Passport, though they're a little more expensive.

✔ Your laptop's main mass-storage device is the hard drive. In Windows, it's referred to as *C:* or *Drive C.*

Doing an initial backup

Your Windows Vista backup adventure begins in the Backup and Restore Center window, shown in Figure 18-2. That's where you can view the current backup status as well as set up and configure your laptop for backup.

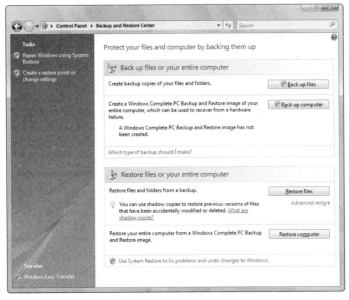

Figure 18-2:
The Backup
and Restore
Center
window.

If the Backup and Restore Center window on your laptop looks different from the one shown in Figure 18-2, backup may already be configured for your laptop. In that case, you see a status report of the last backup. There's nothing else you need to do.

If backup has yet to be configured on your laptop, follow these steps to set things up and back up the laptop's hard drive for the first time:

1. **Ensure that an external hard drive is attached and operational.**

   You can confirm that the external drive has been properly mounted by opening the Computer window and looking for its icon.

2. **Open the Control Panel window.**

3. **From the Control Panel Home, click the link Back Up Your Computer, which is found beneath the System and Maintenance title; from the Control Panel Classic View, open the Backup and Restore Center icon.**

   The Backup and Restore Center window appears (refer to Figure 18-2).

4. **Click the Back Up Files button.**

   Because the button is adorned with a shield icon, you can expect a User Account Control (UAC) warning.

5. **Click the Continue button or type the administrator's password to continue.**

   Your laptop scans for backup devices.

6. **Ensure that the option On a Hard Disk, CD, or DVD is chosen.**

7. **Choose your external hard drive from the drop-down menu.**

   Yes, you could use the laptop's optical drive, but those discs just don't have the capacity you need.

8. **Click the Next button.**

   The next screen you see allows you to choose which types of files to back up. I recommend keeping everything selected.

9. **Click the Next button.**

10. **Set a regular backup schedule using the three drop-down menus.**

    Set a time when you know the laptop will be connected to the external hard drive *and* when the laptop isn't turned off.

11. **Click the Save Settings and Start Backup button.**

    The backup proceeds. You can sit and watch, but it's boring. If you want, do something else with the laptop: Browse the Internet, catch up on e-mail, or actually get work done.

12. **Click the Close button in the Back Up Files window when the backup operation is complete.**

    A pop-up balloon from the notification area alerts you in case you're doing something else.

13. **Close the Backup and Restore Center window.**

The only time to return to the Backup and Restore Center window is in the future, when you need to confirm that a backup has taken place or to run a restore operation. Restoring is covered in the next section.

✔ The first backup takes the longest. After that, Windows merely keeps the backup copy fresh, backing up only those files you added or changed since the last backup.

✔ You can pull a manual backup at any time by clicking the Back Up Files button in the Backup and Restore Center window.

✔ Don't take the backup hard drive with you! It might be stolen. And, when you want to be truly security-minded, lock up the backup drive in a fire safe when you're not using it.

✔ Windows displays a warning dialog box when you miss a regularly scheduled backup. It's annoying but a useful reminder.

✔ You can modify the backup schedule by clicking the Change Settings link in the Backup and Restore Center window.

Restoring from a backup

Having that safety copy of your data doesn't mean anything unless you can get at the data. The operation for retrieving backed-up files is *restore*. You can restore one file or all files on the entire laptop's hard drive. Here's how that works:

1. **Attach the external hard drive to your laptop.**

   You can't restore files unless the backup hard drive is available.

2. **Open the Backup and Restore Center window.**

   Refer to Steps 2 and 3 from the preceding section.

3. **Click the Restore Files button.**

   The Restore Files window appears. It lists plenty of options for not only recovering a single file but also restoring your laptop's data in case of disk disaster.

4. **Select the appropriate file-restore option, such as Files From the Latest Backup.**

5. **Click the Next button.**

6. **Use the Add Files or Add Folders button to populate the list of files to restore.**

   The buttons let you browse for files and folders on the backup drive. Only those files or folders you choose are restored to the laptop's hard drive.

7. **Click the Next button after choosing which files to restore.**

8. **Choose a location for the restored file.**

9. **Click the Start Restore button.**

   The information is copied from the backup hard drive to your laptop's hard drive.

10. **Click the Finish button, and close the Backup and Restore Center window.**

The odds of safely recovering all your laptop's data depend on how often you back up the hard drive. I back up my desktop systems once a day. The laptop, I back up once a week.

Chapter 19

Meeting Expectations

· ·

In This Chapter

▷ Preparing for your presentation

▷ Setting up the video projector

▷ Configuring Windows Meeting Space

▷ Joining a meeting

· ·

1'm one of those laptop users who enjoys the freedom that portable computing brings. It's refreshing to have the option of taking my work with me, of choosing where and when I drop my bones and open the laptop. To me, that means anywhere from the den to a trendy, overpriced coffee shop to the middle seat of some endless overseas flight. You may enjoy your laptop for a similar reason, or you might be one of those road warriors who takes a laptop with you for — dare I say it? — *business*. Ick.

One of the main reasons some laptop users hit the road is to take their laptops to meetings. I find such a mundane thing so outrageously exciting that I decided to write a whole chapter on the laptop-meeting thing. Two topics come to mind: the ecstasy of the PowerPoint presentation and the mysterious thrill of Windows Meeting Space. How can this single chapter possibly contain such explosive excitement?

Presentation Information

Yes, I've given PowerPoint presentations using my laptop — many times. A laptop with PowerPoint software coupled with a video project can be a powerful, influential tool. It can also induce narcolepsy. Regardless, you might find the information in this section useful.

✔ *PowerPoint* is a presentation or slide show application developed by Microsoft. It's often included with Microsoft Office.

✔ These days, it's often not necessary to bring a laptop to a presentation. Merely having the presentation files on an optical disc or media card is sufficient.

The dog-and-pony show

To inform the masses, you need a laptop with PowerPoint software installed. PowerPoint creates documents generically referred to as *slide shows.* Each slide can contain text, graphics, or pictures or a combination of each one. You can add animations and sound effects, plus interesting fades and transitions between the slides.

Of course, the PowerPoint program isn't the point. The point is the information you put on the slides. If you're clever, you can assemble your important information in an informative, entertaining, and memorable way. As someone who has slept through and been bored by hundreds of PowerPoint presentations, I know that doing things well is an exception, not the rule.

PowerPoint is a fairly easy program to figure. Even schoolkids use it with no fuss to make reports and, generally, waste time — just like professional salespeople! Often better! Here are some generic PowerPoint suggestions and tips:

- ✔ PowerPoint must be installed on your laptop. Although . . .

- ✔ . . . Microsoft offers the PowerPoint viewer, which lets you play, but not edit, PowerPoint presentations. The viewer comes in handy when you create a presentation using your desktop PC and then copy it to your laptop for a road show. This viewer program can be obtained from the Microsoft Web site (`www.microsoft.com`) in the Downloads area.

- ✔ PowerPoint takes advantage of sounds, fonts, and animation on your computer. If the same font or sound files don't exist on the laptop, your presentation doesn't look the same. My advice is to create the PowerPoint presentation on the same laptop you plan to use for making the presentation. If that's not possible, don't employ special fonts or sounds in your presentation.

- ✔ One trick I use to keep a presentation from getting too boring is to engage the audience during the show. Ask questions or have the audience fill in the blanks. That strategy not only makes the show more lively but also helps keep people awake and on their toes.

- ✔ Another way to spread the word is to provide hard copies of the slide show. You don't need to put one slide on each page. Instead, put six slides on a page to save paper. (This technique also avoids the crush of fans who want a copy after the presentation.)

- ✔ The first slide of any presentation I make isn't the first slide shown. Instead, the first slide is used to help set up the laptop and video projector (covered in the next section). On that slide I have a logo or my contact information to test the focus. It also helps to employ some sort of sound effect so that I can test the audio system.

> ✔ Yes, it's an *excellent* idea to create a backup copy of your presentation on an optical disc or media card. That way, if you lose the laptop or suddenly discover an incompatibility, you can use the disc or media card with someone else's computer to deliver the talk.

Setting up your presentation

I suppose that the most nerve-wracking part about giving a presentation is ensuring that everything works. When the laptop, projector, and software work correctly, the speech itself should go smoothly, right? Even when well prepared, few folks enjoy speaking before large groups, especially groups of businessfolk who are used to — and often unimpressed by — computer presentations.

In most circumstances, you're allowed to set up your laptop and run through a test to ensure that everything works before giving your presentation to an audience. A technician might be available and even do everything to set it up for you. That's great. But it still doesn't make the situation any less nerve-racking.

For a presentation before a handful of people, viewing the PowerPoint slide show on your laptop screen and sitting at the end of a table is perfectly fine. Most of the time, however, you connect your laptop to a video projector. The video projector works like a combination second monitor and projector.

Modern laptops automatically assume that your laptop has two monitors. The second monitor is available via the VGA expansion port found on the side or the back of your monitor. Refer to Chapter 5, and specifically Table 5-1, for more information.

To connect the external monitor, follow these general steps:

1. **Turn on your laptop!**

   Plug it in, if you can. Start it up. Log in.

2. **Connect your laptop's external video connector to the video projector.**

   The video projector determines the connection you use. Most often it's a standard VGA connector. If a digital connector or S-Video connection is available, you can choose to use it instead.

3. **Connect the laptop's audio-out port to the projector or to the location's sound system.**

   Chapter 5 helps you find that audio-out jack. Note that it might also double as the headphone jack.

At this point your laptop might be smart enough to instantly use the external monitor. The laptop's desktop shows up as the projected video image. If so, that's great. You're done. If not, you may need to coax your laptop into using the external monitor exclusively or in a dual-monitor setup. Continue:

4. **Right-click the desktop and choose Personalize from the pop-up menu.**

   The Personalization window opens.

5. **Choose Display Settings.**

   The Display Settings dialog box, shown in Figure 19-1, confirms that your laptop's hardware is working and that it recognizes the external "monitor" or video projector.

   If the external monitor isn't recognized, click its icon in the Display Settings dialog box, identified by the number 2 (refer to Figure 19-1). Check the option Extend the Desktop onto This Monitor. That should fix things.

6. **Check the image.**

   At first, the projector may just show the Windows desktop. That's not why people are coming to the meeting, though. Still, it proves that the image shows up.

7. **Run your PowerPoint presentation.**

   Take your presentation for a "pre-run." Load the main slide and ensure that it shows up on the screen.

If your presentation has sound effects, preview them as well to ensure that the sound system is working.

Figure 19-1:
This laptop is ready to make presentations.

Video projector suggestions

Most locations where you give presentations might already have a video projector. If not, you need to bring your own. As with buying a laptop, choosing a video projector can be frustrating and intimidating. Here are my suggestions:

✔ You need a more powerful (and expensive) video projector when you frequent larger auditoriums. Most low-end projectors handle small rooms well.

✔ Resolution is an issue. If you plan on projecting to a larger screen, you need a higher resolution than 1024 by 768. Then again, don't go overboard with very high resolutions (greater than 2048) when your presentations don't need it.

✔ Buy an extra bulb — if you can afford it. Nothing sucks more than having a bulb burn out before a presentation. But, dang, those bulbs are expensive. Half of what you pay for the projector is probably the price of the bulb. And you cannot find replacement bulbs in the hotel's sundry store.

8. Close the laptop's lid, and go mingle or sit at the dais and wait to be introduced.

I leave my laptop at the podium, lid closed, ready to go. When I open the lid, the presentation is ready to run. Only when too many people are around and security is a concern do I take the laptop with me.

Some laptops sport a special function (Fn) key on the keyboard, used to activate the external video port. You may need to press this key to switch the display over to the video projector. It's easier than using the Display Properties dialog box (refer to Figure 19-1).

Refer to this book's Cheat Sheet for some handy PowerPoint-presentation keyboard shortcuts.

Close Encounters of the Laptop Kind

Despite being untethered, your laptop has a yearning to be social. Windows Vista has some special tools to help you form an ad hoc network and begin sharing information wirelessly (or wired, but wireless is so sexy). Two software things are involved:

✔ People Near Me
✔ Windows Meeting Space

People Near Me is a way to identify yourself and others for a potential digital rendezvous. It sets up a virtual identity you can use for invites to a cyberspace meeting.

The cyberspace meeting takes place using the Windows Meeting Space program. After you identify people to invite (from People Near Me), you can set up a single program to share with everyone or share your entire laptop.

This section explains the details, if you wish to experience close encounters of the laptop kind.

- ✔ An *ad hoc* network is simply an as-it-happens type of thing. Ad hoc is a Latin term meaning *for this purpose.* Wireless networking devices have the ability to form an ad hoc network by simply connecting with each other. No base station or server or even Internet access is needed to form an ad hoc network.

- ✔ Windows Meeting Space isn't available with all editions of Windows Vista. You can find it in Windows Vista Ultimate, Windows Vista Business, and Windows Vista Enterprise.

- ✔ Windows Meeting Space isn't the same thing as accessing your desktop PC remotely. That's *Remote Desktop Connection,* and it's covered in Chapter 16.

Annoying people near you

Before you can use Windows Meeting Space and do the ad hoc close encounter, you must set up something in Windows Vista called People Near Me. Believe me, even if you don't do this, you're prompted to get it done when you run the Windows Meeting Space program. So it's best to get it done now. Mind these steps:

1. **Open the Control Panel window.**

2. **From the Control Panel Home, choose Network and Internet, and then choose People Near Me; from the Control Panel Classic View, open the People Near Me icon.**

   The People Near Me dialog box appears, as shown in Figure 19-2.

3. **Type your public name.**

4. **Share a picture, if you like.**

   Place a check mark by the option Make My Picture Available. That way, others see your account picture. And, if you don't like the account picture, use the Change Picture button to choose a new, sexier image.

5. **Click the OK button to dismiss the dialog box.**

Figure 19-2:
The People
Near Me
dialog box.

To make your presence known, you can stand on your chair and thump your chest or you can open the People Near Me dialog box again, click the Sign In tab, and choose the option Sign In to People Near Me.

After signing in, you can await an invite from someone who is running Windows Meeting Space. Or, you can start up your own Windows Meeting Space, as described in the following section.

Starting Windows Meeting Space

The Windows Meeting Space program has been described as a whiteboard on which multiple users from separate computers can electronically scribble. That's an okay definition. To see whether it fits, you can set up or join a Windows Meeting Space event happening near you.

To create your own Windows Meeting Space event, follow these steps:

1. **Pop up the Start button menu.**

2. **Choose All Programs⇨Windows Meeting Space.**

    You might be prompted to set up Windows Meeting Space. If so, continue. Eventually, you see the Windows Meeting Space window, shown in Figure 19-3.

3. **Choose Start a New Meeting.**

4. **Give the meeting a name.**

Figure 19-3:
The
Windows
Meeting
Space
startup
screen.

5. **Set a password.**

   Yes, it must be at least eight characters long.

   You give out this password to others who are invited to the meeting. Do not use one of your regular passwords.

6. **Click the green arrow button to create the meeting.**

Refer to the next section for information on how to get people to attend your meeting.

✔ When a meeting has already started, you can join by starting the Windows Meeting Space program and choosing the meeting on the right side of the window. After you type the meeting password, you're "in" the meeting.

✔ To stop the meeting and quit the Windows Meeting Space program, click the Meeting button on the toolbar. Choose the Exit command.

✔ Windows Meeting Space may show up in the Start menu's list of recent programs, under the name *Windows Collaboration*. I haven't quite figured that one out yet.

Getting people to join a meeting

I don't believe that the definition of *meeting* means just one person. Nope, to have a successful meeting, other laptop users must be in attendance. In an office setting, the person in charge of the meeting can use the subtlety of intimidation and the threat of job loss to motivate meeting attendance. With Windows Meeting Space, you must provide for more clever means.

After creating your meeting, you have two options:

You can sit and wait for people to join. (You can sit a lot longer when you don't give them the meeting's password.) When people join, you see their names appear on the right side of the Windows Meeting Space window.

If you don't want to wait, you can send out an invitation. Follow these steps:

1. **Click the Invite button on the toolbar.**

   A list of people near you (get it?) appears, as shown in Figure 19-4.

2. **Put check marks by those whom you want to invite.**

3. **Click the Send Invitations button.**

   The people you invited receive a notice inviting them to the meeting.

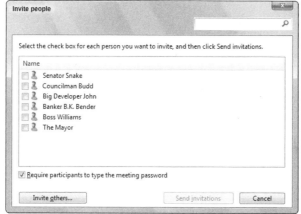

Figure 19-4:
A list of folks
who are
available for
invitation.

Of course, whether they choose to come is up to them.

✔ Only people logged in to People Near Me appear on the Invite list.

✔ You must give your attendees the password if you don't send them an invitation to the meeting.

Doing a meeting

The person who starts the meeting is in charge of what happens, and what happens takes place on that person's computer. Everyone else attending the electronic meeting can either watch or actively participate. Whether they can actively engage in the meeting or not depends on the person setting up the meeting.

To start the meeting, follow these steps in the Windows Meeting Space window:

1. **Choose the link Share a Program or Your Desktop.**

2. **If a warning appears, click the OK button to continue.**

3. **Choose something to share: a program that you're running or the desktop, or use the Browse option to open a specific application.**

   A toolbar appears at the top of the screen, which is how you control the meeting. Figure 19-5 describes the toolbar's options.

Figure 19-5:
Controlling a
meeting tak-
ing place on
your laptop.

Meeting name

Stop sharing

Let others use
your laptop

4. **(Optional) Give control to another user.**

   Choose the user from the Give Control drop-down list.

   You can press the Esc key on the laptop's keyboard to resume control at any time.

5. **To stop sharing, click the toolbar's Stop button.**

6. **Close the Windows Meeting Space window when you're done.**

Whether the others have left the meeting or not, closing the window ends the meeting.

✔ To leave a meeting, click the Meeting button on the toolbar and choose the Leave Meeting command.

✔ If everyone needs to see the screen, choose the Connect to Projector command from the toolbar's Options menu. Of course, it helps to have a video projector connected to the laptop before you do that.

Part V
Troubleshooting

The 5th Wave By Rich Tennant

"I tell him many times—get lighter laptop. But him think he know better. Him have big ego. Him say 'Me Tarzan, you not!' That when vine break."

In this part . . .

Some things just predictably go together: the jock and the cheerleader; peanut butter and jelly; nickels and dimes; war and pestilence, misery and marriage; fat and lean; politicians and hookers; and, most relevantly, computers and trouble.

The notion that a computer works flawlessly all the time without any muss or fuss is poppycock. There are always things you can do to keep any computer in the best shape possible. Even then, and despite your best efforts, there will always be seemingly unpredictable things that go wrong with your laptop. This part of the book addresses that frustration.

Chapter 20

Major Trouble and General Solutions

In This Chapter

▶ Restarting Windows to fix things

▶ Using System Restore

▶ Setting a restore point

▶ Restoring your system

▶ Using Safe mode to find problems

▶ Fixing common problems

▶ Maintaining your laptop

What is it about computers that causes trouble? Oh, that's easy: *Change.* Odds are really good that when your laptop is having problems, it's because *something has changed.* It might seem obvious — I mean, duh! The thing doesn't work any more! But, usually, some change took place *before* the trouble started and is to blame. Therefore, the entire goal of troubleshooting is to either figure out and fix what caused the change or undo the change in the first place. That's the thrust of this chapter, and of all computer troubleshooting.

✔ Changing or modifying your data files (such as Word documents or MP3 or JPEG files) isn't the type of change that causes trouble. No, changing or modifying *programs* or parts of Windows is what can lead to trouble.

✔ For more information on PC troubleshooting, I highly recommend my book *Troubleshooting Your PC For Dummies,* from Wiley Publishing and available exclusively on Planet Earth.

No, you don't need to reinstall Windows

Industry-wide, the average call for tech support must be less than 12 minutes. When the call reaches 10 minutes, tech-support people are advised to direct you to simply reinstall the Windows operating system to fix your problem. Does this advice fix your problem? That's not the issue. It fixes *their* problem, which is to get you off the phone.

I've been troubleshooting and fixing computers for years. Only a handful of times has reinstalling Windows been necessary to fix a problem — and that's usually because the user deleted parts of the Windows operating system either accidentally or due to a virus or other computer disaster. Beyond that, with patience and knowledge, any computer problem can be solved without replanting the operating system.

Reinstalling Windows is like rebuilding your home's foundation when all you need to do is fix a leaky faucet. When someone tells you to reinstall Windows, run. No, better: Scream, and then run. Try to find another source of help. *Remember:* Only in drastic situations is reinstalling Windows necessary. If you can find someone knowledgeable and helpful enough, he can assist you without having to reinstall Windows.

The Universal Quick-Fix

Before dropping into that deep pit of high-tech despair, there's one thing you should try first: Restart Windows. Often times, restarting Windows unclogs the drain and allows your computer to work properly again. If there were a "take two aspirin and call me in the morning" laptop fix, restarting Windows would be it.

Refer to Chapter 4 for information on restarting Windows.

System Restore to the Rescue!

Thanks to the handy program System Restore, you can take Windows and your laptop back in time. You can restore your computer system to the state it was in just before trouble reared its unwelcome head, before you installed new hardware or software or made that fatal change. System Restore is the time-travel pod you take on your journey toward fixing your laptop.

Enabling System Restore

Before you can take advantage of System Restore, you have to ensure that it's turned on. Waddle through these steps:

1. **Open the Control Panel window.**

2. **From the Control Panel Home, choose System and Maintenance and then System; from the Control Panel Classic View, open the System icon.**

   The System window appears.

3. **Click the link on the left that reads Advanced System Settings.**

4. **In the User Account Control dialog box, click the Continue button or type the administrator's password.**

   Finally, you arrive at the System Properties dialog box.

5. **In the System Properties dialog box, click the System Protection tab.**

   You see the part of the System Properties dialog box that deals with System Restore, as shown in Figure 20-1.

6. **Ensure that there's a check mark by each disk drive you want protected with System Restore.**

   Removing the check mark disables System Restore for that drive.

7. **Click OK to confirm your settings and (optional) close the Control Panel window.**

Figure 20-1:
The System
Restore
control
center.

System Restore is turned on in Windows Vista automatically. The only reason to turn it off is to save disk space. I believe, however, that System Restore protection is more vital to running your laptop than any disk space savings offered.

✔ There's no need to run System Restore protection on an external backup hard drive.

✔ In older versions of Windows, turning off System Restore was a way to prevent virus attacks. That's no longer true in Windows Vista.

Setting a restore point

System Restore works by creating a *restore point.* It's like a mini-backup of important system information and settings in Windows. The notion is that by saving that information, you can, in the future, effectively restore your laptop to its prior, working state.

To get the most from System Restore, a restore point must be set any time something is changed. This change includes modifying Windows, installing an update, adding new hardware, or changing a system setting. That way, if anything weird happens, you can attempt to recover using System Restore.

In Windows Vista, System Restore is run automatically at least once a day (if you keep your laptop on or in Sleep mode all the time). A restore point is also set any time you update Windows or install new software.

To manually set a restore point, for example, before a hardware upgrade, follow Steps 1 through 5 in the preceding section. You need to open the System Properties dialog box and click the System Protection tab. Once there, follow these steps:

6. **Click the Create button.**

7. **Type a name for the restore point.**

   I use an event name, such as Installing New Memory or Video Driver Update. Note that the current date and time are automatically appended to whatever name you specify.

8. **Click the Create button.**

   Windows creates a restore point. In a few moments, you see a success dialog box.

9. **Click OK.**

10 **Close the System Properties dialog box, and (optional) the Control Panel window.**

With the restore point set, you can go ahead and make whatever change you were planning to make on your laptop: Add hardware, install new software, or change a setting or configuration option in Windows.

 ✔ Create a restore point before installing new hardware.

 ✔ Create a restore point before removing hardware.

 ✔ Create a restore point before adding or updating a new hardware driver.

 ✔ Create a restore point before installing any programs you download from the Internet.

 ✔ Be sure to create a restore point before you decide to toil with network configurations. That will really save your butt.

 ✔ If you neglect to set a restore point, don't fret! Windows itself automatically sets restore points at key times. You should be fine.

Restoring your system

When the computer starts acting goofy, you need to ask yourself, "What has changed recently?" Even when nothing has changed, I recommend giving a system restore a chance.

To complete its job, System Restore must restart your laptop. Ensure that you quit any programs and save any files before you start. Also, please plug in your laptop so that it doesn't poop out in the middle of an important operation.

Follow these steps to restore your laptop:

1. **From the Start button menu, choose All Programs➪Accessories➪ System Tools➪System Restore.**

2. **Click the Continue button or type the administrator's password to get past the User Account Control dialog box.**

   The System Restore window shows up, as illustrated in Figure 20-2. If you see a restore point that you set as the Recommended Restore (say, before an upgrade), go to Step 6.

3. **Choose the option Choose a Different Restore Point.**

4. **Click the Next button.**

   A list of recent restore points is displayed.

5. **Choose a restore point from the list.**

6. **Click the Next button.**

Figure 20-2:
An artful
depiction of
the System
Restore
window.

7. Click the Finish button.

Scary-warning time! That's okay; System Restore cannot be interrupted while it's restoring your system. That means if you're running other programs now, you should close them. If you're running the laptop on battery power, try to plug in to continue. If you cannot plug in or stop other programs, click the No button and start over. Otherwise:

8. Click the Yes button.

Windows restores itself to an earlier point in time. As part of that process, the laptop shuts down and then restarts. You're informed of the progress on the screen.

9. Log in after Windows restarts.

Eventually, you see a notice on the screen, explaining that the system has been restored to the point you specified.

10. Click the Close button to dismiss the System Restore notice.

Your system has been restored. Any changes you made between the date and time of the restore point and the present have been undone. Hopefully, that fixed the problem. If not, you can try an earlier restore point.

✔ System Restore doesn't delete any new files you created. It affects only the operating system and installed software.

✔ System Restore lets you reset the system back only a few days or so. Attempts to use a restore point earlier than a week before generally don't meet well with success.

> ✔ You also have an emergency startup System Restore option. You may see a text menu when the laptop restarts, identifying a potential problem. If so, choose the option Last Known Good Configuration or whichever option allows for a System Restore.

Safe Mode

When you need to do serious troubleshooting, Windows offers a special mode of operation called *Safe mode.* I question the name. Doesn't it imply that normally Windows is *not* in Safe mode? What is it then? *Unsafe mode?* But I digress. . . .

Safe mode helps determine one major thing: whether the problem is with Windows or with other software. In Safe mode, only the most basic programs required to run Windows are loaded on startup. The rest of the stuff — those troublesome drivers — aren't loaded. Then, if the problem is gone in Safe mode, the problem is *not* to be blamed on Windows.

Entering Safe mode

Safe mode happens in a number of ways. Most annoyingly, your laptop starts in Safe mode when something is awry and Windows cannot start normally. See the later section "Testing in Safe mode" to find out what to do, as well as the even later section "My laptop always starts in Safe mode!"

You can manually enter Safe mode in one of two ways:

First, by pressing the F8 key when the laptop starts, you see a text-based startup menu. One of the options presented is Safe mode. Choose that option to continue starting the computer in Safe mode.

Second, a more reliable way to start your laptop in Safe mode is by using the System Configuration Utility, also known as MS Config. This utility helps you troubleshoot startup problems by selectively disabling various startup services and programs.

To configure the computer to start up in Safe mode, use the System Configuration Utility:

1. **Choose the Run command from the Start button menu.**

   Or, press the Win+R keyboard shortcut; or, choose All Programs⇨ Accessories⇨Run.

2. **Type MSCONFIG into the text box, and then click OK.**

3. **Click the Continue button or type the administrator's password when you're confronted with the User Access Control dialog box.**

   The System Configuration dialog box appears.

4. **Click the Boot tab.**

5. **Put a check mark by the item labeled Safe Boot.**

6. **Click OK.**

   Wait a few seconds. The computer is "thinking."

7. **Click the Restart button.**

   Your laptop restarts in Safe mode.

By making this change, you're configuring your laptop to always start in Safe mode. Refer to the next section for what to do in Safe mode.

Testing in Safe mode

In Safe mode, Windows doesn't load common device drivers or extensions to the computer system. Therefore, the screen has a very low resolution, and some hardware features you're used to working with aren't available: Forget about networking. Forget about the Internet.

Your job in Safe mode is trying to repeat the error. Do whatever it is that's causing your trouble. If the problem persists in Safe mode, it's most likely a Windows problem. If not, and when everything seems okay, the problem is with something else on your computer — some software program or piece of hardware.

When you're done troubleshooting, restart Windows. If the problem has been fixed, the laptop starts normally.

If you manually went into Safe mode by following the steps in the preceding section, follow these steps before restarting Windows to undo that change:

1. **Start the System Configuration Utility in Safe mode.**

   Refer to Steps 1 through 3 in the preceding section.

2. **On the General tab, choose Normal Startup.**

3. **Click the OK button to dismiss the System Configuration dialog box.**

4. **Click the Restart button.**

Windows restarts normally.

✔ Do not try to use your computer in Safe mode. Don't get work done; don't run your word processor. Don't play a game. Safe mode is for fixing the problem, not for doing anything else.

✔ When the problem is with Windows itself, which is evident in Safe mode, you should visit the Windows tech support Web site to find a solution. Restart the computer in Normal mode and visit the Microsoft Knowledge Base:

```
http://support.microsoft.com/
```

Type a few keywords to search the Knowledge Base for your problem. A solution should quickly be at hand.

"My laptop always starts in Safe mode!"

When your laptop starts in Safe mode, it means that something is wrong. Some piece of hardware or software has told Windows that it just can't function, so the system starts in Safe mode — first, to alert you to the problem; and second, to give you the opportunity to fix things.

In most cases, the problem's description appears on the screen, and you can address the issue by reading the text that's displayed.

Common Problems and Solutions

It would be nearly impossible for me to mention every dang doodle problem your laptop can experience. So, rather than list every dang doodle one of them, or even 1,000 or even 100, I narrowed the list to 5. Each of them is covered in this section.

"The keyboard is wacky!"

This problem happens more often than you would imagine, based on the e-mail I receive. The solution is generally simple: You accidentally pressed the Num Lock key on your keyboard, and half the alphabet keys on your keyboard are acting like numbers.

The solution is to press the Num Lock key and restore your keyboard to full alphabetic operation.

Touchpad touchiness

Mouse

Some laptop touchpads seem to operate merely by looking at them. I call them touchy-touchpads. Rather than be frustrated, simply adjust the touchpad's sensitivity. Visit the Mouse Properties dialog box to fix things: From the Control Panel Home, choose Mouse under Hardware and Sound; from Control Panel Classic View, open the Mouse icon.

You don't have to use the touchpad. You can disable it in the Mouse Properties dialog box. If so, use an external mouse, which will probably make you happier.

Making the mouse pointer more visible

When you're having trouble seeing the mouse pointer on your laptop's screen, visit the Pointers or Pointer Options tab in the Mouse Properties dialog box. Refer to directions in the preceding section on how to summon that dialog box. The following suggestions can help you make the mouse pointer more visible:

✔ On the Pointers tab, you can choose larger mouse pointers than the set normally used by Windows. In the Scheme drop-down list, choose Windows Standard (extra large) for some supersize mouse pointers.

✔ On the Pointer Options tab, use two of the options in the Visibility area to help you find a mouse pointer on the screen. Specifically, try Pointer Trails or the Ctrl-key click option.

✔ Pointer Trails adds a comet-tail effect to the mouse in Windows, helping you locate the mouse pointer as you move it around.

✔ When the mouse plays *Where's Waldo?,* you can find it with the Ctrl-key click option by pressing either Ctrl key on your keyboard. A series of concentric rings surrounds and highlights the mouse pointer's location.

"My laptop won't wake up"

A snoozing laptop can mean that the battery is dead. Consider plugging in the laptop and trying again.

When the laptop has trouble waking from Stand By mode — and you have to turn it off and then turn it on again to regain control — you have a problem with the power-management system in your laptop. See the next section.

Power-management woes

When your laptop suddenly loses its ability to go into Stand By or Hibernate mode, it means that there might be a problem with the power-management hardware or software.

First, check with your computer manufacturer's Web page to see whether you can find any additional information or software updates.

Second, ensure that power management is properly enabled, as described in Chapter 9.

Finally, confirm that other hardware or software isn't interfering with the power-management software. If so, remove the interfering software or hardware, or check for updates that don't mess with your laptop's power-management system.

"The battery won't charge"

Batteries die. Even the modern smart batteries are good for only so long. When your battery goes, replace it with a new one. When the battery goes unexpectedly, consider replacing it under warranty if it proves defective.

Rules and laws govern the disposal of batteries. Be sure to follow the proper procedure for your community to safely dispose of or recycle batteries.

Maintenance

There is really nothing to laptop maintenance, especially when using Windows Vista. Most common maintenance chores happen automatically. These include running disk tune-up and defragmentation programs. As long as you haven't disabled any of those activities, consider your laptop's storage system to be adequately maintained.

- ✔ If you disabled automatic disk defragmentation or error-checking, I'll rely on you to use that same knowledge to reenable it. Or, if you need extra directions, consider picking up a copy of my book *Troubleshooting Your PC For Dummies* (Wiley Publishing).

- ✔ Refer to Chapter 8 for information on keeping your laptop clean, which is another part of general maintenance.

✔ Also see Chapter 18, which covers using the Backup program in Windows. Backing up your important files and information is yet another aspect of good, ongoing computer maintenance.

✔ No, unlike with an automobile, you have no reason to take your laptop into the dealer or a repair place for regular check-ups. When someone tells you that you need such a thing, and nothing is otherwise wrong with your laptop, you and your money will soon be parted (if you catch my drift).

Chapter 21

Upgrading Your Laptop

. . . .

In This Chapter

▶ Updating your software

▶ Updating Windows

▶ Adding hardware

. . . .

*Y*our laptop is based upon the most popular computer design in history. The key to that success has been a relatively open standard and an abundant selection of software and hardware. The term is *upgrade*. Both desktop and laptop PCs have more hardware and software upgrades available to them than any other computer system ever built. That's good because it gives you choices. Of course, having the choice isn't the issue; what's important is making the right choice. This chapter helps you make the right choice when it comes to upgrading your laptop.

How 'bout Some New Software?

Generally speaking, I don't recommend upgrading software. In the olden days, upgrades were necessary to add new features and expand on the abilities of older programs. But today's software is so advanced that even a program developed half a dozen years ago would still serve you well today.

Upgrading your software

I recommend upgrading your software only when the newer version of the program offers features you need or fixes problems you have. Otherwise, my motto is "If it ain't broke, don't fix it!"

I'm serious: You can avoid a lot of trouble by not upgrading. I've seen too many stable computers become unstable after simple upgrades. I've seen printers suddenly not work. Worse yet, I've seen the chain reaction of having to upgrade more than one application just to keep things compatible. That can be expensive, but it's a tough choice: The newer version of the application can boost your productivity. The key is to be prepared for anything.

✔ Before upgrading, set a *restore point*. It helps you recover things in case the upgrade doesn't work properly. Refer to Chapter 20.

✔ Upgrading is as easy as sticking the new program's disc into your laptop's optical drive. Everything after that should run automatically, with your input required to answer a few simple questions.

✔ You don't need to uninstall the previous version of a program when you're installing an update. The only exception is when you're specifically advised to uninstall any older versions.

✔ Refer to Chapter 8 for information on removing software from your computer.

Updating Windows

Microsoft routinely updates Windows — weekly, in fact. As bugs are fixed or security issues are addressed, updates are made available. They can be automatically installed as your laptop accesses the Internet, or they can be manually installed by visiting the Windows Update service on the Internet or obtaining the occasional update disc directly from Microsoft.

When your computer is configured for automatic updates, Windows goes to the Microsoft update site and downloads the updates in the background when you're connected to the Internet. As new updates are available, they're provided to you. Then you're informed of the updates and given the option to install them, depending on which settings you choose when you configure automatic updates (see the next two sections).

To ensure that your laptop is configured for automatic updates, follow these steps:

1. **Pop up the Start button's menu.**

2. **Choose All Programs⇨Windows Update.**

   The Windows Update window appears, as shown in Figure 21-1. If any updates are pending, you see them categorized and listed.

3. **On the left side of the window, click Change Settings.**

4. **To activate automatic updates, select the first option at the top, Install Updates Automatically (Recommended).**

   You can peruse the other options, if you like, though I highly recommend the first one.

Upgrades versus updates

Computer jargon can be confusing enough without having to deal with vague terms that also exist in English. Prime examples are the words *upgrade* and *update.* They might seem like the same thing, but in the computer world, they're not.

Upgrade means to install a newer version of a program you already own. For example, you upgrade from version 2.1 of a program to version 2.2. Specifically, that's referred to as a *minor* upgrade. From version 4.0 to version 5.0 is a *major* upgrade.

Update means to improve an existing program, but not change its version or release number. For example, Microsoft routinely releases security updates for Windows. These updates, or *patches,* are applied to your version of Windows to improve features, address security issues, or fix bugs.

In some universe somewhere, this stuff all makes sense.

5. **Choose a proper time for the updates to take place.**

   Ideally, your laptop is turned on and connected to the Internet.

6. **Click OK.**

7. **If prompted with a User Account Control, click the Continue button or type the administrator's password.**

 When updates for your laptop are pending, the Start menu's power button appears with a tiny shield icon, as shown in the margin. The icon is your clue that an update is pending, one that requires you to restart Windows.

Figure 21-1:
The
Windows
Update
window.

Upgrading to a new version of Windows

I highly recommend against upgrading your laptop's operating system. Specifically, I recommend against upgrading Windows. Once upon a time, upgrading the operating system was a good idea. But today the improvements and changes that upgrades make to Windows are just too great to risk the stability of your computer — specifically, a laptop.

Rather than upgrade Windows, the next best thing is simply to wait until you need to buy a new laptop. Then get the latest version of Windows preinstalled. That way, you're assured that all the hardware is compatible with the new version and that it's robust enough to handle the new version of Windows. When you're upgrading an older computer, you just can't be assured of those things, so it's a risk. I don't recommend risking the investment you made in your laptop.

✔ One thing you might not get with the update are *drivers,* or specific software that controls various parts of your laptop. These parts include the mousepad, the wireless and Ethernet network adapters, the display, the power-management hardware — essentially, all the things that make your laptop easy to use.

✔ Sure, if you want to upgrade Windows, go ahead. I can't stop you. But I highly recommend against upgrading Windows.

Giving Your Laptop New Hardware

If you're fortunate enough to have an upgradeable laptop, by golly, you should take advantage of it someday!

Internal expansion options are somewhat limited on laptops. Even so, on many laptops, it's possible to replace or upgrade the hard drive and memory (RAM). Most other items on the laptop cannot be upgraded; the processor, video circuitry, networking adapter, modem, and other hardware are often all integrated into the laptop's main circuitry board, or *motherboard.* It's cheaper to buy an entirely new laptop than to try to upgrade anything on the motherboard.

If your laptop is equipped with a handy method for adding more memory, do so! Memory chips are available far and wide, though my favorite place to shop for RAM is the online memory store at www.crucial.com. The site has a configuration program that helps you select the exact amount of memory you need. The program is very handy, plus the memory chips come with good instructions on how to install them in your computer.

Some laptops allow for the hard drive to be replaced or upgraded. The easiest way to do this is when the laptop has a drive bay option. For example, you can use an optical drive, media card reader, or hard drive in the drive bay. So, if your computer came with an optical drive and you want to replace the drive with a second hard drive, the operation is not only possible but also relatively easy to accomplish. The bad news is that the extra drives are available only from the manufacturer and are often quite pricey.

Beyond those few basic items, your laptop is essentially a closed box, and no further upgrades are offered. Don't despair! Refer to Chapter 10 for various ways to expand your laptop without using a screwdriver.

Refer to the documentation that came with your hardware to find out exactly how to configure it. Note that sometimes the software that comes with your device might need to be installed first, before you install the hardware. Other times, it's vice versa.

Part VI
The Part of Tens

"They won't let me through security until I remove the bullets from my Word document."

In this part . . .

There's been some debate about why people who put things into lists seem to group them into ten items. My argument is that we humans have ten fingers and ten toes. Well, all except for polydactyl people. Rumor has it that Anne Boleyn had six fingers on one hand. If that were true for everyone, we'd probably see more lists of 11 than 10. Regardless, we won't know for certain until we're conquered by an alien civilization with 16 fingers. So if they group lists into 16 items, I'm spot-on.

To keep with the ten-items-in-a-list tradition, I present you with this, the final part of *Laptops For Dummies:* The Part of Tens. In this part, you'll find chapters that list ten items. They're tricks, hints, and helpful bits of information that just fit best in a ten-item list format.

Chapter 22

Ten or So Battery Tips and Tricks

In This Chapter

▶ Avoiding battery perils

▶ Draining the battery

▶ Using less battery power

▶ Preventing virtual memory swapping

▶ Cleaning the battery terminals

▶ Storing the battery

▶ Understanding that the battery drains itself over time

*Y*our laptop sports everything found on a desktop computer, all shrunk down to a miniature version or sporting special power- and heat-saving abilities. But there's one thing your laptop has that a desktop PC lacks: a battery.

This chapter contains tips and tricks to help you use your laptop and its battery in the most productive manner possible. Note that these aren't the standard battery tips. I'm assuming, for example, that you know better than to put your laptop's battery into your mouth. Furthermore, I assume that you won't suddenly desire to put your laptop's battery on a campfire "to see what happens." Finally, I assume that you'll never go anywhere near your laptop's battery with a can opener or soldering iron — unless it's your dying wish to see your grieving relatives try to explain your stupidity to a television news crew.

Don't Drop the Battery, Get It Wet, Short It, Play Keep-Away with It, Open It, Burn It, or Throw It Away

Enough said.

Scary lithium-ion battery trivia

Lithium-ion batteries are what many of us humans aspire to be: smart and popular. But there's a scary side to the lithium-ion battery. Consider this frightening lithium-ion battery information designed to literally shock you away from any thought of messing with your laptop's battery:

✔ When a lithium-ion battery is overcharged, it gets hot. Then it explodes.

✔ There's an increased risk of explosion when the battery gets too hot.

✔ The lithium metal in the battery burns inside water.

✔ The acid inside the battery is not only highly caustic but also flammable.

✔ I'm sure that the acid is poisonous as well, but — golly — that last sentence had me at "caustic."

✔ You cannot recycle a used lithium-ion battery, so don't ever think of buying or using a "recycled" battery.

Every Few Months, Drain the Battery All the Way

To keep your laptop's battery nice and healthy, remember to drain it completely at least once every few months.

Most laptops use modern, intelligent lithium-ion batteries. Unlike the "memory effect" batteries of the past (NiCad and NiMH), you can recharge your lithium-ion batteries at any time, and they still maintain full capacity. Even so, let the battery completely drain about once every two or three months. Then recharge the battery nice and slow; overnight is best. That keeps your battery healthy and happy.

Turn Down the Monitor's Brightness

To save a bit on battery life on the road, lower the brightness on your monitor just a hair — or perhaps as low as you can stand. That definitely saves the juice.

✔ Buttons near the laptop's LCD monitor control the brightness.

✔ Sometimes, the brightness is controlled by using special Fn-key combinations.

✔ Your laptop's power manager might automatically dim the screen when the laptop is on battery power.

✔ Screen dimming can be done in the Control Panel's Mobility Center.

✔ Check the Power Options window to see whether your laptop has any advanced or specific settings for disabling or saving power used by the display.

Power Down the Disk Drives

The motors in your laptop consume the most power — specifically, the motors that keep the hard drive continually spinning. When you're using a program that continually accesses the hard drive, such as a database, it's more efficient to keep the drive continually spinning. But when you're working on something that doesn't require constant disk access, save some juice by "sleeping" an idle hard drive.

✔ Also consider turning off or disabling the laptop's optical drive.

✔ Refer to Chapter 9 for more information on hard drive timeouts.

Add RAM to Prevent Virtual Memory Disk Swapping

One way that the hard drive conspires with the operating system to drain the battery quickly is when the virtual memory manager pulls a disk swap. The way to prevent it is to add memory (RAM) to your laptop.

Virtual memory has nothing to do with virtue. Instead, it's a chunk of hard drive space that Windows uses to help supplement real memory, or RAM. Mass chunks of information are swapped between RAM and your laptop's hard drive, which is why you never see any Out of Memory errors in Windows. But all that swapping drains battery juice.

Windows does a great job of managing virtual memory. Although you can fine-tune the virtual memory manager, I don't recommend it. Instead, test the virtual memory manager this way:

1. **Run three or four of your most-often-used programs.**

   Start up each program, and get its window up and ready on the screen, just as though you're about to work on something. In fact, you can even load a document or whatever, to ensure that the program is occupied.

2. **Watch the hard drive light; wait for it to stop blinking.**

   Wait until the hard drive light on the laptop (refer to Chapter 5) stops blinking. That means hard drive access has stopped and the computer is simply waiting.

3. **Press Alt+Esc.**

   The Alt+Esc key combination switches from one program (or window) to another.

4. **Watch the hard drive light.**

5. **Repeat Steps 3 and 4 until you cycle through all programs and windows at least once.**

   What you're looking for is hard drive access. If you detect a noticeable pause or the hard drive light blinks as you switch between programs, it can be a sign that virtual memory is being used, by swapping from RAM to disk. Yes, your system is working harder than it should, and it affects battery life.

The idea isn't really to adjust virtual memory as much as it is to add RAM to your laptop and prevent virtual memory from ever taking over in the first place.

- ✔ A good amount of RAM to have with Windows Vista is 1GB, although 2GB is even better.

- ✔ To see how much memory is installed in your laptop, view the System window (from the Control Panel). The amount of memory that's installed appears along with other information about your computer.

Keep RAM Empty

Even when you cannot add to RAM to your laptop, it can save battery life by economically using the RAM you have.

To optimize performance, I recommend running only a few programs at a time on your laptop when you're using the battery. For example, you might be reading e-mail in your e-mail program, browsing the Web, editing a document in your word processor, and keeping a game of Spider Solitaire going in another window. All that activity is unnecessary, and shutting down the programs you're not using helps save battery life.

It may seem trivial, but by not setting a background image or wallpaper, Windows spends less time updating the screen. And, time is battery life! Consider setting a solid color background image on your laptop: use the Personalization window's Desktop Background link to set the image.

Guard the Battery's Terminals

Like a big-city airport or a bus station or Frankenstein's neck, your laptop's battery has terminals. People don't traverse a battery's terminals; but, like Frankenstein's neck, electricity does. The terminals are usually flat pieces of metal, either out in the open or recessed into a slot.

- ✔ Keep your battery in the laptop.

- ✔ Outside the laptop, keep the battery away from metal.

- ✔ Keep the terminals clean; use a Q-tip and some rubbing alcohol. Do this whenever you succumb to the temptation to touch the terminals, even though you shouldn't be doing that.

- ✔ Do not attach anything to the battery.

- ✔ Do not attempt to short the battery or try to rapidly drain it.

- ✔ The terminals appear in different locations on the battery, depending on who made the battery and how it attaches to the laptop.

Avoid Extreme Temperatures

Batteries enjoy the same type of temperatures you do. They don't like to be very cold, and they don't like hot temperatures, either. Like Goldilocks, the battery enjoys temperatures that are *just right.*

Store the Battery If You Don't Plan to Use It

Don't let a battery sit. If you keep the laptop deskbound (and nothing could be sadder), occasionally unplug the thing and let the battery cycle, just to keep the battery healthy. That's the best thing to do.

When you would rather run your laptop without the battery inside, or when preparing a spare battery for storage, run down the battery's charge to about 40 percent or so, and then put the battery in a nonmetallic container. Stick the container in a nice, cool, clean, dry place.

- ✔ Like people, batteries need exercise! Cycle your battery every two months or so whether you're using the laptop remotely or not.

- ✔ The recommended storage temperature for lithium-ion batteries is 59 degrees Fahrenheit or 15 degrees Celsius.

✔ Also refer to the next section.

 ✔ A lithium-ion battery has an expiration date! After several years, the battery dies. This is true whether you use the battery or store it.

Understand That Batteries Drain Over Time!

No battery keeps its charge forever. Eventually, over time, the battery's charge fades. For some reason, this surprises people. "That battery was fully charged when I put it into storage six years ago!" Batteries drain over time.

Yet, just because a battery has drained doesn't mean that it's useless. If you stored the battery properly, all it needs is a full charge to get it back up and running again. So, if you store a battery (see the previous section), anticipate that you'll need to recharge it when you want to use it again. This works just like getting the battery on the first day you bought your laptop; follow those same instructions for getting the stored battery up and running again.

Deal with the Low-Battery Warning

Thanks to smart-battery technology, your laptop can be programmed to tell you when the juice is about to go dry. In fact, you can set up two warnings on most laptops. (Refer to Chapter 9.) The idea is to act fast on those warnings when they appear — and to take them seriously! Linger at your own risk. It's your data that you could lose!

The real trick, of course, is to ration the battery power you do have. Here's a summary of tips, some of which are found elsewhere in this book:

 ✔ **Be mindful of power-saving timeouts.** Setting a Stand By timeout for 15 minutes may work well in the office, but on the road you may want to adjust those times downward. Refer to Chapter 9.

 ✔ **Modify the display to use a lower resolution or fewer colors on the road.** In fact, for most computing, a resolution of 800 x 600 with 16-bit color is fine. This setting uses less video memory, which requires less power to operate and keep cool.

 ✔ **Mute the speakers!** This strategy not only saves a modicum of power but also prevents the ears of those next to you from hearing the silly noises your laptop makes.

✔ **Disable unused devices.** If you're not using the modem, turn it off. If you don't need the optical drive, remove its disc. Speaking of which. . . .

✔ **If your laptop's optical drive is removable, consider removing it when you go on the road.** That saves a bit on weight as well as on power usage.

✔ **Save some stuff to do when you get back home or reconnect to a power source.** Face it: Some things can wait. If that 200K file upload isn't needed immediately, save it for when you're connected to the fast Internet line back at the hotel or your office.

✔ **Hibernate!** When time is short and your laptop has the Hibernation smarts, just hibernate. Refer to Chapter 9.

Chapter 23

Ten Handy Laptop Accessories

In This Chapter

▶ Getting a laptop bag or case

▶ Adding a spare battery

▶ Expanding the laptop with a port replicator

▶ Keeping the laptop cool with a cooling pad

▶ Cleaning with a minivac

▶ Illuminating with a USB lamp

▶ Enjoying a full-size keyboard and mouse

▶ Adding an ID card

▶ Installing theft prevention

*O*ne thing that keeps the computer industry alive is that a computer purchase never stops with the computer itself. First comes software. Then follows more hardware and even more hardware. Peripherals! Gizmos! Gadgets! And then there are accessories, like mousepads and tchotchkes to sit atop the monitor. The computer is an endless expense.

Feast your eyes, dear reader, and stretch your pocketbook on the following ten fun or must-have items to expand your laptop universe. (Go to Chapter 10 to find out more about other peripheral devices you can use with your laptop.)

Laptop Bag or Travel Case

Buy yourself and your laptop a handsome laptop bag. Chapter 17 offers some great suggestions and recommendations.

Spare Battery

Nothing cries "Freedom!" to the laptop road warrior more than an extra battery. Having a bonus battery doubles the time you can compute without that AC wall-socket umbilical cord. Some laptops even let you hot-swap from one battery to another while the laptop is still running, which means that the total length of time you can use your battery greatly exceeds your capacity to do work.

Ensure that the spare battery is approved for your laptop, coming either directly from the manufacturer or from a source that is reliable and guarantees compatibility. Using the wrong battery in your laptop can be disastrous.

Docking Station or Port Replicator

The way to expand your laptop's options is to add special nonportable options, such as a docking station or port replicator.

Port replicator: A port replicator, snaps on to a special expansion connector on your laptop, adds some common desktop connectors to your laptop, plus maybe more copies of ports that the laptop has too few of. The port replicator can plug into the wall and supply the laptop with power, or it can just be a "cling-on" that snaps on to the laptop's rump for added expansion.

Docking station: A docking station is a more sophisticated (and expensive) version of the port replicator. As with the port replicator, it allows you to add peripherals and expand the power of your laptop, although it's more of a base station or permanent location than a port replicator is. Some docking stations are even shaped like desktop PCs, but with open maws into which you slide the laptops. Some even allow you to add expansion cards, which make the laptops even more like stationary, desktop PCs.

- ✔ When you're ready to go back on the road, pop out the laptop and you're gone!

- ✔ A port replicator also gives your laptop more ports and more expandability options than the laptop might be supplied with on its own.

- ✔ The docking station and port replicator aren't generic add-ons. You must get one specific to your laptop, from either your laptop's manufacturer or your computer dealer.

Cooling Pad

The ideal accessory for any well-loved laptop is a cooling pad. It's a device, similar to the one shown in Figure 23-1, on which your laptop sits. The *cooling pad* contains one or more fans and is powered by either the laptop's USB port or standard AA batteries. Your laptop sits on the pad, and the fans help draw away the heat that the battery and microprocessor generate. The result is a cooler-running laptop, which keeps the laptop happy.

- ✔ Note that the cooling pad runs from the power supplied by the USB port or from its own batteries. That means it's portable.

- ✔ If you're getting a USB-powered cooling pad, try to buy a model that has a pass-through USB port so that you don't lose a USB port when you add a cooling pad.

- ✔ Some cooling pads also double as USB hubs.

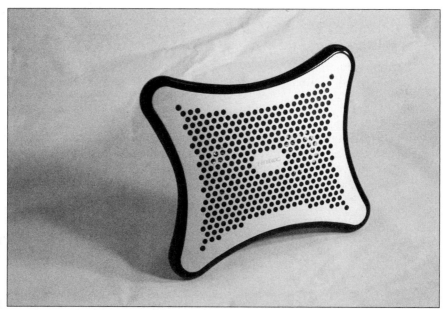

Figure 23-1:
A cool
cooling pad.

Minivac

Useful for cleaning your laptop, especially the keyboard, is the minivac. This item is found in most office-supply stores, and many are portable (battery powered). You'll be surprised (and disgusted) by the gunk that the minivac can suck from your laptop.

USB Lamp

Your laptop's LCD screen is illuminated and even shows up in the dark. Sadly, however, most laptop keyboards don't light up. To help you see the keyboard as well as other important areas around your laptop, you can light things up with a USB-powered lamp.

The lamp plugs into a standard USB port on your laptop. It has either a stiff, bendable cord or a clamp so that you can position it. Flip the switch and let there be light!

Note that some laptops might already have built-in keyboard lights. Some Lenovo models, for example, feature a lamp mounted atop the LCD screen. The key combination Fn+Page Up turns the lamp on or off.

Full-Size Keyboard

Although you might not want to tote one around with you, there's a certain pleasure to be had when you're using a laptop with a comfy, full-size keyboard. Especially if you rely on the numeric keypad, for either numbers or cursor control, it's a joy to use a full-size, USB keyboard on a laptop.

In addition to (or perhaps, instead of) using a USB full-size keyboard, you can select any of a number of fun and different keyboards for your laptop. You can find keyboards with special Internet buttons, ergonomically designed to make typing easier on the human bod, as well as wireless keyboards. Because your laptop didn't come with a full-size keyboard, it's a buyer's paradise as far as choosing one for your laptop. Or, if all you need is that numeric keypad, you can get special USB numeric keypads for your laptop.

External Mouse

The only problem I have with using an external mouse on my laptop is that I neglect it. I'm so trained to use the touchpad that I forget about the full-size, comfy, and easy-to-use mouse right next to my laptop.

As with a keyboard, you aren't limited to your choice of an external mouse for your laptop. You can get a basic mouse, a space age, optical glowing mouse, a mouse with lots of buttons, a weird mouse that you can hover in the air and use like a TV remote, a wireless mouse, a trackball mouse, a tiny laptop mouse, and the list goes on and on.

Although you can disable the touchpad on your laptop, I recommend keeping it active when you use an external mouse. When I'm browsing the Web or just reading a document, I typically revert to the touchpad rather than use the external mouse. (I'm hard to train.)

ID Card or Return Service Sticker

Way back when, your mom would probably write your name on your laptop, just like she wrote your name on your underwear. Today you know why that's important, and you can probably guess why it's necessary.

It's common for businesspeople to simply tape their business cards somewhere on the inside of their laptops, such as just to one side of the touchpad.

The idea here is not only to claim ownership of the laptop but also to pray that if it's ever lost or stolen, the laptop will be recognizable as your own. A good citizen will phone you up and offer to return the laptop that he or she found with your name emblazoned on an ID card.

- ✔ While you're at it, attach a business card to other portable devices you might leave behind, like a portable printer, the power supply, video projector, and so on.

- ✔ A better solution is to use a return service and take advantage of its tamper-resistant asset tags. Refer to Chapter 18 for more information.

Theft-Prevention System

The perfect gift for your dear laptop: some type of cable to keep your laptop from walking off, one of those annoyingly loud my-laptop-has-been-moved alarms, or that special software that tries to "phone home" when the laptop is purloined. Ease your fears! Also refer to Chapter 18 for more information on laptop security — specifically, these types of devices.

Chapter 24

Ten Things to Throw in Your Laptop Case

In This Chapter

▶ The laptop's power cord

▶ A spare battery

▶ An external mouse

▶ Something to clean the laptop

▶ Security devices

▶ Removable media

▶ A set of headphones (or two)

▶ Handy tools

▶ Cables, cables, and more cables

Some people who know that they're going to be away from home just don't know how to pack. For example, although they recognize the need to cook out in the wild, they don't see the impracticality of toting around every cast iron pot, pan, and skillet they own. They probably don't know that lightweight and resourceful camping cooking gear exists. The same holds true for a laptop user set upon taking to the wild.

It comes down to experience. The toil and trials of toting around cast iron cookware every weekend begs for a solution. Likewise, you want to pack your laptop carrying case with the items you need and no more — especially no cast iron peripherals. Plus, you might be unaware of some handy things to pack. To help in your education, this chapter presents ten handy, useful, and necessary items you should consider including in your laptop carrying case.

Power Cord and Brick

This item is one that even I forget. Sometimes I think, "Oh, I'm only going to be gone for an hour, and the battery lasts for three hours, so I don't need the power cord." Then an appointment is canceled, and I have more time but regret not taking the power cord with me.

Always take your power cord and its adapter, or *"brick,"* in your laptop case. You just never know when a wall socket will appear. Take advantage of it!

Spare Battery

If you're blessed with a spare battery for your laptop, bring it!

✔ Don't forget to charge the spare battery before you leave.

✔ Also refer to Chapter 9 for more information on your laptop's battery.

Mouse

Anyone who's used to a real mouse probably won't forget to throw it in the laptop's case, but you never know. I highly recommend using a real (*external, not furry*) mouse with your laptop, especially if your laptop sits somewhere on a table or desk with room for the mouse.

Screen Wipes and Cleaner

Go to the office-supply store and buy some screen wipes and a small, portable bottle of cleaner. Toss 'em in your laptop bag and keep them there. If you can find screen wipes in a smaller, portable size, buy them. Make them a permanent part of your laptop bag.

Laptop Lock

Don't forget your laptop's antitheft device. Whether it's a cable you can connect to something solid or one of those loud, loud audio alarms, you probably want to pack it in your laptop bag.

Refer to Chapter 18 for more information on laptop security.

Removable Media

Saving your stuff to the laptop's hard drive often isn't enough. It helps to have an assortment of alternatives to get that information out of the computer, especially when your laptop isn't connected to a network for easy file transfer. Two such options are optical discs and media cards.

✔ I often toss a few DVD-R discs into my laptop bag when I'm away for a while. For short trips, I use a Secure Digital card.

✔ The discs or media cards can also be used for backing up important data.

✔ When your laptop lacks a media card reader, get a USB thumb drive.

Headphones

The computer is a musical machine! Why bring along an MP3 player when all you really need is that digital music? The music on your laptop, plus some basic earbud headphones, means that your music is wherever you and the laptop are.

I also pack an audio splitter in my laptop case, plus a second pair of headphones. That way, when I go traveling with a companion, we can share the audio from the laptop and enjoy music or a movie together.

Some Necessary Utensils

Consider packing a small "handyman" kit with your laptop. Or, include in your laptop case at least a small regular screwdriver and a Phillips-head screwdriver, a pair of pliers, and a small wire cutter. I also recommend a small utility knife; however, such a thing is likely to be confiscated by airport security.

Cables, Cables, Cables

Cables are good. When you can, bring spare Ethernet, phone, USB, IEEE 1394 (FireWire), S-Video, power, and any other type of spare cables you can muster. You might never use them, but then again, you never know.

✔ You never know where the Internet lurks! Taking along a goodly length of Ethernet cable with your laptop is always a good idea. Then you can instantly connect to any available Ethernet network without having to wait for or (worse) rent a cable.

   ✔ A goodly length is about 6 feet long.

   ✔ Cables don't have to be all tangly, either. If you don't like wrapping up your cables, look for those cables that come with retractable spools at any office-supply store.

   ✔ Another cable to have, if it's available for your laptop, is an automobile "cigarette lighter" DC adapter.

Not the End of the List

You can pack your laptop bag full of so much stuff that the bag will eventually weigh more than you do. There's only so much you can take: portable printers, USB hubs, PC Cards, external disk drives — and the list goes on.

The items mentioned in this chapter are good to *always* have in your laptop bag. Add the other stuff as you need it. Or, when you're traveling, consider putting those things in your checked luggage so that you're not toting the extra weight.

Chapter 25

Ten Tips from a PC Guru

In This Chapter

▶ Remember that you're in charge

▶ Realize that computer nerds love to help

▶ Use antivirus software

▶ Don't fret over upgrading software

▶ Don't reinstall Windows to fix things

▶ Perfectly adjust your monitor

▶ Unplug your PC when you open its case

▶ Subscribe to a computer magazine

▶ Avoid the hype

▶ Don't take this computer stuff too seriously

I don't consider myself a computer expert or genius or guru, though many have called me those nasty names. I'm just a guy who understands how computers work. Or, better than that, I understand how computer people think. They may not be able to express an idea, but I can see what they mean and translate it into English for you. Given that, here are some tips and suggestions so that you and your PC laptop can go off on your merry way.

Remember That You Control the Computer

You bought the computer. You clean up after its messes. You feed it CDs when it asks for them. You control the computer — simple as that. Don't let that computer try to boss you around with its bizarre conversations and funny idiosyncrasies. It's really pretty dopey; the computer is an idiot.

If somebody shoved a flattened can of motor oil in your mouth, would you try to taste it? Of course not. But stick a flattened can of motor oil into a CD drive, and the computer tries to read information from it, thinking that it's a CD. See? It's dumb.

You control that mindless computer just like you control an infant. You must treat it the same way, with respect and caring attention. Don't feel that the computer is bossing you around any more than you feel that a baby is bossing you around during 3 a.m. feedings. They're both helpless creatures, subject to your every whim. Be gentle. But be in charge.

Realize That Most Computer Nerds Love to Help Beginners

It's sad, but almost all computer nerds spend most of their waking hours in front of a computer. They know that it's kind of an oddball thing to do, but they can't help it.

Their guilty consciences are what usually make them happy to help beginners. By passing on knowledge, they can legitimize the hours they while away on their computer stools. Plus, it gives them a chance to brush up on a social skill that's slowly slipping away: the art of *talking* to a person.

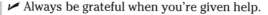

✔ Always be grateful when you're given help.

✔ Avoid relatives who claim to be nerds and desire to "fix" your laptop for you. Don't try to be nice to them; treat your laptop like your wallet. You wouldn't hand it over to anyone, right? Remember, it's easier to sue someone you don't know.

Use Antivirus Software

It's a sad statement, but to really enjoy your laptop, you have to invest in some antivirus software. You really need the protection that such a program offers — even if you're careful. Every PC that's running Windows and connected to the Internet is at risk. There are no exceptions.

✔ See Chapter 18 for more computer security advice.

✔ Yes, pay the money and buy the annual subscription to keep your antivirus software up to date.

✔ Some antivirus programs come with other Internet security software as well, including spyware protection and perhaps a firewall. Yes, those things are worth the cost.

✔ There's no need to run two antivirus (or spyware or firewall) programs at once. One program is enough to do the job.

Understand That Upgrading Software Isn't an Absolute Necessity

Just as the models on the cover of *Vogue* change their clothes each season (or maybe I should say "change their *fashions*" each season), software companies issue perpetual upgrades. Should you automatically buy the upgrade?

Of course not! If you're comfortable with your old software, you have no reason to buy the new version. None!

The software upgrade probably has a few new features in it (although you still haven't had a chance to check out all the features in the current version). And, the upgrade probably has some new bugs in it too, making it crash in new and different ways. Feel free to look at the box, just as you stare at the ladies on the cover of *Vogue*. But don't feel obliged to buy something you don't need.

Don't Reinstall Windows

A myth floating around tech-support sites says that the solution to all your ills is to reinstall Windows. Some suspect that tech-support people even claim that it's common for most Windows users to reinstall at least once a year. That's rubbish.

You *never* need to reinstall Windows. All problems are fixable. It's just that the so-called tech-support people are lazy and resort to a drastic solution as opposed to trying to discover what the true problem is. If you press them, they *will* tell you what's wrong and how to fix it.

In all my years of using a computer, I have never reinstalled Windows or had to reformat my hard drive. It's not even a good idea just to refresh the bits on the hard drive or whatever other nonsense they dish up. There just isn't a need to reinstall Windows ever. Period.

Refer to my book *Troubleshooting Your PC For Dummies* (Wiley Publishing) for all the various solutions you can try instead of reformatting your hard drive or reinstalling Windows.

Perfectly Adjust Your Monitor

I don't have much explaining to do here. Keeping the monitor turned up too brightly is bad for your eyes, and it wears out your monitor more quickly.

To adjust your monitor to pink perfection, turn the brightness (the button with the little sun) all the way up and adjust the contrast (the button with the half moon) until the display looks pleasing. Then, turn the brightness down until you like what you see. That's it!

Unplug Your Laptop When You Upgrade Hardware

If you should need to open the case to upgrade or add an expansion card, you should unplug the laptop before you open it for upgrading.

You don't need to unplug the laptop or even turn it off when you add a USB or FireWire device. (You need to unplug it if you add a USB expansion card, however.)

Subscribe to a Computer Magazine

Oh, why not? Browse the stacks at your local coffeehouse-slash-music-store-slash-bookstore. Try to find a computer magazine that matches your tastes.

- One magazine that seems to be worthy for computer beginners is *SmartComputing*. Look for it in a magazine stand near you.

- What sells me on a magazine are the columns and the *newsy* stuff they put up front.

- Some magazines are all ads. That can be great if you like ads, or it can be boring.

- Avoid the nerdier magazines, but I probably didn't need to tell you that.

Shun the Hype

The computer industry is rife with hype. Even if you subscribe to a family-oriented computer magazine, you still read about the latest this or the next-biggest-trend that. Ignore it!

My gauge for hype is whether the thing that's hyped is shipping as a standard part of a laptop. I check the ads. If they're shipping the item, I write about it. Otherwise, it's a myth and may not happen. Avoid being lured by the hype.

- ✔ When hype becomes reality, you read about it in this book.
- ✔ Former hype I have successfully ignored: Pen Windows, push technology, Web channels, Shockwave, Microsoft Bob, and Windows CE.
- ✔ Hype that eventually became reality: USB, CD-R, shopping on the Web (or *e-commerce*), DVD drives, digital cameras, and home networking.

Don't Take It So Seriously

Hey, simmer down. Computers aren't part of life. They're nothing more than mineral deposits and petroleum products. Close your eyes and take a few deep breaths. Listen to the ocean spray against the deck on the patio; listen to the gurgle of the marble Jacuzzi tub in the master bedroom.

Pretend that you're driving a convertible through a grove of sequoias on a sunny day with the wind whipping through your hair and curling over your ears. Pretend that you're lying on the deck under the sun as the Pacific Princess chugs south toward the islands where friendly, wide-eyed monkeys eat coconut chunks from the palm of your hand.

You're up in a hot air balloon, swirling the first sip of champagne and feeling the bubbles explode atop your tongue. Ahead, to the far left, the castle's spire rises through the clouds, and you can smell Chef Claude's awaiting banquet.

Then slowly open your eyes. It's just a dumb computer. Really. Don't take it too seriously.

Index

• *Symbols and Numerics* •

3M Laptop Privacy Filter, 258
802.11 networking protocols, 177–178

• *A* •

abacus, 8
AC (alternating current)
  defined, 131, 261
  keeping battery installed while using,
    138–139
accessories
  case
    cleaning, 126
    manufacturer's, 36, 252–253
    overview, 251–252
    packing, 328–330
    recommended brands, 254–255
    recommended features, 253–254
    security and, 269
  cooling fan pad, 147, 150, 323
  docking station, 29, 38, 322
  external keyboard, 158–159, 324
  external mouse, 77–78, 160, 325, 328
  ID card, 325
  minivac, 324
  port replicator, 29, 38, 66, 322
  return service sticker, 325
  spare battery, 322
  theft-prevention system, 326
  USB lamp, 324
account, user
  Administrator, 46
  choosing, 47–48
  configuring, 114–115
  Guest, 274
  modifying, 95

activity timer, 54
ad hoc network
  People Near Me feature, 286–287
  Windows Meeting Space, 287–290
adapter
  legacy, 147
  power, 261, 328
  wireless networking, 146, 179, 259
Ad-Aware program, 223
Add Files button, 280
Add Folders button, 280
Add Printer Wizard, 123, 173–175
Administrator account, 46
Adobe Acrobat (PDF) file, 125
Advanced System Settings link, 295
Advanced tab, 202
Advantages of laptop, 19–21
air travel
  airplane mode, 259–260
  carry-on luggage, 257
  inflight power, 260–261
  inflight usage, 260
  inspection of laptops, 257–258
  onboard storage, 258
alcohol, 127
alkaline battery, 130
All Programs menu, 80
alphanumeric keys, 69
Alt+Esc key combination, 316
alternating current (AC)
  defined, 131, 261
  keeping battery installed while using,
    138–139
AltGr (Alternative Graphic) key, 69
Always Available Offline dialog box,
    240, 243
AMD Mobile Sempron processor, 26

AMD Turion 64 processor, 26
anti-spyware software, 214, 222–223
antivirus software
   checking for, 219–220
   defined, 214
   disabling, 221
   overview, 218–219
   protecting from viruses, 221
   scanning for viruses, 220
AOL Call Alert, 205
arcade games, 112, 147
area code, 205–207
Area Code Rules tab, 205
Ask Me Later button, 217
asset tag, 268–269
audio hardware, 28, 100, 147, 329
audio note, 112
audio splitter, 329
automatic synchronization, 243
automatic updates, 306–307
Avast! Antivirus software, 219
AVG Anti-Virus software, 219

• *B* •

Back Up Files button, 278–279
Back Up Files window, 279
Back Up Your Computer link, 278
background, 49–50, 93, 115–116
backpack, 255
Backspace key, 109
Backup and Restore Center icon, 278
Backup and Restore Center window,
   278, 280
backup copy, 276
backups
   initial, 277–279
   overview, 276–277
   preparing for, 277
   restoring from, 280
   schedule, 279

bag for laptop
   cleaning, 126
   manufacturer's, 36, 252–253
   overview, 251–252
   packing, 328–330
   recommended brands, 254–255
   recommended features, 253–254
   security and, 269
bar-code asset tag, 269
base station, wireless, 179
battery
   charging, 38–39, 137, 255
   disk drives, 315
   disposal of, 139
   draining, 134, 314, 318
   icons, 132–133, 135
   keeping installed while using AC power,
      138–139
   life of, 17, 116, 129
   light, 67, 133
   locating, 131–132
   low-battery warning, 135–136, 318–319
   monitor brightness, 314–315
   monitoring, 132–134
   pre-purchase considerations, 25
   protecting terminals, 317
   RAM, 315–316
   spare, 137–138, 322, 328
   storing, 138, 317–318
   temperature, 132, 317
   troubleshooting, 303
   types of, 130–131
   what to avoid, 313–314
   when power gets low, 134–135
biometric device, 48, 100
BIOS Setup program, 45
bits per second (bps), 198
Bluetooth wireless networking, 67, 179
booting, 44
boxes, 36. *See also* unpacking laptops
bps (bits per second), 198

brand names
  considering, 24
  laptop bags, 255
Briefcase feature, 238
brightness level, 142–143
broadband access
  disconnecting, 192
  overview, 189–190
  public networks, 190–191
broadband modem, 190
Browse dialog box, 114
browser, wireless network, 181
bugs, 306
buttons
  Add Files, 280
  Add Folders, 280
  Ask Me Later, 217
  Back Up Files, 278–279
  Change Default Preferences, 208
  Change Settings, 208
  Disconnect, 185, 192, 195
  Edit, 205
  function, 101
  Keep Blocking, 217
  moon, 43
  power
    controlling, 59–60
    locating, 43–44
    software, 55, 59–60
    on Tablet PC, 100
    using, 44
  pray-and-press, 43
  Properties, 273
  Receive a Fax Now, 212
  Restore Files, 280
  Save Settings and Start Backup, 279
  sleep, 43, 53
  Start, 50
  Sync All, 241
  Unblock, 217
  wheel, 75

buying laptops
  communications choices, 28
  core computer parts, 25–27
  docking station, 29
  energy management hardware, 28–29
  key items, 24–25
  optical discs, 27–28
  overview, 23
  port replicator, 29
  process of, 30
  service, 29–30
  support, 29–30
  unnecessary items, 23–24
  warranties, 30

● **C** ●

C: (Drive C), 277
cable
  Ethernet, 165, 196, 264, 329
  packing, 329–330
  security, 66, 270–271
  USB, 123, 149
café computing, 261–263
calculator, 8
call waiting, 205
Calling Card tab, 207
camera
  digital, 146
  video, 66, 147
  webcam, 100, 147
Canon Bubble Jet portable printer, 121
Caps Lock state, 67
carrier code, 200
case, laptop
  cleaning, 126
  manufacturer's, 36, 252–253
  overview, 251–252
  packing, 328–330
  recommended brands, 254–255
  recommended features, 253–254
  security and, 269

Cat 5 (Ethernet) cable, 165, 196, 264, 329
CD (compact disc) drives, 27
cellular modem, 198
central processing unit (CPU), 25, 27
Centrino Duo processor, 26
Centrino technology, 26
CF (CompactFlash) media card, 157
Change Default Preferences button, 208
Change Settings button, 208
Change Settings link, 279
Character Pad mode, 107, 108
charging batteries, 38–39, 67, 137, 255
check boxes
    Check for New Messages Every [blank]
        Minutes, 232
    To Disable Call Waiting Dial, 204
    Disconnect a Call If Idle for More
        Than, 208
    Send Messages Immediately, 232
    Use Dialing Rules, 207
Check for New Messages Every [blank]
    Minutes check box, 232
checklist, travel, 255–256
chipset, 45
Choose a Different Restore Point
    option, 297
cigarette lighter power, 261
clamshell design, 13
cleaning
    case, 126
    keyboard, 127
    screen, 127, 328
clicking, stylus, 105
client-server network, 169
closing programs, 51
cold boots, 44
colleges, laptop use in, 21
color coding, keyboard, 69
communication features
    modem
        broadband, 190
        cellular, 198

dialup, 193–195, 203–207
dialup access, 203–208
disabling, 140–141
in early laptops, 12
fax, 208–212
overview, 28, 197–198
ports for, 65
setting up, 199–203
networking
    accessing printers, 172–175
    accessing storage, 171–172
    finding other computers on network,
        170–171
    hardware, 164–166
    overview, 28, 163, 237
    peer-to-peer network, 169–170
    sharing folders, 175–176
    software, 166–169
overview, 28
wireless networking
    connecting, 179–182
    disconnecting, 185–186, 192
    hardware, 178–179
    lease, 184
    light, 67
    MAC address, 183–184
    overview, 28
    pay-service wireless network, 185
    protocol, 177–178
    SSID, 182–183
compact disc (CD) drives, 27
CompactFlash (CF) media card, 157
Compaq III computer, 12–13
Compaq SLT computer, 13–14, 72
compressed air, 127
Compressed Folder attachments, 221
computer description, 167
computer name, 167
Computer Name/Domain Changes dialog
    box, 167, 169
Computer window, 83–84, 87
computrace.com, 276

configuring
  dialup access, 193–194
  displays, 115–116
  fingerprint readers, 48
  laptops, 37
  modems, 199–203
  presentations, 283–285
  Remote Desktop, 244–245
Connect to a Network window, 180, 185, 192–193, 195
Connect To command, 195
Connect to Projector command, 290
connecting. *See also* disconnecting
  desktops and laptops
    overview, 235–236
    Remote Desktop, 244–247
    synchronization, 238–243
    via cables, 236–237
    via Ethernet, 237
    via portable media, 236
  dialup access, 194–195
  printers, 123
  to wireless networking, 179–182
connection speed, 195
Connection tab, 231
Control Panel
  modems, setting up, 199–200
  Network and Sharing Center, 94
  overview, 89–90
  Personalization window, 93–94
  Phone and Modem Options, 95
  Power Options window, 94–95
  Printers window, 95
  Start menu, 90–91
  Tablet PC settings, 93, 102–104
  user accounts, modifying, 95
  Windows Mobility Center, 92–93
Control Panel Classic View, 90
Control Panel Home, 89–90
Control Panel item, 81
convertible Tablet PC, 98, 102
cooling fan pad, 147, 150, 323

Core Duo chip, 26
cost
  laptop, 24, 30
  Tablet PC, 99
counting board, 8
CPU (central processing unit), 25, 27
credit card, 30
Critical battery action item, 136
Critical battery level item, 136
crucial.com, 308
cursor control pad, 100
cursor-control keys, 69
custom folder, 86
custom port, 64
customization questions, 46
Customize link, 191
cyberspace meeting, 286
cycling power, 44

• D •

data, protecting
  Guest account, 274
  Setup password, 271–272
  Windows account password, 272–274
  Windows locking command, 275
data thief, 271
DC (direct current), 131, 261
default printer, 124
defragmentation, 303
Dell 320LT laptop, 16
desktop, Windows
  overview, 49–50, 80
  placing home folder on, 86
Desktop Background link, 316
desktop computer
  versus laptops, 19–20
  mice for, 78
desktop-laptop connections
  overview, 235–236
  Remote Desktop, 244–247
  synchronization, 238–243

desktop-laptop connections *(continued)*
  via cables, 236–237
  via Ethernet, 237
  via portable media, 236
Device Manager window, 140–141
Dialing Rules tab, 203–204
dialog boxes
  Always Available Offline, 240, 243
  Browse, 114
  Computer Name/Domain Changes,
    167, 169
  Display Properties, 285
  Display Settings, 115–116, 284
  Edit Location, 205, 207
  File Download Security Warning, 118
  Location Information, 199
  Mouse Properties, 76–77, 302
  Network Connection Status, 184
  New Area Code Rule, 205
  New Location, 203
  Options, 110, 231–232
  Page Setup, 125
  Pen and Input Devices, 93, 102–104,
    106, 110
  Phone and Modem Options,
    199–203, 205
  Power Options, 59–60, 135–136
  Print, 124–125, 210
  Properties, 141, 196, 201–202, 208
  Remote Desktop Connection, 245–246
  Save As, 119
  System Configuration, 300
  System Properties, 167, 244, 295–296
  User Account Control, 117, 223, 244,
    259, 278, 297, 300, 307
  Windows Firewall Settings, 216, 245
dialup access
  area codes, 205–207
  calling card info, 207
  configuring, 193–194
  connecting, 194–195
  disconnecting, 195
  location, 203–205
dialup modem, 197

digital audio output, 28
digital camera, 146
digital stylus
  gestures and flicks, 109–110
  Input Panel, 106–109
  training, 104–106
  using finger as, 110–111
digital subscriber line (DSL), 190
digital video connector, 283
digital video port, 65
digitizer pen
  gestures and flicks, 109–110
  Input Panel, 106–109
  training, 104–106
  using finger as, 110–111
direct current (DC), 131, 261
disabling
  antivirus software, 221
  automatic e-mail checking, 231–232
  modems, 140–141
disadvantages, laptop, 21
discarding laptops, 36
Disconnect a Call If Idle for More Than
    check box, 208
Disconnect button, 185, 192, 195
disconnect timeout, 207–208
disconnecting
  after retrieving e-mail, 231
  broadband access, 192
  dialup access, 195
  wireless networking, 185–186
dishwashing liquid, 126
disk defragmentation, 303
disk storage, networked, 171–172
display
  angle of, 42
  brightness of, 314–315
  cleaning, 127, 328
  LCD, 12–13, 24–25, 127
  pre-purchase considerations, 24–25
  setting up, 115–116
  Tablet PC, 99–100
Display Properties dialog box, 285
Display Settings dialog box, 115–116, 284

disposal, battery, 139
distraction ploys, 270
Do Not Download It from the Server option, 234
Do Nothing option, 59
docking station, 29, 38, 322
Documents folder, 86
double clicking, stylus, 105
downloading programs, 118–119
downstream cable end, 149
dragging
  with digital stylus, 105
  with touchpads, 74
draining batteries, 134, 314, 318
Dreaded Memory Effect, The, 134
Drive C (C:), 277
driver, 52, 123, 308
drives
  cleaning around, 126
  flash, 148, 157, 182
  hard, 25–27, 272, 309
  microdrive, 158
  optical, 27, 62, 119, 152
  powering down, 315
  removable, 152–154, 156
DSL (digital subscriber line), 190
DVD drives, 27
Dynabook computer, 8–9

• E •

ebags.com, 255
Eddie Bauer soft briefcase, 254
Edit button, 205
Edit Location dialog box, 205, 207
802.11 networking protocols, 177–178
ejecting
  optical discs, 62
  PC Cards, 63–64
e-mail
  accessing from another computer, 229–230
  disabling automatic checking, 231–232
  disconnecting after retrieving, 231

forwarding, 230–231
  group mailings, 232
  overview, 227–228
  password, 273
  reading on Web, 228
  skipping messages over given size, 233–234
  Web-based account, 188, 229
EmPower DC power, 261
endlessly forwarding loop, 230
energy management
  battery
    charging, 38–39, 137, 255
    disk drives, 315
    disposal of, 139
    draining, 134, 314, 318
    icons, 132–133, 135
    keeping installed while using AC power, 138–139
    life of, 17, 116, 129
    light, 67, 133
    locating, 131–132
    low-battery warning, 135–136, 318–319
    monitor brightness, 314–315
    monitoring, 132–134
    pre-purchase considerations, 25
    protecting terminals, 317
    RAM, 315–316
    spare, 137–138, 322, 328
    storing, 138, 317–318
    temperature, 132, 317
    troubleshooting, 303
    types of, 130–131
    what to avoid, 313–314
    when power gets low, 134–135
  hardware for, 28–29
  plan for
    creating, 142–143
    using, 141–142
  power-saving tricks and tips, 139–141
  software for, 54
  troubleshooting, 303
engraving tool, 268
Enter Initialization Commands box, 202

Enter key, 109
error-checking, 303
Ethernet
  cable, 165, 196, 264, 329
  overview, 237
  port, 28, 65
Eudora e-mail program, 234
euro symbol, 69
Exceptions tab, 245
expansion
  external keyboard, 158–159
  external mouse, 160
  media card, 157–158
  PC Card, 154–156
  second monitor, 159–160
  via USB port, 145–154
exploding laptops, 131
Extend the Desktop onto This Monitor
  option, 284
extension, filename, 120
extension cables, USB, 149
external keyboard, 158–159
external media backups, 276
external monitor, 283–285
external mouse, 77–78, 160, 325, 328
external optical drive, 119, 152
external USB storage
  adding, 152–153
  overview, 146
  removing, 153–154
external video port, 285

• F •

F1-F12 (function) keys, 69
Fax Central window, 211
fax icon, 209
fax machine, 125
fax modem
  Fax Central window, 211
  finding, 209

  overview, 208–209
  receiving faxes, 212
  sending faxes, 210–211
Fax Setup window, 210
File Download Security Warning dialog
  box, 118
filename extension, 120
files
  defined, 84
  sharing, 175–176
  synchronizing, 241–243
  zip, 221
Find Gold in Windows Vista, 240
fingerprint reader, 48, 100, 276
firewall
  monitoring, 217–218
  overview, 214–215
  using, 215–217
FireWire standard, 65, 151
flash drive, 148, 157, 182
flash media card slot, 62
flash memory card, 157–158, 276, 329
flash memory card reader, 152
flicking, stylus, 109–110
Flicks tab, 110
Fn (function) key, 71–72, 285
folders
  custom, 86
  defined, 84
  home, 85–86
  Program Files, 87–88
  read-only, 172
  sharing, 171–172, 175–176
  special, 86
forwarding e-mail, 230–231
fuel cell, 19, 132
full computer name, 167
full-size keyboard, 324
function (F1-F12) keys, 69
function (Fn) key, 71–72, 285
function buttons, 101

• G •

game controller, 147
games, 112, 147
GB (gigabyte), 26
General tab, 232
general timeout, 208
generic battery, 138
gestures, stylus, 109–110
GHz (gigahertz), 26
gigabyte (GB), 26
gigahertz (GHz), 26
Gmail, 229
Guest account, 274
Guest Account icon, 274

• H •

handyman kit, 329
Hang Up after Sending and Receiving
    option, 231
hard drive
  backups
    initial, 277–279
    overview, 276–277
    preparing for, 277
    restoring from, 280
  pre-purchase considerations, 25–27
  replacing, 309
  stealing information from, 272
hardware
  compatibility, 17
  energy management, 28–29
  networking, 164–166
  Tablet PC, 99–102
  unpacking, 35
  upgrading, 308–309
  wireless networking, 178–179
Hardware and Sound option, 199
hardware firewall, 215–217
headphone port, 65

headphones, 146, 329
hexidecimal, 184
hibernation, 54–55, 59, 303, 319
hijacking, 214, 223–224
history of laptop
  advantages of, 19–21
  disadvantages of, 21
  early, 13–14
  future, 18–19
  luggables, 10–11
  lunch buckets, 12–13
  Model 100, 11–12
  notebooks, 15–17
  Osborne 1, 9
  portability, 7–8
  Tablet computer, 17–18
  weight of, 14–15
  Xerox Dynabook, 8–9
home folder, 84
hot batteries, 132
hot swapping, 150
hotels, 264–265
Hotmail, 229
hub
  USB, 150–151
  wireless network, 164–165, 181
hybrid sleep mode, 52
hybrid Tablet PC models, 98–99

• I •

IBM compatibility, 10–11
icons
  Backup and Restore Center, 278
  battery, 132–133, 135
  Control Panel, 90
  desktop, 49–50, 86
  fax, 209
  Input Tablet, 108–109
  Install program, 119
  Network, 88

icons *(continued)*
Networking Guys, 94
notification area, 82
padlock, 51, 56, 275
Phone and Modem Options, 95
Safely Remove Hardware, 156
Security Center, 219
Setup, 119
shield, 52, 116
shortcut, 80
Sync Center, 237–240, 243
Turn Off the Guest Account, 274
used in book, 3–4
Windows, 80
Windows Firewall, 215–217
Wireless Network Connection, 196, 259
ID card, 325
Idle Time before Hanging Up option, 208
IEEE 1394 standard, 65, 151
If My Computer Is Not Connected at This
    Time drop-down list, 232
image, account, 114
inactivity timer, 54
inflight laptop usage, 260–261
information storage, 83. *See also* storage
infrared communication, 28
initial backups, 277–279
InkBall game, 112, 147
input, 84, 235–236
Input Panel, 106–109
Input Tablet icon, 108
input/output (I/O), 235–236
inspection, airport, 257–258
Install program icon, 119
installing
    external mouse software, 78
    software, 117–119
    updates, 52
    Windows, 46
instructions, unpacking, 34
Intel Centrino Duo processor, 26
Intel Centrino technology, 26
Intel Core Duo processor, 26

Intel Pentium M processor, 26
internal expansion options, 24, 308
Internet, 188
broadband access, 189–192
dialup access, 193–195, 203–207
e-mail
    accessing from another computer,
        229–230
    disabling automatic checking, 231–232
    disconnecting after retrieving, 231
    forwarding, 230–231
    group mailings, 232
    overview, 227–228
    password, 273
    reading on Web, 228
    skipping messages over given size,
        233–234
    Web-based account, 188, 229
installing programs from, 118–119
mobility, 187–188
offline Web browsing, 226–227
security
    firewall, 214–218
    malware, 219, 222–224
    phone home capability, 275–276
    spyware, 214, 222–223
    virus, 214, 218–221
shared access, 196
Web sites
    anti-spyware solutions, 223
    antivirus software, 219
    author's, 4
    batteries, 138
    e-mail programs, 229, 234
    incoming call monitors, 205
    laptop cases, 255
    memory, 308
    Microsoft, 282, 301
    phone-home services, 276
    power adapters, 261
    Real Virtual Network Computing, 247
    screen cleaning products, 127
    STOP program, 269

Internet Explorer toolbar, 226
Internet service provider (ISP), 188
Into the Comet short story, 8
invoices, shipping, 34
I/O (input/output), 235–236

• J •

jack, 198
Journal program, 111
JumpDrive, 148

• K •

Kaspersky antivirus protection, 219
Keep Blocking button, 217
Kensington Security Slot (K-Slot), 66
keyboard
  alphanumeric keys, 69
  Alt+Esc key combination, 316
  AltGr key, 69
  Backspace key, 109
  cleaning, 127
  cursor-control keys, 69
  custom keys, 72–73
  Enter key, 109
  external, 158–159
  full-size, 324
  function (F1-F12) keys, 69
  function (Fn) key, 71–72, 285
  layout, 68–69
  Num Lock key, 67, 70–71, 301
  numeric keypad, 69–71, 147, 159
  Shift key, 69
  Space key, 109
  Tab key, 109
  troubleshooting, 301
  Win key, 275
  Windows key, 275
keypad, numeric, 69–71, 147, 159
Klear Screen, 127
K-Slot (Kensington Security Slot), 66

• L •

lamp, USB, 147, 324
LAN (local-area network), 170–171, 189
Laptop Privacy Filter, 258
laptops
  advantages of, 19–21
  buying, 23–30
  disadvantages of, 21
  disposing of, 36
  exploding, 131
  marking, 268–269
  portability, 7–8
  turning on/off, 41–44, 51–58
  unpacking, 33–37
  waking up, 44
  weight of, 14–15
Last Known Good Configuration
    option, 299
LCD monitor, 12–13, 24–25, 127
lead acid battery, 130
lease, wireless networking, 184
Leave Meeting command, 290
legacy adapter, 147
lid
  opening, 42–43
  shutting options, 56–58
lightning storm, 39
lights, 67–68, 133
Li-ion (lithium-ion) battery, 130, 134,
    137, 314
line in port, 65
line jack, 198
line out port, 65
links
  Advanced System Settings, 295
  Back Up Your Computer, 278
  Change Settings, 279
  Customize, 191
  Desktop Background, 316
  Manage Another Account, 274
  Scan, 222
  Share a Program or Your Desktop, 290

lint-free cloth, 127
lithium-ion (Li-ion) battery, 130, 134, 137, 314
local-area network (LAN), 170–171, 189
location
    dialup access, 203–204
    laptop, 37–38
Location Information dialog box, 199
lock, laptop, 328
locking Windows, 56, 275
logging in/on to Windows, 46–49
logging off Windows, 55–56
lojackforlaptops.com, 276
long distance numbers, 205
Low battery action item, 136
Low battery level item, 136
Low battery notification item, 136
low-battery warning, 135–136, 318–319
luggable computers, 10–11
lunch bucket computers, 12–13

• *M* •

MAC address, 183–184
maintenance, laptop, 303–304
Make My Picture Available option, 286
malware, 219, 222–224
Manage Another Account link, 274
Manage Network Connections option, 196, 259
manual, laptop, 35
manual network connections, 182–183
marking laptops, 268–269
mass storage, 25–27, 153. *See also* hard drive
MB (megabyte), 26
McAfee VirusScan software, 219
media card, 157–158, 276, 329
media card reader, 152
media card slot, 62
Meeting Space software, 286
meetings, 285–290
megabyte (MB), 26

memory, pre-purchase considerations, 25
memory card, 157–158, 276, 329
memory card reader, 152
memory card slot, 62
memory chips, 272, 308
Memory Stick Duo media card, 157
Memory Stick/PRO media card, 157
menus
    All Programs, 80
    Shutdown, 53
    Start, 80–82, 90–91
mice
    external, 77–78, 160, 325, 328
    overview, 73
    pointer, 76–77, 302
    thumball, 73
    touchpad, 74–75
    TrackPoint, 75–76
    wheel button, 75
microcomputers, 41
microconnector, 149
microdrive, 158
microphone, 100
microphone port, 65
Microsoft PowerPoint program, 281–283
Microsoft Windows
    account password, 272–274
    configuring user account, 114–115
    Control Panel
        modems, setting up, 199–200
        Network and Sharing Center, 94
        overview, 89–90
        Personalization window, 93–94
        Phone and Modem Options, 95
        Power Options window, 94–95
        Printers window, 95
        Start menu, 90–91
        Tablet PC settings, 93, 102–104
        user accounts, modifying, 95
        Windows Mobility Center, 92–93
    desktop, 49–50, 80, 86
    folders, 84–86
    installing, 46

locking, 56, 275
logging in, 46–49
logging off, 55–56
notification area, 82
overview, 45, 79–80
Program Files folder, 87–88
restarting, 52, 294
setting up display, 115–116
Start menu, 80–82
storage, 83–84
UACs, 116–117
updating, 306–307
upgrading, 307–308
WinNT folder, 87
Microsoft Windows Backup
  initial, 277–279
  overview, 276–277
  preparing for, 277
  restoring from, 280
Microsoft Windows Collaboration, 288
Microsoft Windows Defender, 222–223
Microsoft Windows Firewall
  monitoring, 217–218
  overview, 214–215
  using, 215–217
Microsoft Windows Journal program, 111
Microsoft Windows Mail
  accessing from another computer,
    229–230
  disabling automatic checking, 231–232
  disconnecting after retrieving, 231
  forwarding, 230–231
  group mailings, 232
  overview, 227–228
  password, 273
  skipping messages over given size,
    233–234
Microsoft Windows Meeting Space,
  286–290
Microsoft Windows Mobility Center,
  92–93, 239, 315
Microsoft Windows Security Center, 219
Microsoft Windows Sidebar, 50, 133

Microsoft Wireless Notebook Laser
    Mouse 6000, 78
miniconnector, 149
minivac, 324
MMC (MutliMediaCard), 157
mobile CPU, 26
mobile Internet use, 187–188
mobile phone recharger, 147
Mobile Sempron processor, 26
Mobility Center, 92–93, 239, 315
Model 100 computer, 11–12
modem
  broadband, 190
  cellular, 198
  dialup
    area codes, 205–207
    calling card info, 207
    configuring, 193–194
    connecting, 194–195
    disconnecting, 195
    location, 203–205
  dialup access, 203–208
  disabling, 140–141
  in early laptops, 12
  fax
    Fax Central window, 211
    finding, 209
    overview, 208–209
    receiving faxes, 212
    sending faxes, 210–211
  overview, 28, 197–198
  ports for, 65
  setting up, 199–203
Modem tab, 201–202
modem-timeout value, 208
monitor
  angle of, 42
  brightness of, 314–315
  cleaning, 127, 328
  LCD, 12–13, 24–25, 127
  port, 65
  pre-purchase considerations, 24–25
  second, 159–160
  Tablet PC, 99–100

monitoring
  battery, 132–134
  Windows firewall, 217–218
moon button, 43
motherboard, 308
mouse
  external, 77–78, 160, 325, 328
  overview, 73
  pointer, 76–77, 302
  thumball, 73
  touchpad, 74–75
  TrackPoint, 75–76
  wheel button, 75
Mouse Properties dialog box, 76–77, 302
mouse/fingerprint reader, 276
MS Config (System Configuration Utility),
    299–300
Music folder, 86
muting modems, 202
MutliMediaCard (MMC), 157
My Book external USB hard drive, 277
My Location item, 204–205
MyWay Mail, 229

• *N* •

NEC UltraLite laptop, 14–15
NetBook computer, 19
Network and Internet item, 286
Network and Sharing Center window, 94,
    167, 191, 196, 259
Network Connection Status dialog
    box, 184
network interface card (NIC), 164
Network window, 88, 239–240, 243
networking
  accessing printers, 172–175
  accessing storage, 171–172
  finding other computers on network,
    170–171
  hardware, 164–166
  overview, 28, 163, 237
  peer-to-peer network, 169–170
  sharing folders, 175–176
  software, 166–169
  wireless
    connecting, 179–182
    disconnecting, 185–186, 192
    hardware, 178–179
    lease, 184
    light, 67
    MAC address, 183–184
    overview, 28
    pay-service wireless network, 185
    protocol, 177–178
    SSID, 182–183
Networking Guys icon, 94
New Area Code Rule dialog box, 205
New Location dialog box, 203
New Message Rule window, 233
NIC (network interface card), 164
nickel-cadmium (NiCad) battery, 130
nickel-metal hydride (NiMH) battery,
    130–131
Norton AntiVirus software, 219
notebook computers, 15–17
notes, 112
notification area, 50, 82
Num Lock key, 67, 70–71, 301
numeric keypad, 69–71, 147, 159

• *O* •

oakley.com, 255
Offline Files folder, 242
Offline Files Sync Schedule Wizard, 243
Offline Files window, 240
offline Web browsing, 226–227
on-off switch, 41
On-screen Keyboard mode, 107, 108
opening laptop lid, 42–43
operating system, Windows
  account password, 272–274
  configuring user account, 114–115
  Control Panel
    modems, setting up, 199–200
    Network and Sharing Center, 94
    overview, 89–90

Personalization window, 93–94
Phone and Modem Options, 95
Power Options window, 94–95
Printers window, 95
Start menu, 90–91
Tablet PC settings, 93, 102–104
user accounts, modifying, 95
Windows Mobility Center, 92–93
desktop, 49–50, 80, 86
folders, 84–86
installing, 46
locking, 56, 275
logging in, 46–49
logging off, 55–56
notification area, 82
overview, 45, 79–80
Program Files folder, 87–88
restarting, 52, 294
setting up display, 115–116
Start menu, 80–82
storage, 83–84
UACs, 116–117
updating, 306–307
upgrading, 307–308
WinNT folder, 87
optical disc, 27, 35, 62, 329
optical drive
external, 119, 152
overview, 27
tray-type, 62
Options dialog box, 110, 231–232
Osborne 1 computer, 9–10
output, 84, 235–236

• *P* •

packing laptop cases
cables, 329–330
handyman kit, 329
headphones, 329
lock, 328
mouse, 328
power cord and brick, 328

removable media, 329
screen wipes and cleaner, 328
spare battery, 328
padlock icon, 51, 56, 275
Page Setup dialog box, 125
passive virus scan, 220
pass-through USB device, 151
password
administrator, 46
network storage, 171–172
Setup, 271–272
Windows account, 272–274
Password text box, 273
patches, 307
pay-service wireless network, 185
PC Card, 151, 154–156, 198
PCs For Dummies, 263
PDF (Adobe Acrobat) file, 125
peer-to-peer network, 169–170, 189
pen, digitizer
gestures and flicks, 109–110
Input Panel, 106–109
training, 104–106
using finger as, 110–111
Pen and Input Devices dialog box, 93,
102–104, 106, 110
pen tether, 102
Pen Windows, 99
Pentium M processor, 26
People Near Me feature, 286–287
personal information manager (PIM), 238
Personalization window, 93–94, 115,
284, 316
Phillips-head screwdriver, 329
phishing, 223–224
Phone and Modem Options dialog box,
199–203, 205
Phone and Modem Options icon, 95
phone home capability, 275–276
phone jack, 194, 198
phone port, 65
Physical Address item, 184
Pictures folder, 86

PIM (personal information manager), 238
pin-on area, 80
pliers, 329
plugging in, 38–39
Pointer Options tab, 77, 302
Pointers tab, 302
port replicator, 29, 38, 66, 322
portability, computer, 7–8
portable printer, 121
ports
  types of, 64–66
  USB, 146–147
power adapter, 261, 328
power brick, 16, 328
power button
  controlling, 59–60
  locating, 43–44
  software, 55, 59–60
  on Tablet PC, 100
  using, 44
power cord, 38, 328
power management
  battery
    charging, 38–39, 137, 255
    disk drives, 315
    disposal of, 139
    draining, 134, 314, 318
    icons, 132–133, 135
    keeping installed while using AC
      power, 138–139
    life of, 17, 116, 129
    light, 67, 133
    locating, 131–132
    low-battery warning, 135–136, 318–319
    monitor brightness, 314–315
    monitoring, 132–134
    pre-purchase considerations, 25
    protecting terminals, 317
    RAM, 315–316
    spare, 137–138, 322, 328
    storing, 138, 317–318
    temperature, 132, 317
  troubleshooting, 303
  types of, 130–131
  what to avoid, 313–314
  when power gets low, 134–135
hardware for, 28–29
plan for
  creating, 142–143
  using, 141–142
power-saving tricks and tips, 139–141
software for, 54
troubleshooting, 303
Power Options dialog box, 59–60,
  135–136
Power Options System Settings window,
  57–58
Power Options window, 57–58, 94–95,
  141–143, 315
power port, 65
power sockets, 263
power up, 44
powered hub, 151
powering laptops on/off
  hibernation, 54–55
  locking Windows, 56
  logging off, 55–56
  opening lid, 42–43
  overview, 41–42
  power button, 43–44
  properly, 51–52
  restarting Windows, 52
  shutting down, 51–52
  shutting lid options, 56–58
  Sleep mode, 52–54
  software power button, 55
  when laptop won't cooperate, 58
PowerPoint program, 281–283
pray-and-press button, 43
preinstalled software, 121
presentations
  overview, 281–282
  PowerPoint program, 282–283
  setting up, 283–285

prices
  laptop, 24, 30
  Tablet PC, 99
Print command, 210
Print dialog box, 124–125, 210
Print to File option, 125
printer
  connecting to laptop, 123
  default, 124
  displaying Printers window, 122
  network, 172–175
  nonprinter suggestions, 125
  overview, 121
  Print dialog box, 124–125
Printers window, 95, 122, 124, 172–173,
      209–210
processor, pre-purchase
      considerations, 25
Program Files folder, 87–88
programs
  blocking, 218
  installing, 117–119
  uninstalling, 120–121
projector, 285
Properties button, 273
Properties dialog box, 141, 196,
      201–202, 208
protecting data. *See also* security
  Guest account, 274
  Setup password, 271–272
  Windows account password, 272–274
  Windows locking command, 275
protocol, wireless networking, 177–178
Public folder, 175–176
public network, 180–181, 190–191
purchasing laptops
  communications choices, 28
  core computer parts, 25–27
  docking station, 29
  energy management hardware, 28–29
  key items, 24–25
  optical discs, 27–28

overview, 23
port replicator, 29
process of, 30
service, 29–30
support, 29–30
unnecessary items, 23–24
warranties, 30

• *Q* •

quitting options, 82

• *R* •

Radio Shack Model 100 computer, 11–12
RAM
  adding, 315–316
  pre-purchase considerations, 27
  saving battery life, 316
read-only folder, 172
Real Virtual Network Computing
      (VNC), 247
rebooting, 44
Receive a Fax Now button, 212
Recently Used Programs area, 80
recordable optical drive, 27
registering laptops, 269
registration card, 269
Remember This Password option, 194
Remote Desktop
  accessing on network, 245–247
  setting up for, 244–245
Remote Desktop Connection dialog box,
      245–246
removable drive, 152–154, 156
removable media, 62–63, 329
removable storage device
  adding, 152–153
  removing, 153–154
repairing laptops, 29–30
replicator, port, 29, 38, 66, 322

resetting laptops, 44
resolution
  display, 115
  projector, 285
resources, network, 165
restarting
  laptops, 44
  Windows, 52, 294
Restore Files button, 280
restore point, 296–297, 306
restoring from backups, 280
return service sticker, 325
right-clicking, stylus, 105
right-dragging, stylus, 105
RJ-45 port, 65
root port, 151
router, 164–165, 190

• *S* •

Safe mode
  entering, 299–300
  starting laptops in, 301
  testing in, 300–301
Safely Remove Hardware icon, 156
satellite Internet service, 190
Save As dialog box, 119
Save Settings and Start Backup
    button, 279
saving work, 51
Scan link, 222
scanners, 146–147
Scheme drop-down list, 302
schools, laptop use in, 21
screen
  angle of, 42
  brightness of, 314–315
  cleaning, 127, 328
  LCD, 12–13, 24–25, 127
  pre-purchase considerations, 24–25
  Tablet PC, 99–100
screen saver, 116, 143
screwdriver, 329

SD (Secure Digital) media card, 157, 329
second computer, 20
second monitor, 159–160
Secure Digital (SD) media card, 157, 329
security
  backups
    initial, 277–279
    overview, 276–277
    preparing for, 277
    restoring from, 280
  cables, 66, 270–271
  cases, 269
  fingerprint reader, 48, 100, 276
  firewall
    monitoring, 217–218
    overview, 214–215
    using, 215–217
  malware, 219, 222–224
  marking laptops, 268–269
  password, 46, 171–172, 271–274
  phone home capability, 275–276
  protecting data
    Guest account, 274
    Setup password, 271–272
    Windows account password, 272–274
    Windows locking command, 275
  registering laptops, 269
  Setup program, 45
  shared folders, 175–176
  spyware, 214, 222–223
  theft, 268–271
  UACs, 116
  USB devices for, 147
  virus
    antivirus software, 214, 218–219, 221
    checking for, 219–220
    protecting from, 221
    scanning for, 220
  vulnerabilities, 267–268
Security Center icon, 219
Security Tracking of Office Property
    (STOP) program, 269
security-screening procedures, 257–258

Send and Receive Messages at Startup option, 232
Send Messages Immediately check box, 232
Send tab, 232
serial number, 269
Servers tab, 273
service contract, 30
service plan, 24
servicing laptops, 29–30
Set Network Location window, 190–191
Set Network Location Wizard, 191
Set Up a Connection or Network option, 193
Set Up a Dial-Up Connection option, 193
setting up
  dialup access, 193–194
  displays, 115–116
  fingerprint readers, 48
  laptops, 37
  modems, 199–203
  presentations, 283–285
  Remote Desktop, 244–245
Setup icons, 119
Setup password, 271–272
Setup program, 45, 271
Share a Program or Your Desktop link, 290
shared Internet access, 196
shared resources, 171–172
shield icon, 52, 116
Shift key, 69
shipping invoice, 34
shopping for laptops
  communications choices, 28
  core computer parts, 25–27
  docking station, 29
  energy management hardware, 28–29
  key items, 24–25
  optical discs, 27–28
  overview, 23
  port replicator, 29
  process of, 30
  service, 29–30
  support, 29–30
  unnecessary items, 23–24
  warranties, 30
shortcut icon, 80
shorting batteries, 137
Shut down option, 59
Shutdown menu, 53
shutting lid, 56–58
shutting off laptops
  hibernation, 54–55
  locking Windows, 56
  logging off, 55–56
  properly, 51–52
  restarting Windows, 52
  shutting down, 51–52
  shutting lid options, 56–58
  Sleep mode, 52–54
  software power button, 55
  when laptop won't cooperate, 58
Sidebar, 50, 133
silicon disk, 15
size, laptop, 24
slate Tablet PC model, 98–99
sleep button, 43, 53
Sleep mode
  versus hibernation, 54
  light, 67
  overview, 52–53
  waking up from, 53–54
Sleep option, 59
slide shows, 282
slot, memory card, 158
SmartMedia (SM) card, 157
social engineering, 218
software
  adding, 117–120
  anti-spyware, 214, 222–223
  antivirus, 218–221
  discs, 36
  external mouse, 78

software *(continued)*
  for function keys, 73
  installing, 117–119
  networking, 166–169
  power management, 54
  removing, 120–121
  Tablet PC, 111–112
  uninstalling, 120–121
  upgrading, 305–308
  USB device, 150
software power button, 55, 59–60
sound hardware, 28, 100, 147, 329
Space key, 109
space-saving computer systems, 20
spare battery, 137–138, 322, 328
speakers, 28, 100, 147
spike protection, 39
Spybot Search & Destroy software, 223
spyware, 214, 222–223
SpywareBlaster software, 223
SSID, 180, 182–183
Stand By mode, 302–303
Stand By timeout, 318
Start button, 50
Start menu, 80–82, 90–91
starting laptops
  opening lid, 42–43
  overview, 41–42
  power, 43–44
status light, 101
Sticky Notes, 112
STOP (Security Tracking of Office
    Property) program, 269
storage
  battery, 138, 317–318
  external USB, 152–154
  laptop, 38, 258
  mass, 25–27, 153
  network, 171–172
  removable, 62–63
  in Windows, 83–84
strong password, 272–273

students, laptop use by, 21
stylus
  gestures and flicks, 109–110
  Input Panel, 106–109
  training, 104–106
  using finger as, 110–111
subfolder, 86
subnotebook, 16
sunlight, 37
support, technical, 29–30
surge protection, 39
S-Video connection, 65, 160, 283
Switch user option, 56
symbols
  light, 67–68
  port, 64–66
  power, 43
Sync All button, 241
Sync Center, 238–240
Sync Center icon, 237–240, 243
Sync Center window, 240–242
sync partnership, 240
synchronization
  defined, 20
  ending, 243
  files, 241–242
  reviewing, 240–241
  scheduling automatic, 243
  Sync Center, 238–240
System and Maintenance option, 244, 295
System Configuration dialog box, 300
System Configuration Utility (MS Config),
    299–300
System Properties dialog box, 167, 244,
    295–296
System Protection tab, 295–296
System Restore
  enabling, 295–296
  restore point, 296–297
  restoring system, 297–299
System window, 166–167

• T •

Tab key, 109
Tablet PC
  Control Panel settings, 93, 102–104
  hardware, 99–102
  overview, 17–18, 97–99
  power, 43
  software, 111–112
  stylus, 104–111
tabulae ceratea, 18, 97
targus.com, 255
taskbar, 50
technical terminology, 26
temperature, extreme, 265, 317
terminals, battery, 317
Text File option, 227
theft prevention, 268–271, 326
thenorthface.com, 255
3M Laptop Privacy Filter, 258
throwing out laptops, 36
thumb ball mouse, 73
thumb drive, 148, 157, 182
timeouts, 142–143, 207–208, 318
To Disable Call Waiting Dial check
    box, 204
Touch tab, 110
touchpad, 73–75, 302, 325
tracking service, 275
TrackPoint, 75–76
Transportation Security Administration
    (TSA), 257
travel
  air
    airplane mode, 259–260
    carry-on luggage, 257
    inflight power, 260–261
    inflight usage, 260
    inspection of laptops, 257–258
    onboard storage, 258

café computing, 261–263
case
  cleaning, 126
  manufacturer's, 36, 252–253
  overview, 251–252
  packing, 328–330
  recommended brands, 254–255
  recommended features, 253–254
  security and, 269
checklist, 255–256
hotels, 264–265
overview, 20–21
temperature, 265
tray-type optical drive, 62
Trojan horse, 219
troubleshooting
  battery, 303
  keyboard, 301
  maintenance, 303–304
  mouse pointer, 302
  power-management, 303
  restarting, 294
  Safe mode, 299–301
  Stand By mode, 302
  System Restore, 295–299
  touchpad, 302
Troubleshooting Your PC For Dummies,
    213, 223, 277, 293, 303
TSA (Transportation Security
    Administration), 257
Turion 64 processor, 26
Turn Off the Guest Account icon, 274
turning laptops on/off
  hibernation, 54–55
  locking Windows, 56
  logging off, 55–56
  opening lid, 42–43
  overview, 41–42
  power, 43–44
  properly, 51–52
  restarting Windows, 52
  shutting down, 51–52

turning laptops on/off *(continued)*
    shutting lid options, 56–58
    Sleep mode, 52–54
    software power, 55
    when laptop won't cooperate, 58
typewriter keys, 69

• *U* •

UACs (User Account Controls), 116–117
UltraLite laptop, 14–15
Ultra-Mobile PCs (UMPCS), 19
Unblock button, 217
Uninstall command, 121
uninstalling software, 120–121
uninterruptible power supply (UPS), 39,
    138–139
universal security slot (USS), 66, 270–271
Universal Serial Bus (USB)
    adding external storage, 152–153
    cables, 123, 149
    devices, 27, 48, 119, 147–148, 150,
        324, 329
    hubs, 150–151
    overview, 145–146
    plugging in, 149–150
    ports, 65–66, 146–147
    removing external storage, 153–154
universities, laptop use in, 21
unpacking laptops
    keeping boxes, 36
    overview, 33–34
    sending in warranty, 36–37
    setting up, 37
    sorting items, 34–36
unpowered hub, 151
unsecured network, 180–181
updates
    automatic, 306–307
    installing, 52
upgrading
    hardware, 308–309
    software, 305–308

UPS (uninterruptible power supply), 39,
    138–139
upstream cable end, 149
USB (Universal Serial Bus)
    adding external storage, 152–153
    cables, 123, 149
    devices, 27, 48, 119, 147–148, 150,
        324, 329
    hubs, 150–151
    overview, 145–146
    plugging in, 149–150
    ports, 65–66, 146–147
    removing external storage, 153–154
Use Dialing Rules check box, 207
user account
    Administrator, 46
    choosing, 47–48
    configuring, 114–115
    Control Panel, 95
    Guest, 274
    modifying, 95
User Account Control dialog box, 117,
    223, 244, 259, 278, 297, 300, 307
User Account Control warning, 116, 196,
    208, 216, 245
User Account Controls (UACs),
    116–117
User Accounts window, 114–115,
    273–274
user profile, 46
User Profile folder, 84–85
USS (universal security slot), 66, 270–271

• *V* •

vacuuming keyboard, 127
ventilation, 67
video camera, 66, 147
video projector, 283
Videos folder, 86
View Sync Partnerships task, 241–242
View Sync Results task, 240–241
virtual memory manager, 315–316

virus
  antivirus software, 214, 218–219, 221
  checking for, 219–220
  protecting from, 221
  scanning for, 220
VNC (Real Virtual Network Computing),
    247

• W •

waking up laptops, 44, 53–54
wallpaper, 49–50, 115–116
warm booting, 44
warnings
  low-battery warning, 135–136, 318–319
  UAC, 116, 196, 208, 216, 245
warranty, 30, 36–37
WDS (Wireless Distribution System), 181
Web Archive, Single File (*.mht) option,
    226
Web browsing, offline, 226–227
Web Page, Complete (*.htm, *.html)
    option, 226
Web Page, HTML Only (*.htm, *.html)
    option, 226
Web sites
  anti-spyware solutions, 223
  antivirus software, 219
  author's, 4
  batteries, 138
  e-mail programs, 229, 234
  incoming call monitors, 205
  laptop cases, 255
  memory, 308
  Microsoft, 282, 301
  phone-home services, 276
  power adapters, 261
  Real Virtual Network Computing, 247
  screen cleaning products, 127
  STOP program, 269
Web-based e-mail, 188, 229
webcam, 100, 147

weight
  of accessories, 16
  of lunch buckets, 12–13
  of modern laptops, 17
  NEC UltraLight laptop, 14–15
  pre-purchase considerations, 24
Western Digital Passport, 277
wheel button, 75
Where the Message Size Is More Than
    Size option, 233
Win (Windows key), 275
Windows
  account password, 272–274
  configuring user account, 114–115
  Control Panel
    modems, setting up, 199–200
    Network and Sharing Center, 94
    overview, 89–90
    Personalization window, 93–94
    Phone and Modem Options, 95
    Power Options window, 94–95
    Printers window, 95
    Start menu, 90–91
    Tablet PC settings, 93, 102–104
    user accounts, modifying, 95
    Windows Mobility Center, 92–93
  desktop, 49–50, 80, 86
  folders, 84–86
  installing, 46
  locking, 56, 275
  logging in, 46–49
  logging off, 55–56
  notification area, 82
  overview, 45, 79–80
  Program Files folder, 87–88
  restarting, 52, 294
  setting up display, 115–116
  Start menu, 80–82
  storage, 83–84
  UACs, 116–117
  updating, 306–307
  upgrading, 307–308
  WinNT folder, 87

Windows Backup
  initial, 277–279
  overview, 276–277
  preparing for, 277
  restoring from, 280
Windows Collaboration, 288
Windows Defender, 222–223
Windows Fax and Scan window, 212
Windows Firewall
  monitoring, 217–218
  overview, 214–215
  using, 215–217
Windows Firewall icon, 215–217
Windows Firewall Settings dialog box,
    216, 245
Windows Firewall window, 245
Windows Journal program, 111
Windows key (Win), 275
Windows Mail
  accessing from another computer,
    229–230
  disabling automatic checking,
    231–232
  disconnecting after retrieving, 231
  forwarding, 230–231
  group mailings, 232
  overview, 227–228
  password, 273
  skipping messages over given size,
    233–234
Windows Meeting Space, 286–290
Windows Mobility Center, 92–93,
    239, 315
Windows Security Center, 219
Windows Sidebar, 50, 133
Windows Update window, 306
WinNT folder, 87
wire cutter, 329
wired network, 164, 192

Wireless Distribution System (WDS), 181
wireless keyboard, 159
wireless network adapter switch, 259
Wireless Network Connection icon,
    196, 259
wireless networking
  connecting, 179–182
  disconnecting, 185–186, 192
  hardware, 178–179
  lease, 184
  light, 67
  MAC address, 183–184
  overview, 28
  pay-service wireless network, 185
  protocol, 177–178
  SSID, 182–183
wireless networking card, 155
Wireless Notebook Laser Mouse 6000, 78
wireless router, 230
workgroup name, 167–170
workgroup networking, 189
worm, 214, 218
Writing Pad mode, 107–108

• X •

xD-Picture Card, 157
Xerox Dynabook, 8–9
X-ray machine, 258
xtool.com, 276

• Y •

Yahoo! Mail, 229

• Z •

zip file, 221
ztrace.com, 276

BUSINESS, CAREERS & PERSONAL FINANCE

Accounting For Dummies, 4th Edition*
978-0-470-24600-9

Bookkeeping Workbook For Dummies†
978-0-470-16983-4

Commodities For Dummies
978-0-470-04928-0

Doing Business in China For Dummies
978-0-470-04929-7

E-Mail Marketing For Dummies
978-0-470-19087-6

Job Interviews For Dummies, 3rd Edition*†
978-0-470-17748-8

Personal Finance Workbook For Dummies*†
978-0-470-09933-9

Real Estate License Exams For Dummies
978-0-7645-7623-2

Six Sigma For Dummies
978-0-7645-6798-8

Small Business Kit For Dummies, 2nd Edition*†
978-0-7645-5984-6

Telephone Sales For Dummies
978-0-470-16836-3

BUSINESS PRODUCTIVITY & MICROSOFT OFFICE

Access 2007 For Dummies
978-0-470-03649-5

Excel 2007 For Dummies
978-0-470-03737-9

Office 2007 For Dummies
978-0-470-00923-9

Outlook 2007 For Dummies
978-0-470-03830-7

PowerPoint 2007 For Dummies
978-0-470-04059-1

Project 2007 For Dummies
978-0-470-03651-8

QuickBooks 2008 For Dummies
978-0-470-18470-7

Quicken 2008 For Dummies
978-0-470-17473-9

Salesforce.com For Dummies, 2nd Edition
978-0-470-04893-1

Word 2007 For Dummies
978-0-470-03658-7

EDUCATION, HISTORY, REFERENCE & TEST PREPARATION

African American History For Dummies
978-0-7645-5469-8

Algebra For Dummies
978-0-7645-5325-7

Algebra Workbook For Dummies
978-0-7645-8467-1

Art History For Dummies
978-0-470-09910-0

ASVAB For Dummies, 2nd Edition
978-0-470-10671-6

British Military History For Dummies
978-0-470-03213-8

Calculus For Dummies
978-0-7645-2498-1

Canadian History For Dummies, 2nd Edition
978-0-470-83656-9

Geometry Workbook For Dummies
978-0-471-79940-5

The SAT I For Dummies, 6th Edition
978-0-7645-7193-0

Series 7 Exam For Dummies
978-0-470-09932-2

World History For Dummies
978-0-7645-5242-7

FOOD, GARDEN, HOBBIES & HOME

Bridge For Dummies, 2nd Edition
978-0-471-92426-5

Coin Collecting For Dummies, 2nd Edition
978-0-470-22275-1

Cooking Basics For Dummies, 3rd Edition
978-0-7645-7206-7

Drawing For Dummies
978-0-7645-5476-6

Etiquette For Dummies, 2nd Edition
978-0-470-10672-3

Gardening Basics For Dummies*†
978-0-470-03749-2

Knitting Patterns For Dummies
978-0-470-04556-5

Living Gluten-Free For Dummies†
978-0-471-77383-2

Painting Do-It-Yourself For Dummies
978-0-470-17533-0

HEALTH, SELF HELP, PARENTING & PETS

Anger Management For Dummies
978-0-470-03715-7

Anxiety & Depression Workbook For Dummies
978-0-7645-9793-0

Dieting For Dummies, 2nd Edition
978-0-7645-4149-0

Dog Training For Dummies, 2nd Edition
978-0-7645-8418-3

Horseback Riding For Dummies
978-0-470-09719-9

Infertility For Dummies†
978-0-470-11518-3

Meditation For Dummies with CD-ROM, 2nd Edition
978-0-471-77774-8

Post-Traumatic Stress Disorder For Dummies
978-0-470-04922-8

Puppies For Dummies, 2nd Edition
978-0-470-03717-1

Thyroid For Dummies, 2nd Edition†
978-0-471-78755-6

Type 1 Diabetes For Dummies*†
978-0-470-17811-9

---

* Separate Canadian edition also available

† Separate U.K. edition also available

Available wherever books are sold. For more information or to order direct: U.S. customers visit www.dummies.com or call 1-877-762-2974.
U.K. customers visit www.wileyeurope.com or call (0)1243 843291. Canadian customers visit www.wiley.ca or call 1-800-567-4797.

INTERNET & DIGITAL MEDIA

AdWords For Dummies
978-0-470-15252-2

Blogging For Dummies, 2nd Edition
978-0-470-23017-6

**Digital Photography All-in-One
Desk Reference For Dummies, 3rd Edition**
978-0-470-03743-0

Digital Photography For Dummies, 5th Edition
978-0-7645-9802-9

**Digital SLR Cameras & Photography
For Dummies, 2nd Edition**
978-0-470-14927-0

**eBay Business All-in-One Desk Reference
For Dummies**
978-0-7645-8438-1

eBay For Dummies, 5th Edition*
978-0-470-04529-9

eBay Listings That Sell For Dummies
978-0-471-78912-3

Facebook For Dummies
978-0-470-26273-3

The Internet For Dummies, 11th Edition
978-0-470-12174-0

Investing Online For Dummies, 5th Edition
978-0-7645-8456-5

iPod & iTunes For Dummies, 5th Edition
978-0-470-17474-6

MySpace For Dummies
978-0-470-09529-4

Podcasting For Dummies
978-0-471-74898-4

**Search Engine Optimization
For Dummies, 2nd Edition**
978-0-471-97998-2

Second Life For Dummies
978-0-470-18025-9

**Starting an eBay Business For Dummies,
3rd Edition†**
978-0-470-14924-9

GRAPHICS, DESIGN & WEB DEVELOPMENT

**Adobe Creative Suite 3 Design Premium
All-in-One Desk Reference For Dummies**
978-0-470-11724-8

**Adobe Web Suite CS3 All-in-One Desk
Reference For Dummies**
978-0-470-12099-6

AutoCAD 2008 For Dummies
978-0-470-11650-0

**Building a Web Site For Dummies,
3rd Edition**
978-0-470-14928-7

**Creating Web Pages All-in-One Desk
Reference For Dummies, 3rd Edition**
978-0-470-09629-1

**Creating Web Pages For Dummies,
8th Edition**
978-0-470-08030-6

Dreamweaver CS3 For Dummies
978-0-470-11490-2

Flash CS3 For Dummies
978-0-470-12100-9

Google SketchUp For Dummies
978-0-470-13744-4

InDesign CS3 For Dummies
978-0-470-11865-8

**Photoshop CS3 All-in-One
Desk Reference For Dummies**
978-0-470-11195-6

Photoshop CS3 For Dummies
978-0-470-11193-2

Photoshop Elements 5 For Dummies
978-0-470-09810-3

SolidWorks For Dummies
978-0-7645-9555-4

Visio 2007 For Dummies
978-0-470-08983-5

Web Design For Dummies, 2nd Edition
978-0-471-78117-2

Web Sites Do-It-Yourself For Dummies
978-0-470-16903-2

Web Stores Do-It-Yourself For Dummies
978-0-470-17443-2

LANGUAGES, RELIGION & SPIRITUALITY

Arabic For Dummies
978-0-471-77270-5

Chinese For Dummies, Audio Set
978-0-470-12766-7

French For Dummies
978-0-7645-5193-2

German For Dummies
978-0-7645-5195-6

Hebrew For Dummies
978-0-7645-5489-6

Ingles Para Dummies
978-0-7645-5427-8

Italian For Dummies, Audio Set
978-0-470-09586-7

Italian Verbs For Dummies
978-0-471-77389-4

Japanese For Dummies
978-0-7645-5429-2

Latin For Dummies
978-0-7645-5431-5

Portuguese For Dummies
978-0-471-78738-9

Russian For Dummies
978-0-471-78001-4

Spanish Phrases For Dummies
978-0-7645-7204-3

Spanish For Dummies
978-0-7645-5194-9

Spanish For Dummies, Audio Set
978-0-470-09585-0

The Bible For Dummies
978-0-7645-5296-0

Catholicism For Dummies
978-0-7645-5391-2

The Historical Jesus For Dummies
978-0-470-16785-4

Islam For Dummies
978-0-7645-5503-9

**Spirituality For Dummies,
2nd Edition**
978-0-470-19142-2

NETWORKING AND PROGRAMMING

ASP.NET 3.5 For Dummies
978-0-470-19592-5

C# 2008 For Dummies
978-0-470-19109-5

Hacking For Dummies, 2nd Edition
978-0-470-05235-8

Home Networking For Dummies, 4th Edition
978-0-470-11806-1

Java For Dummies, 4th Edition
978-0-470-08716-9

**Microsoft® SQL Server™ 2008 All-in-One
Desk Reference For Dummies**
978-0-470-17954-3

**Networking All-in-One Desk Reference
For Dummies, 2nd Edition**
978-0-7645-9939-2

**Networking For Dummies,
8th Edition**
978-0-470-05620-2

SharePoint 2007 For Dummies
978-0-470-09941-4

**Wireless Home Networking
For Dummies, 2nd Edition**
978-0-471-74940-0

OPERATING SYSTEMS & COMPUTER BASICS

iMac For Dummies, 5th Edition
978-0-7645-8458-9

Laptops For Dummies, 2nd Edition
978-0-470-05432-1

Linux For Dummies, 8th Edition
978-0-470-11649-4

MacBook For Dummies
978-0-470-04859-7

**Mac OS X Leopard All-in-One
Desk Reference For Dummies**
978-0-470-05434-5

Mac OS X Leopard For Dummies
978-0-470-05433-8

Macs For Dummies, 9th Edition
978-0-470-04849-8

PCs For Dummies, 11th Edition
978-0-470-13728-4

Windows® Home Server For Dummies
978-0-470-18592-6

Windows Server 2008 For Dummies
978-0-470-18043-3

**Windows Vista All-in-One
Desk Reference For Dummies**
978-0-471-74941-7

Windows Vista For Dummies
978-0-471-75421-3

Windows Vista Security For Dummies
978-0-470-11805-4

SPORTS, FITNESS & MUSIC

Coaching Hockey For Dummies
978-0-470-83685-9

Coaching Soccer For Dummies
978-0-471-77381-8

Fitness For Dummies, 3rd Edition
978-0-7645-7851-9

Football For Dummies, 3rd Edition
978-0-470-12536-6

GarageBand For Dummies
978-0-7645-7323-1

Golf For Dummies, 3rd Edition
978-0-471-76871-5

Guitar For Dummies, 2nd Edition
978-0-7645-9904-0

**Home Recording For Musicians
For Dummies, 2nd Edition**
978-0-7645-8884-6

**iPod & iTunes For Dummies,
5th Edition**
978-0-470-17474-6

Music Theory For Dummies
978-0-7645-7838-0

Stretching For Dummies
978-0-470-06741-3

Get smart @ dummies.com®

- **Find a full list of Dummies titles**
- **Look into loads of FREE on-site articles**
- **Sign up for FREE eTips e-mailed to you weekly**
- **See what other products carry the Dummies name**
- **Shop directly from the Dummies bookstore**
- **Enter to win new prizes every month!**

* Separate Canadian edition also available
† Separate U.K. edition also available

Available wherever books are sold. For more information or to order direct: U.S. customers visit www.dummies.com or call 1-877-762-2974.
U.K. customers visit www.wileyeurope.com or call (0) 1243 843291. Canadian customers visit www.wiley.ca or call 1-800-567-4797.